The Road to Inner Joy & Peace

Including:

Prosperity is Your Birthright!

Destined for Great Things!

Words of Inspiration!

Walk the path leading to peace, joy, wealth, health and prosperity!

Dr. Mia Y. Merritt

Copyright © 2010
by Mia Y. Merritt, Ed.D
THE ROAD TO INNER JOY & PEACE
*Walk the path leading to peace, joy, wealth,
health and prosperity!*

INCLUDING:
Prosperity is Your Birthright!
Destined for Great Things!
Words of Inspiration
Golden Nuggets for the Wise at Heart

All rights reserved. No part of this book may be reproduced
in any form without permission in writing
from the author or publisher.

All biblical references/scriptures are taken from the
Original King James Version of the Bible

ISBN #978-0-9720398-6-4

Library of Congress Control
in-Publication Data

First Printing June 2010
In the USA
Merritt, Mia

Foreword

The road leading to inner joy and peace is not a smooth one. There are roadblocks, obstacles, barricades, and distractions along the way; but if you will persevere, endure, and persist in your pursuit of joy, peace and prosperity, you will be sure to find it.

This book, **The Road to Inner Joy and Peace** *contains three books in one. The first book, entitled,* **Prosperity is Your Birthright** *outlines in specific detail the principles that must be applied in your life in order to achieve meaningful prosperity and success. The use of your gifts is emphasized throughout the book. Allowing yourself to be a conduit for God to express Himself through is a sure way to walk in the unfolding of your destiny. This book is a step by step guide to bringing into fruition your heart's desires. If you are tired of living in mediocrity, and are ready to take your life to another level, then this book is for you!*

The Second Book, **Destined for Great Things** *details the struggles and hardships that the author endured as she was evolving into the person that God would have her to be. As the forces of evil pulled her in the direction leading to destruction, her unmitigated faith and fight pulled her in the direction leading to joy and peace. Eventually the fight subsided and, although left with many wounds she persevered and did not allow God's gifts in her to be aborted. If you are in a place in your life where you do not understand why fiery darts keep getting thrown at you, why tribulations and struggles keep knocking on your door, or why it seems as though God is against you, then Destined for Great Things is the book for you to read in this season.*

The third book, **Words of Inspiration** *contains simple quotes, mostly taken from the book Prosperity is Your Birthright. They are reminders for how to learn life's lessons. If repeated and placed in your spirit, they will spring up when needed and hopefully allow you to apply their words of wisdom when the time arises. Enjoy the books!*

Book 1

Prosperity is Your Birthright!

Affirm Your Spiritual Inheritance!

*Walk in the
Unfolding
of
Prosperity, Peace,
&
Abundance!*

~~~~~~~~~~~~~~~~~

Dr. Mia Y. Merritt

Copyright © 2009
by Mia Y. Merritt, Ed.D
PROSPERITY IS YOUR BIRTHRIGHT!

All rights reserved. No part of this book may be reproduced
in any form without permission in writing
from the author or publisher.

All biblical references/scriptures are taken from the
Original King James Version of the Bible

ISBN #978-0-9720398-2-6

Other Books by Mia Y. Merritt:
Destined for Great Things!
Destined for Great Things Workbook

Library of Congress Control #2009910133
in-Publication Data

First Printing October 2009
In the USA

Merritt, Mia

Contents

CHAPTER 1 1
Prosperous People Plan for Success

CHAPTER 2 15
Remarkable Manifestations Appear to Visionaries

CHAPTER 3 29
Open Your Mind to the Influx of Miracles

CHAPTER 4 39
Share Your Gifts With the World

CHAPTER 5 51
Prepare to Receive What You Believe

CHAPTER 6 65
Expand Your Consciousness

CHAPTER 7 83
Remind Yourself of Your Worth and Power

CHAPTER 8 93
Integrity Should Guide Your Actions

CHAPTER 9 109
Train Your Mind to Think Positively

CHAPTER 10 122
Your Prayers Make A Difference

1
PROSPEROUS PEOPLE PLAN FOR SUCCESS

> *The secret to productive goal setting is establishing clearly defined goals, writing them down and then focusing on them several times a day with words and emotions as if you've already achieved them.*
> Denis Waitley

Abundant prosperity is waiting to break forth in your life in a mighty and powerful way! It is God's desire for you that you would be prosperous even as your soul prospers. I believe that everyone wants to be prosperous, happy, healthy, wealthy, and at peace with themselves and the world, but very few people make the mental and physical sacrifices required in order to achieve and maintain those things to a noteworthy degree. Prosperity is an outward manifestation of an inward reality. True prosperity on the outside is evidence of prosperity on the inside. This is the result of having an expanded consciousness and enlarged vision. An expanded consciousness does not simply widen for those who only wish for it. It comes to those who begin to realize that they posses a power within to accomplish the goals they have set out to achieve. One must recognize and take ownership of the power they posses within. Prosperity to one person may be totally different from prosperity to another person. It is a relative term that does not declare that "this" is prosperous and "that" is not. It can be defined as success, accomplishment, good fortune or wealth. However, it is a word that is often associated with money in the minds of most people, but money is only a fraction of what it means to be prosperous. Prosperity most often does encompass money, but it also includes peace, good health, affluence, love, joy, happiness, and abundance. It should therefore be one's desire to have all of these assets along with having Good wealth. After all, what is the purpose of being financially wealthy if you are sick, unhappy, and miserable? Do not be deceived into thinking that just because a person holds a high position, drives a luxurious car, lives in an extravagant home and appears to have lots of money that he or she is prosperous. It may appear that way on the outside, but on the inside that person could very well be the most unhappy, dissatisfied, miserable person you could ever meet.

Prosperity is Your Birthright!

You fall into error when you judge someone based on where you think they are. Never judge a book by its cover and always remember that prosperity encompasses more than just material things. Keep in mind the following:

    There is wealth under the blessing of God.
    There is wealth under the curse of God.
    There is poverty under the blessing of God.
    There is poverty under the curse of God.

    Success and prosperity does not happen by chance and are not given to a select group of individuals only. When you look around, you see prosperous, rich and successful people from all walks of life. They come from different races, cultures, and creeds. So we dare not say that only a specific group of people are prosperous, those who were born into families of riches and wealth within their culture or race or who were educated at the finest institutions, or those who won the lottery. Prosperous people are just ordinary folks like you and me who have developed belief and confidence in themselves and found the power within them to do what they set their minds and hearts to do. If you were to research, you would discover that the origin of wealthy people came from very humble backgrounds with little-to-no education. Many were underprivileged and had no early advantages. However, they discovered a creativity and a power inside of them. They took hold of that power and used it to manifest prosperity. No one just stumbled into success and prosperity.

    It sometimes appears as though prosperity comes to certain people very easily, some with much toil and struggle, and then still to some not at all. We seem to wonder why this is so. The answer certainly could not lie in physical strength, appearance, health, or intelligence because tall, strong, and muscular people become prosperous as well as short, weak, and scrawny people. Intellectually brilliant people become prosperous and average people become prosperous. Physically healthy individuals become prosperous and weak and degenerate people also become prosperous. Therefore prosperity is not contingent upon anything physical, conditional, or intellectual. It is dependant upon a mind that has learned how to tap into ingenuity, creativity, and power, which is a combination of developed mental and spiritual faculties. They then used that mind to properly and strategically guide that ingenuity, creativity, and power into the direction they chose. Later in the book, we will explore how to develop both of these kinds of power. But for now, we will look at one of the main commonalities that prosperous people share, which is their commitment to planning.

COMMITMENT TO PLANNING

We have always heard that if you fail to plan, you plan to fail. It has been said that only three percent of Americans set goals through planning. Three percent is not a whole lot compared to the number of people in this world. Yet, we wonder why the top three percent of the wealthiest people in the nation own more than half the wealth in America. They did not get there by accident that's for sure. They planned for it. Planning ahead is a major attribute of wealthy, successful, organized, productive people of the world. It requires self-discipline and has many benefits. Let's look at some of those benefits below:

Planning ahead helps one to:

- Be more organized and feel more competent
- Feel more confident and prepared
- Relax and be at ease
- Not worry about having to rush or strain
- Reduce stress
- Know the direction in which to go
- Know the right road to take to get there
- Always know what the desired outcome is

Show me a person who plans and I will show you a person who has an organized and orderly life. When we look at order, we reflect on God's way of doing things. He is a God of order. Look at the methodical manner in which He created the world. Everything was organized and strategically executed. He did not create the entire world in one day, although He could have. He properly planned each day knowing exactly what was to be implemented in each. He did not overextend the duties of the day and He certainly did not start one thing before He was completely finished with another. Everything He started, He completed with excellence, precision, diligence, and accuracy. Each creation was divinely connected to the next, which was light and darkness, earth and sea, grass and trees, sun and moon, land creatures and sea creatures, man. That which was created before the next, was for the benefit of what was to come afterwards. When man was created on the sixth day, everything he needed for his continued existence and sustenance was already there, and so it still is today. Everything we need, want, or desire is already here waiting for you to take hold of. God is a God of order, accuracy, and precision, and so, as we are made in His image and likeness, we must also be orderly.

IMPLEMENT YOUR PLAN

Your goals are a stimulating pursuit. It is extremely important that you begin to strategically plan out your life in a courageous manner and execute your goals fearlessly. Recognize yourself as a person worthy of accomplishing great things. Endeavoring to accomplish goals is exciting and gives you something to always strive for. When you develop goals, you are actually planning how you want your life to unfold in terms of what you want to see manifested. Plans are like a road map showing you where you want to go and telling you approximately how long it will take to get there. Plans are the "what" of goal setting. Action plans are the "how". They delineate the steps you need to take along the way to arrive at your destination. Not only does writing your goals down help you to visualize clearly what it is that you aspire to do, have, or be, but seeing them written also motivates you and strengthens that power within you that causes those goals to be manifested. Once you have taken the time and effort to write specifically what you want to achieve, the power to accomplish those goals emerges inside of you. There is power in writing things down on paper. The Bible puts it this way: *"Write the vision, and make it plain upon tables, that he may run that reads it. For the vision is yet for an appointed time, but in the end it shall speak, and not lie: though it tarry, wait for it; because it will surely come, it will not tarry."* (Habakkuk 2:2).

There is a resurgence of taking on the world that overpowers you once you see your vision on paper. When you set goals and make plans for their accomplishment, you have actually solidified the vision by means of writing. You must now manifest the vision out of the mental into the natural. Once you get your goals down on paper, you have to consistently keep them before you so that they may always be at the forefront of your mind. Spend time examining your goals and work on them daily. You have everything you need inside of you to accomplish them with precision and power. The only thing that can stop you from pursuing your goals is YOU! You are the master of your own destiny. You are the captain of your own ship. Planning is the key! Properly setting goals can be incredibly motivating. As you get into the habit of setting and achieving goals, you will find that your self-confidence increases quickly. A sure way to increase self-esteem is by achieving one goal after the next, and as Maxwell Maltz quotes, *"Real self-esteem does not result from the great things that you have done or the things you won or the mark you've made, but in an appreciation of yourself for what you are."* Goal setting techniques are used by countless individuals all over the world and in all professions. The size of your belief determines the size of your accomplishments. You are much bigger than you think you are. People who dare to aim high and work towards accomplishing those aims are big thinkers with enlarged conscienceness'. They are experts in creating positive and forward-looking images in their minds and in the minds of others. Don't concern yourself too much with *how* and *when* you are going to achieve your goals after you have written your plan for executing them. Leave that completely to God. The desire to accomplish them is the power within you seeking to manifest. Look at things not as they are, but as they will be. Visualization adds value to your aspirations. A person who strategically plans, always visualizes what will be done in the future. A planner looks beyond the present. The reward is great if you persist until you succeed.

PLANT THE SEEDS IN GOOD SOIL

However you decide to plan your life is exclusively up to you. The key is to plan. As mentioned earlier, when you fail to plan, you plan to fail. The majority of people meet with failure because of their lack of planning or their lack of persistence in creating new plans to take the place of the ones that may have failed. When they don't see instant results, they become discouraged and quit. Giving up and quitting should never be an option when it comes to the pursuit of your dreams. Discouragement destroys hope, so naturally the enemy of your faith tries to discourage you. You may not see immediate results because of detours or obstacles, but that is okay. Your job is to have faith and continue planting the seeds that will reap a bountiful harvest. When a gardener plants a seed in the ground, he or she does not

Prosperity is Your Birthright!

instantly see a result. A plant is not even seen after a few days or a few weeks, but that does not mean that there is no seed there. The gardener is not concerned that he or she can not see a plant yet. He or she has faith that the seed is there and so they water that area, cultivate that area, and makes sure that the place where the seed is planted has plenty of sunshine and air. Eventually, something begins to appear in the very spot where the seed was planted. As the plant continues to burst forth out of the ground, the gardener continues to cultivate, water, and nurture until the plant is fully visible and eventually healthy and strong. Initially, there was no indication in the natural realm that a plant even existed where the seed was sown, but there were powerful forces at work underneath the surface. As the manifestation appeared, it was evident that the one seed, in the process of growing, multiplied, proving that inherent in the law of growth, there is a law of multiplicity. It also proves that you not only reap what you sow, but you get a surplus (or double for the trouble) for the time, effort, and sacrifice that was put into sowing, cultivating, nurturing, and watering the seed. In due season, you shall reap what you have planted according to the nature of the seed. You must therefore be sure before you plant a seed that you are going to be satisfied with the harvest you get back. If you plant a tomato seed, you will reap tomato plants. You will get exactly what you have planted. You can not plant a tomato seed and get a turnip plant. You can not sow hatred, discord, conflict, and dissension and get back love, peace, happiness and harmony. You have no right to expect to reap what you have not sown. The law works with astounding accuracy. You reap exactly what you sow.

    We live in a microwave, fast-paced world. Everybody wants instant results and immediate solutions to problems, but nature teaches that things take time. There are some things that just can not be rushed. Even when you know that you have been called to do a specific task, there is a season for when you are to step into the position. When David was anointed as King, there was a very long wait before he actually took the throne. The time between the calling and the actual commission is an essential time of preparation. Many theologians believe that David was 20 years old when Samuel anointed him as King. We know that he was 30 years old when he actually took the throne because the Bible states that. So there was about a ten year wait between the calling and the actual appointment to the throne. I am sure that after a few years had passed David began to doubt the veracity of the prophecy, but there was a reason for the ten year wait.

During that time, David should have been preparing himself for kingship by acquiring wisdom, knowledge, understanding and leadership skills through fasting and praying. There were essential things that needed to be done within that ten year time frame. Had David tried to take the throne from King Saul before the appointed time, he could have severely obstructed God's divine purpose for making him king, and the people of Israel and Judah would have suffered. It is critical that you wait until your season has arrived before you step out to assume the role for which you have been called. Stepping out before the appointed time may obstruct God's plan for your life. *"There is a time and a season for every purpose under the sun." (Ecclesiastes 3:1).* If your desire is noble, your goals identified, action plans carried out, and cultivating and nurturing of the desire has taken place, then all there is left to do is wait with patience, faith, expectation, and receptivity. The longer the wait, the greater the harvest will be.

A LESSON ON WAITING

As I talk to you about waiting, let's take a look at the Chinese Bamboo Tree. Like most seeds, when the seed for this tree has been planted, nothing is seen in the first season. Regular seeds begin to sprout within the first year, but not the Chinese Bamboo Tree seed. Nothing is seen after the first season or the second season or the third season. After four years, nothing has appeared. It is as though no seed was ever planted in four years. But here comes year five. In the fifth year, something begins to emerge in the spot where the seed was planted. In this fifth year the Chinese Bamboo Tree seed begins to break forth from the ground and grows, and grows, and grows up to eighty feet tall! All this growth happens in one year! Now the question is this: Did the tree grow eighty feet tall
in one year or five years? Think about your answer for a second. The answer is five years. It took five years for that seed to develop a strong root system to be able to support the eighty foot tree. While underground, unseen forces were at work strengthening the foundation for what was to be the outward manifestation. Had the seed not developed a strong unseen foundation, it would never have been able to support this eighty foot tree. If the gardener had dug up the soil every year to see what was going on with the seed, there would never have been a tree. He would have stunted the tree's growth, but the gardener had faith that the seed would one day sprout.

Prosperity is Your Birthright!

Therefore the gardener continued to water that area where the seed was planted. He nurtured that area, cultivated it, and took very good care of it, knowing that one day he was going to reap what he had sown. Nature in turn gave him a surplus (or double for his trouble). Had he neglected the seed that was planted by not watering, cultivating, or nourishing the area, the seed would have died under ground. Mother Nature knew that the gardener had been faithful to that seed for five years and so she rewarded him for his patience with a beautiful eighty foot tree. Nature is very good to us.

And so it is with prosperity. We set the goals, develop the plans, work at the execution of the plans, plant the seed of faith, water the seed with labor, and nurture the seed with expectation. We may not immediately see a harvest, but in due season, we shall reap a harvest, if we faint not. It is in DUE SEASON. We must never give up. There will be some failure, but that is okay. Temporary defeat is not permanent failure. It is in you to succeed. No one succeeds without overcoming obstacles and opposition. There would be no <u>test</u>-imony if there were no <u>test</u>. Giving up is not an option! Doubt and fear have no place in your heart, mind, or consciousness. Faith is the key that expands your belief. Out of every adversity comes an equal or greater opportunity. Success requires heart and soul effort. You can only put your heart and soul into something you really desire. Just continue to plan your work and work your plan.

In order for you to receive a strong and healthy harvest, you must ensure that the cultivation is frequent and ongoing. The seed must be planted in good soil. There can be no neglect after you plant the seed of desire. Carefully ensure that your seed is being properly nourished and cultivated until it comes into fruition. Do not allow thoughts of doubt and fear to enter the field where you have planted your seed. You must have faith, hope, and expectation. If you don't, you will never see the manifestation of your desires. Your seed is your earnest desire. Hold that desire in your mind everyday until it becomes a reality in your life. A strong and healthy desire is clear and distinctive, not vague. The cultivation of that desire is the small things you do each day toward bringing that desire nearer to you. When you develop goals centered around your desire and develop action plans by setting target dates and quotas for yourself, then you are cultivating that desire. Good soil is your good, honest and noble motive for wanting this desire. The motive should not be only for money, recognition, or the acquiring of material things, but for wisdom through the process and also to help others reach their highest good. Your faith that the desire will be accomplished is the power of belief that will bring it to you. Whatever your desire is, you must mentally feel that you have it until it begins to take form around you. As you visualize it in the mental realm, begin to enjoy it and act as though it has already arrived. Before you know it, you will be touching and experiencing your desires in your daily living environment.

ABUNDANCE FOR ALL

There is plenty in the world for everyone. Just look around and notice the profusion everywhere. Look at the number of trees in the world, the number of sand on the seashore, the quantity of water in the ocean, the number of fish in the sea, the amount of animals on the land, and the vast amount of plants and flowers everywhere. There is never a limit of nature's resources. The earth contains incalculable riches and the air is effervescent with power. The flower never runs out of smell, the ocean never runs out of water, the birds never run out of songs to sing, the butterfly never runs out of colors, the clouds never run out of rain and the cemetery never seems to run out of space. The world never runs out of books to read, clothes and shoes to wear, people to entertain them, television shows, actors and actresses, music, etc. There is more than enough of everything in this world. Things are always being replenished and always will be. Man has been taken care of from the beginning of creation until now. There is more than enough money, more than enough cars, boats, houses, jewelry, positions and business opportunities. There is no lack of anything. The only lack there is, is the limit we place on ourselves. God wants you to have everything your heart desires. You do not have to compete or scramble for anything because what rightfully belongs to you will come to you, claim you, and rush to you. You do not have to cheat, steal, or take anything from anybody else. Nothing will run out. If one door closes, another will open. If one job opportunity is taken, another will come along. You do not have to envy anyone else for what they have. You can have the same things, if not better things than they have. Just open your mind to the influx of creativity and ingenuity and bring your desire or creation out of the invisible realm into the visible realm. You are a creator through your mind. If you look around and don't see any opportunities for you, then make your own opportunities.

We are all surrounded by opportunities and ideas. Ideas are the product of the mind. As Emerson put it, *"Do the thing and you shall have your reward."* The supply is never limited. It is God's desire that you have abundance and there is abundance for all. You should be able to eat, drink, and be merry when it is time to do that. You never have to worry about the cupboard going bare. *"A man hath no better thing under the sun, than to eat, and to drink, and be merry." (Ecclesiastes 8: 15).*

God is ready to give you what you have planned for, worked for, meditated for, and prayed for. All you have to do is reach out and grab hold of it. You must be perceptive enough to know when the time has arrived. What if God is pressing abundance upon you, but all you can see and accept is poverty in the midst of abundance? There can be no compromise between poverty and abundance. The roads that lead to poverty and abundance travel in opposite directions. Poverty and bondage is not God-ordained. If you want riches, you must refuse to travel any road that leads toward poverty. Open your spiritual eyes so that you may see your desires all around you. When they come, you must not hoard them. When God blesses you with gifts, they are a blessing for you, but also for you to bless others with. You will never hold on to anything for long if you hoard them. If you tied a rope around your leg, circulation would be cut off after a while and your leg would die. It is the same with things. If there is no circulation, there is no flow. There must be a back and forth flow of going out and coming back in. Life is about giving and receiving. There can be no one-way flow. For this reason, you have two hands, one for giving and one for receiving.

GOOD SUCCESS

God outlined all throughout the Bible what we needed to do to be successful. We just don't apply the principles to our lives. A good example of how God outlined success for us is in the book of Joshua, Chapter 1:8 *"This book of the law shall not depart out of thy mouth; but thou shall meditate therein day and night, that thou may observe to do according to all that is written therein: For then thou shall make thy way prosperous, and then thou shall have good success."* Good success is attaining total peace and fulfillment in every area of your life. God plainly told Joshua how he and the Israelites could have not just success, but "good success" and be prosperous. He said for them to meditate on the Word day and night and do what the Word says. Seems simple enough right? Then why was it so hard to do, and still is today? Because it takes "discipline" to meditate on the Word of God day and night. It takes "discipline" to, *"do according to ALL that is written therein..."* It takes "discipline" to do anything that is worth striving for. Unfortunately, most of us keep our lives so jammed with junk food for the soul and amusement for the flesh that the cost for good success and prosperity is too expensive to pay. God reiterates this same principle in Psalm 1:2, *"...his delight is in the law of the Lord and in his law does he **meditate day and night**; and he shall be like a tree planted by the rivers of the water that brings forth fruit in his season; His leaf also shall not wither, and whatsoever he doeth shall prosper."* There it is again. God says to "meditate" on His Word day and night as a process to get to prosperity. The word also says that in "due season" we shall reap, indicating that there is a waiting period. Prosperity is an ongoing, progressing state of success. God wants us to be prosperous and have "good" successes. You do not hinder another person when you live in prosperity. You harm nobody else by being happy and full of joy. You steal from no one by being wealthy, and you should not have to feel guilty about becoming a success because God has told everybody in His Word what needed to be done to have it. You can have it. I can have it. Discipline and obedience is the key.

KEEP YOUR CONNECTION TO THE ROOT

When prosperity materializes into your life, do not be deceived into thinking that you have arrived. With success and prosperity comes greater responsibility. Keep in mind that a person may rise to great levels of success in the world and even reach high altitudes in the spiritual realm, but fall into weakness, arrogance, and pride by allowing selfish and haughty thoughts to consume their mindset. The higher you get and the more you achieve, the more susceptible you are to being caught up in the superficial world of success. In John Maxwell's book, 'Winning With People' he quotes, *Success can bring many things: power, privilege, fame and wealth. But no matter what else it brings, with success comes options. How we use those options reveals our character. Wealthy people can use their resources to benefit others or only themselves. Leaders can make decisions that affect others positively or negatively."* Stay grounded and remember that you achieve your goals only with the help of other people.

Through goal setting, developing action plans, having faith, walking in confidence, being determined, persistent, and letting patience have her perfect work in the process of achieving your goals, you will receive the desires of your heart and will soon find that you are prosperous beyond your wildest dreams! You will exude prosperity while experiencing the beauty of your surroundings and enjoying the affluent conditions with which you live. It is at this point where many fail to remain humble and end up getting caught up in the glory and pride of the world. Many forget to remember where they came from, put out of their minds the humiliating defeats they encountered along the way, forget about the many nights of crying, and discount the toil and struggle they endured while trying to get where they wanted to be. Arrogance surfaces and pride begins to take over. You are not to allow this to happen to you, but you are to pray for humility over your successes *before* they actualize. You are to ask God to make you a good steward over all the money that is coming to you before it comes. You are to ask for wisdom and good judgment in making important decisions when the time arises. You are to ask for love to spring up in you as you interact with God's people. These are things to pray for as you wait for the manifestation of your desires so that when they come, you are well prepared to be a good steward over them. As mentioned earlier when talking about David and his calling, the time between the goal and the manifestation of the goal is an essential time for preparing. This is the time when praying is extremely necessary.

Let's take a deeper look at the Chinese Bamboo Tree as an analogy for your life. As we know, the Chinese Bamboo Tree grows eighty feet tall in the fifth year of the seed being planted. It is common knowledge that a tree gets its nourishment from the roots. In order for the leaves to receive nourishment from the Chinese Bamboo Tree, the nourishment has to pass all the way up from the root that is deeply imbedded into the ground. The nourishment comes up then out into the branches
extending in the various directions where the leaves are. Although the leaves are a distance from the roots, with a solid foundation and connecting branches, the leaves receive nourishment emanating from the foundation. When it comes to success and prosperity, some people get so high up on the ladder of success that they no longer are able to receive proper nourishment from the Lord. A disconnect happens and God's nourishment is no longer

extending to them. Although it is the Lord, the solid foundation ultimately responsible for the success and prosperity of the person, he or she has distanced themselves so far from the Lord that they are no longer able to accept the fact that had it not been for the Lord, they would not be successful in the first place. Unfortunately, while there is a disconnect, there is no nourishment being received. Eventually, all the nourishment in the reserve from when there was a constant flow is used up and there is nothing left. The individual is left to rely upon his or her own reasoning and guidance and sooner or later falls into error. A humiliating fall usually follows this process. The point here is that no matter how high up you go, you must always stay closely connected to the root, the solid foundation, the Lord. For this is how you get your nourishment of wisdom, guidance, humility, grace, understanding and good judgment. Stay rooted and grounded. Learn from this analogy.

KEEP MOVING FORWARD

As you begin to walk in prosperity and success, you become more knowledgeable about things and people. This knowledge is not always pleasant. *For in much wisdom is much grief: and he that increases knowledge increases sorrow. (Ecclesiastes 1:18).* Sometimes friends and even certain family members begin treating you differently. There will be times when people will say things to deliberately hurt your feelings to try and steal your joy. You must keep moving forward. Those who sincerely and genuinely support you and want to see you succeed will be there no matter what. Those who don't will reveal themselves, and although it may hurt, you must keep moving forward. Watch your actions and reactions during this time. Your actions and reactions reveal what is inside of you. People respond to our actions more than they respond to our words. If the reaction is worse than the action, then the problem usually gets bigger, but if the reaction is less than the action, the problem usually gets smaller. There will be some disappointments, a few failures, a little jealously, and some discouraging days, but you must not focus on the negativity, but keep moving forward. You walk in your integrity by acknowledging the disappointments, identifying where things went wrong, celebrating the successes, and appreciating those who supported you along the way. Part of becoming great is obtaining prosperity with humility and facing failure with dignity. Your eyes should be focused on your goals everyday. You should be working on ways to continue developing yourself, elevating yourself, and progressing. Bring meaning to your life and the lives of others. You can not leave a powerful impact on anybody's life if you have no powerful impact on your own. Move onward and upward. Ask yourself this question right now, *"What significant meaning does my life have besides my family? What have I done for myself?"* If you are not able to identify anything meaningful, then you may start developing goals for yourself today. Make time for your personal goals. If you *have* been able to identify accomplishments, then that is wonderful. Your achievements today are the sum total of your thoughts yesterday, but what goals have you developed to take the place of the ones that have been achieved? No one has ever arrived. Let's keep moving forward.

CHAPTER 1 KEY POINTS:

- ❖ When we look at order, we reflect on God's way of doing things. He is a God of order. Look at the methodical manner in which He created the world. Everything was organized and strategically executed.

- ❖ Your goals are a stimulating pursuit. When you develop goals, you are actually planning how you want your life to be in terms of what you want to see manifested.

- ❖ A strong and healthy desire is clear and distinctive. It is not vague. The cultivation of that desire is the small things you do each day toward bringing that desire nearer to you.

- ❖ God is ready to give you what you have planned for, worked for, meditated for, and prayed for. All you have to do is reach out and grab hold of it.

- ❖ You should be working on ways to continue developing yourself, elevating yourself, and progressing. Bring meaning to your life and the lives of others. You can not leave a powerful impact on anybody's life if you have no powerful impact on your own.

2

REMARKABLE MANIFESTATIONS APPEAR TO VISIONARIES

> *Keep your dreams alive. Understand to achieve anything requires faith and belief in yourself, vision, hard work, determination, and dedication. Remember all things are possible for those who believe.*
>
> *Gail Devers*

Idealization, Visualization, and Manifestation. This is the order in which your desires become a reality. Whether you realize it or not, your life is shaped by the images you have seen and entertained in your mind over the years. You may have consciously entertained these images through mental exercises such as meditation, or unconsciously entertained these images through daydreaming; but you are the one who brought them out of the invisible (your mind) into the visible (your environment) and you are the one who is now dealing with the existence of these thoughts in your life whether they are good or bad. Therefore, it is imperative that you become consciously aware of the thoughts, imaginations, and visions that you entertain on a day to day basis because what you think about today shall become the reality that you shall experience tomorrow, just as what you are experiencing today, is the reality of what you thought about yesterday and in time past. What came to you in the physical world is what already existed in your inner world. When you consistently envision yourself as having self-actualized, meaning you have achieved your highest dreams and are living the life you have always desired while possessing peace, harmony, abundance, and an even flow of love going out and coming in, then you are bringing your highest ideal to you. If you are not yet living your highest ideal, but you can "see" yourself as living this ideal through strategic visualization, then you are on the road to manifestation and will soon kiss the lips of your desires. When you visualize your ideal on a consistent basis through meditation, you are actually using the law of cause and effect.

THE INVISIBLE WORLD

Anything you can see with the natural eye already exists in the physical realm, but it first existed in the mental realm in the form of a thought, then an imagination (seeing a picture in mind), next a vision (concept), followed by an actual object in the natural environment. Someone's imagination created cities, towns, railroads, and shopping malls. The airplane, automobile, boat, computer, I-pod, DVD Player, blackberry, etc. all existed in someone's imagination before they became a physical reality. Nothing ever took material form without first being imaged in the mind. There is no way around that. What you see when you visualize is a reality already existing in the spiritual realm and transitions from one realm into the next. It is important to know and understand that everything seen came from that which is not seen, including you. You came from out of the unseen into the visible world. The only indication that you existed before you were birthed was the fact that your mother's belly grew larger and larger indicating that there was something inside growing. With modern technology today, we can now see a clear image of the baby through an ultrasound, but the fact remains that you began as a conception before you were birthed into the world. Your thoughts work in the exact same way. The thoughts and pictures you see in your mind are conceptions (causes) and the experiences that you encounter are the manifestations (effects). If your thoughts are peaceful, harmonious, constructive, and positive, the manifestations shall be good. If your thoughts are destructive, discordant and negative, the manifestations shall be evil. You must always "image" what you want, which is your inside world. Most people live solely in the outside world, thinking that things come to them externally. But you know better. You know that things, natural or spiritual do not come to you from the outside world. They come *through* you. Be careful of the thoughts you allow to spring up in your mind. If they are of an unpleasant nature, dismiss them immediately and replace them with thoughts of a more positive and productive nature.

All power a person possesses is from within him or her and is developed by a conscious recognition of that power. Most people are clueless of the vast amount of mental power they possess. Professor William James, the famous Harvard Psychologist from the early 1900s estimated that the average human being only uses ten percent of their mental power. That leads one to believe that if we just doubled that percentage, we would achieve extraordinary things in our lives. Can you imagine if we used even 50%? Our mental power can be increased through a perceptive awareness of the use and cooperation with natural laws. When you acquire a clear understanding of cause and effect and then direct that understanding toward manifesting good for yourself and others, you then are able to create any condition that you desire. You will be able to experience in the natural realm those things that you visualize in the mental realm. All thought is creative according to the strength, power, conviction and vitality of the thought.

MEDITATION AND VISION

It is vital that those who desire to tap into their power spend considerable time alone with nothing but their own thoughts. The remarkably successful people in every field take time to commune with themselves. Many people fail to arrive at practical solutions to their problems because they confer with everybody else except themselves. If they only conferred with themselves in the silence, the answers would come to them from God, who knows the answer to every problem. A constructive form of visualization will precede every form of right action. Successful people tap into their creative powers through being alone in the silence, which is where all the power is. Managed solitude pays off. When the mind is peaceful and still, it catches a glimpse of the greater good. Meditation requires strict self-discipline. Removing oneself from the day-to-day hustle and bustle of the job, the phone, the appointments, the Blackberry, the e-mail, the errands, the children, the spouse, the household chores, cooking, preparing for the next day, etc. requires discipline. To actually find the time to be alone with oneself can be invigorating and revitalizing. Silence is a healing, soothing, healthy practice. A very effective technique for obtaining peace is to practice emptying the mind. Practice emptying your mind of worry, frustration, doubt, fear, or insecurities. Make a decision right now to set some time aside each day to be completely alone, undisturbed, and free from distractions and interruptions. Your meditation can be strategic or undirected. In strategic meditation, focus on a specific problem or ideal. Study the ideal or the problem as detailed as you can. If you are seeking a solution, be receptive to the solution and it will come to you. If you are meditating on an ideal, begin to visualize it and mentally see yourself as having it. This will bring the thing near to you. Meditation is connecting the real to the ideal and then receiving insight. Visualize yourself to success. In undirected meditation, you are simply allowing your mind to think about whatever it wants. Let the arbitrary thoughts come out. This is how you empty your mind. You will learn a lot about yourself this way. Once your mind is empty of haphazard thoughts, you can then focus your concentration on a particular ideal or desire.

Consistent visualization through meditation strengthens the mind. When one begins his or her morning or ends his or her day through strategic meditation, it directs the way in the right direction. Meditation frees the mind to think the thoughts desired. Through meditation, one can easily identify negative thoughts and dismiss them accordingly. Arbitrary thoughts are recognized and allowed to pass out of the mind through meditation. The body is relaxed and full control of the physical being is secured. An inflow of energy and power is acquired through mediation. Patience is received and calmness is developed through this process. When one begins to make meditation a habitual action in their life, that person walks with a certain "something" that others see but can not put their hand on. That "something" is called POWER, and can be acquired only in the silence. Power is a silent force that grows stronger as you recognize it and use it for good. It comes when you are at repose. Vigilance is critical during this time. When the mind is empty, something else will enter. It is imperative that once you have freed your mind of unfruitful thoughts, you refill it with thoughts of power, peace, love, success, prosperity and joy.

Like attracts like in the mental and spiritual world. Your thoughts, words and visions are magnets that attract things that are of the same nature of your thought. People, circumstances, and events are arranged in the universe compelling themselves toward you because of the magnetic force exuding from you. When your thought is full of conviction, vitality, and energy, the force going out is strong and things come to you faster. The quality of your thought is the measure of your power. If there is nothing in you to draw towards, nothing can be magnetized to you. There must be a two-way flow going out and coming in. If you are constantly thinking, imaging, feeling, visualizing, meditating, and discussing a specific aspiration, you are creating in the mental and spiritual world those elements that will cause that desire to be attracted to you. When you can see it when you visualize, then it already exists as a real thing in the invisible world. You have already created it with your mind. As you continue to see it in thought and vision, the desire becomes clearer and the strength and force of it becomes stronger. There is now something in your inner world that goes out with magnetic force attracting that desire back to you. That is how it always works. When a businessman wants a skyscraper built, he has to get the plans from the architect. The architect has to get those plans from his imagination. The architect does not have an accurate or complete picture until the businessman gives him very specific details about the way he wants his building constructed. The directions must be clear, concise, detailed, understandable and thorough before the architect can give the businessman exactly what he has asked for. It is the same with you and your desires. What you desire must entail the same clarity when you visualize it. Otherwise, if your desires are vague, unclear, and indistinct, that is what you will get back. You must be clear when you visualize.

      Wishing and hoping for a desire will not bring it into being. You must create what you want in your inner consciousness first. Your inner consciousness is your predominating thought, imagination, vision, labor, discussion, and prayers of a particular ideal desired. You can not concentrate upon your desire for two days a month and think that it is coming to you because of two days of strong wishing and hoping at 15 minutes a time. Your *predominant* thoughts about your desire will bring the thing nearer to you. What you think about the longest becomes the strongest! You must hold that aspiration ever so strongly until it has materialized and dropped right into your circumstances. You must know however, that when your desires come, they will be delivered through people, whose minds would have been unknowingly touched by powers in the universe to navigate circumstances that have been arranged to bring you your desired goal. God uses people as messengers, vessels and instruments to carry out His will and purpose for our lives. Things just don't come to you out of the atmosphere dropping down into your lap. People need people to help get them where they want to go. He uses you to do the same for others. You may not know initially that you are being used and you really don't need to know. Sometimes you never know. That is how God has orchestrated the operation of His universe. Everything you have acquired was given to you with the help of other people. No prosperity or success is ever accomplished by individual effort. It is an utterly obtuse statement to say "I don't need anybody."

THE BENEFITS OF MENTAL EXERCISE

Visualization is a form of imagination. However, the difference between imagination and visualization is that imagination shows you pictures of things, but visualization conceptualizes those pictures and idealizes them. Anyone can drop off into an imagination at any moment not realizing what they are doing at that time. It is comparable to when people drop off into daydreams. Not realizing what is being concentrated upon can predispose one to entertaining negative pictures which have reached them as the result of their mind neglect. He or she is momentarily in a trance, not realizing that they may be attracting disastrous, problematic, negative situations to them by doing this. This can be devastating if those haphazard imaginations manifest. When that happens, people then say that they never envisioned such a horrible situation happening to them. We must remember that "like attracts like." The thoughts we think and the images we focus on consciously or unconsciously bring to us the people, who bring the circumstances, which make the conditions with which we meet. Be careful with random imaginations because what you see, you get. Learn to image only the things that you want to see manifested. Imagination is extremely beneficial when doing it for a purpose. There is much power in strategic imagination, which is watching those moving pictures through the mind's eye. Visualization conceptualizes those images conceived in the mind. Constructive visualization means mental labor and is considered the hardest kind of labor. Most people are mentally lazy, but strategic visualization yields the greatest benefits. All great things in life have come to men and women who have had the courage to be visionaries, to imagine, and to make their dreams come true.

The reward comes to those who are totally committed to achieving success to a very significant degree. Those who want to lift themselves out of the rut of mediocrity and place themselves among the elite, the powerful, and the influential, are the ones who receive what they desire to the exact degree that they have been faithful to their ideal. Those who make the mental, spiritual, and physical sacrifices are those whose creative faculties are widened to a level where they can receive the influx of intuition, ingenuity, and originality when it comes to them. Self-discipline used on a frequent and consistent basis is a sacrifice. This strengthens the mind, body, and spirit.

BALANCING THE MIND, BODY, AND SPIRIT

    As busy as we all are, we are each given the same 24 hours in a day. What we choose to do in those hours determines what we shall have to do in the next 24 hours to come, just as the use we have made in past time has fixed our place in present time. To be prudent and wise is to be able to use time well and when we use time well, we become less stressed about the concerns of tomorrow. To know the right use of the present moment is of extreme importance. Using time to feed your spirit by praying, reading, meditating and fasting, keeps your soul in shape. As you read the Bible to show yourself approved to God, you are actually spending time with God. Keeping a balanced life is essential to walking in prosperity. The mind, body, and spirit must be adequately nourished.

    Mind. The mind guides you and has shaped who you are. In order to keep the mind active, you must fill it with new information on a consistent basis. Reading is one sure way to keep your mind stimulated and active. You could read the newspaper, articles, magazines, journals, books, etc. Reading is a sure way of acquiring knowledge. Keeping abreast of political issues and world news is yet another way; and being aware of current events is yet another. Exposing yourself to other cultures and ways of living is enlightening as well as informative; and traveling to distant lands to learn about the lifestyles of people in other countries is yet another way to keep one's mind stimulated. However, to live solely for the stimulation of the intellect is to be out of balance and out of harmony with God. Satisfying the intellect is only a fraction of what is needed to be well-rounded and balanced.

    Body. Your physical body must also be taken care of adequately because your physical body houses your mind, spirit, and soul. You are actually a spiritual being clothed in a physical body, and although your spirit and soul goes back to God, your physical body does not. Your physical body is temporal, subject to decline, decay, and deterioration. You must do your part in helping to maintain this body until it is ready to completely shut down and return back to the dust. While your spirit resides in your physical body, you must eat, sleep, drink, and breathe accurately and adequately. You must get plenty of exercise and proper nourishment. However, to live solely for the body alone is to be out of balance and out of harmony with God. There is a principle of health in every person and when in full constructive activity, it causes all the voluntary functions of life to perform at optimal levels. When the mind, body, and spirit are sufficiently nourished, there is a balance and a power that you walk with that causes your mental attitude to be positive, harmonious, and constructive. This attitude opens the door for good to be manifested in your life. You are always guided by divine intelligence.

Spirit. Your spirit is who and what you are. You must continuously feed this spirit to keep it healthy just as you do your physical body. Spirit renewal takes place as the Word of God is studied with an open heart led of the Holy Spirit. However, having knowledge of the Word without the Spirit of the Word is ineffective. What does it profit a person to be able to profoundly discourse the Word of God, if he or she is void of the Spirit of God, which leads to humility and a balanced life? Your goal is not just to know the book of the Lord, but to know the Lord of the book. This is why prayer is the foundation upon which every aspect of your life is built. Prayer is keeping the lines of communication open to God, casting all your cares upon Him, praising and honoring Him, and confessing your misdeeds to Him. When there is a balance between prayer, study and fellowship, you can fairly say that you have a pretty balanced spiritual life with some room for improvement. Attending Christian services and fasting for a specific purpose builds upon your spiritual life and further helps to strengthen and feed your soul. However, to live solely in the spirit is to be out of balance and out of harmony with God. Being spiritually strong is only a fraction of living a balanced life. To be overextended in one area is to be weak in another.

Keeping the mind, body and spirit balanced is a necessity and is essential to healthy living. If you find that there is an imbalance, try and rectify it quickly. Many people are over-extended in one area and under extended in another. For instance, some people have a very strong spiritual life, but they have neglected their physical bodies and therefore find themselves having medical and physical challenges. Some people are very much in physical shape. They eat properly and get plenty of exercise, but are malnourished in their soul because of deprivation of prayer, study, and reading the Word. We must stay balanced in order to experience a life of fulfillment and satisfaction. An excess in any one area causes a deficiency in another area. Make sure that you have delegated sufficient time for the growth and development of mind, body, and spirit.

ATTRACTING BIG THINGS

Everything in the universe is God's Spirit manifesting through the things that move. When you get to a place where you have a deep understanding of the power that operates through you, your physical environment and day-to-day affairs will change. Things will begin to form around you according to the predominating power that is magnetizing those things to you. People, circumstances and events will begin shifting themselves towards you in order to fulfill the desires that you have put out into the universe. Results will come to you through your mind. Within your own consciousness is a center from which power flows. That center is the magnet. Toward that center within you will gravitate everything you desire. You must always keep in mind that everything you have, are, and experience came to you through your mind and the only thing you get out of mind is what you have first put into it, therefore, what you think is of the greatest importance.

All manifestation in your life has come to you through you and is backed up by your mental attitude. Life only operates for you by flowing through you, never in any other way. You must always believe that you have received even before you have physically received what you desire. Begin to be receptive and mentally accept things in a big way. Take your desire to the highest possible place it can go mentally in thought. When you believe and direct your thoughts in a certain way, you get results. Your ability to manifest big things depends upon what is in your mind. This is cause and effect. If you are an individual who is accustomed to handling big projects, managing big accounts, interacting with influential, powerful people, and managing huge amounts of money, then you are already attracting big things to you. The center within your consciousness is magnetizing to and exuding from you in an active way already. Like attracts like. If you are not yet operating in this manner then your consciousness needs to be expanded so that you will mentally have the room to receive big things when they come to you.

LIVING WITH THE CONDITIONS THAT YOU HAVE CREATED

If when you look around, you are not satisfied with your home environment, your job, your car, your relationships, or your accomplishments generally, then blame nobody but yourself. Your life is what you have made it. The conditions of your day-to-day living experiences have been created by you. It is true that you had no control over the conditions that you were born into and no control over the things that you saw and heard as a child being raised, but it was up to you to change what you did not like. If your mother or father were alcoholics or drug addicts and neglected you as a child, you had no control over that. You did not ask to be born into those conditions. If you were born into wealth and affluence, attended the finest schools and were exposed to fine culture and art, you did not ask to be born into that either. Fortunately or unfortunately, those things shaped how you perceive situations today and they contribute significantly to your personality. But you reached a point of personal responsibility and you began making decisions that shaped who you became and what you acquired in life thus far. Being born into wealth and affluence did not guarantee that your life would be prosperous and well, just as being born into poverty and lack did not dictate that you would remain poor and deprived. Inequities of life are a reality. Everyone knows and understands that, but God has placed the internal fortitude and strength inside everyone to overcome every obstacle, difficulty, or set-back that the vicissitudes of life may have dealt you. We rejoice to know that the level of your fight is the best indicator as to the level of blessing that waits for you beyond the struggle.

Every person has a higher self and a lower self. The lower self tells you that you are not deserving of greatness, do not have the wherewithal to achieve greatness, and are not smart enough. The lower self tells you that you can only achieve so much and then that's it. This self says that no one else in the family has tried to be better than they are, so why should you? It tells you that you came from nothing and you shall be nothing, that there is a standard made for you and that you should live within that standard only and no higher. Doubt, fear, procrastination, and lack of follow through are the fruits of the lower self and that is what it feeds you with. The higher self tells you that you can be more than you are, do more than you have done, and have more than you have. The higher self nudges you to step out on faith and work at achieving the greater things that you inwardly desire. The higher self craves freedom from lack and limitation, desires abundant living and wants you to walk with character and integrity. The higher self tells you that there is greatness in you, that you are destined for great things and allows you to feel the power inside you. The fruit of the higher self are faith,

courage, perseverance and accomplishment. To thine own self be true. Which self are you going to be true to, the higher or lower self?
A servant can not serve two masters. You will love one and hate the other. Which will you love? Just so you know, the lower self can never change your conditions, only the higher self can.

PRISONERS OF MIND

There are many people in this world who habitually blame everyone else for their lot in life. I have a friend who used to be a social worker at a public assistance agency for economically deprived citizens. She saw many people coming in for a handout on a daily basis. These individuals believed that everybody should help them even though they did not help themselves. My friend was so disheartened by observing these people day to day with no drive, no motivation to get up and make a better life for themselves, no goals, no aspirations, seemingly no hope. They were haphazardly just living from day to day. She prayed and asked the Lord to put her in a position where she could actually talk to the people and convey to them that they could do more and have more with their lives by setting goals for themselves. Her prayer was answered and her position changed. She now had direct contact with clients. When the people complained that they could not secure a job because of lack of money to pay for childcare, the agency provided childcare. When they complained that they could not pay their rent, the agency paid it. When they stated that they had no car, the agency provided transportation to and from their destinations. When they reported that their electricity was getting turned off, the agency paid the light bill. But it was always one excuse after another. My friend soon realized that the vast majority of those individuals did not desire to do any better. It was their way of thinking that was holding them back. When my friend was able to deeply converse with some of them, she discovered that the poverty mindset was so deeply ingrained that she often could not penetrate it. These people were prisoners of their own mind. This puts to mind a quote stated by Franklin D. Roosevelt, which says, *"Men and women are not prisoners of fate, but only prisoners of their own minds."* Unfortunately, there are millions of people who believe that because of some unseen force over which they believe they have no control, they are destined to failure and poverty. Because we manifest what we believe, these people have created their own misfortunes because of

Prosperity is Your Birthright!

this erroneous, negative belief which has been picked up by their subconscious mind. Their mentality has to change before any progress, development, or advancement will take place in their lives. When the frame of mind changes for the better, poverty and prosperity will switch places. Until that happens, they will remain prisoners of poverty in their own minds. Andrew Carnegie says, *"The soundest of all forms of charity is that which helps a man to help himself. That form of help begins by aiding a man to organize his own mind."* When we can reach the poor by penetrating their mind-set, changing their belief system and reprogramming their thought process, then we will see a drastic change in their lives. When they change their belief system, they will change the world, and not just their world, but our world. Why? Because they are in the same world that we are in and the world is changed for the better when people change it through their positive thoughts. The poor do make a difference in this world, just like you make a difference in this world. Success is a mindset. It all goes back to your mental attitude, which stems from your belief system. As each of us change, the whole world changes.

CHAPTER 2 KEY POINTS:

- ❖ Successful people tap into their creative powers through being alone in the silence, which is where all the power is. Managed solitude pays off. When the mind is peaceful and still, it catches a glimpse of the greater good.

- ❖ Prosperity is an outward manifestation of an inward reality.

- ❖ Prosperity is not contingent upon anything that is physical, conditional, or intellectual. It is dependant upon a combination of developed mental and spiritual faculties.

- ❖ Not only does writing your goals down help you to see clearly what it is that you aspire to do, have, or be, but seeing them written motivates you and strengthens that power in you which causes those goals to be manifested.

- ❖ There is a time and a season for everything. Have patience and wait for your season before you step out into your role. Stepping out before the appointed time may obstruct God's plan for your life.

3

OPEN YOUR MIND TO THE INFLUX OF MIRACLES

> *The miracle, or the power that elevates the few is to be found in their mind, application, and perseverance under the prompting of a brave, determined spirit.*
>
> *Mark Twain*

Since the beginning of time there has never been another with your mind, your heart, your spirit, your personality, your eyes, your hair or your mouth. Nobody who came before, no one who lives today, and no one who comes tomorrow will walk or talk or move exactly like you. You are rare, and there is value in rarity, therefore you are valuable! Don't look for miracles because *you* are a miracle. Do not compare yourself with others because you are a unique and beautiful creation. Humanity is made up of millions of individuals, but no two are alike. Every flower, every tree, every blade of grass, every drop of water, every leaf is a little different than its counterparts.

Before we delve into miracles, let's get a clear distinction between the brain and the mind as it relates to receiving miracles. We must clearly understand how and why our beliefs, perceptions, and hereditary tendencies can help or hinder the operation of miracles working in our lives. All too often, these two words, brain and mind are used interchangeably but they are not synonymous terms. The brain is an organ, which is matter. It is that part of the central nervous system that includes all the higher nervous centers enclosed within the skull, which is continuous with the spinal cord. The biggest part of the brain is the cerebrum, which makes up 85% of the brain's weight. The cerebrum is the thinking part of the brain and it controls voluntary muscles. When you are thinking very hard, you are using your cerebrum. Both your short-term and long-term memory lives there. The cerebrum has two halves, one on the left and one on the right side of the head. It has been determined that the right half helps you think about abstract things such as music, colors, and shapes. The left half is said to be more analytical, helping with mathematics, logic, and speech. The left side is commonly used for thought and for the retention of knowledge. Doctors have discovered that the right half of the cerebrum controls the left side of the body, and the left half controls the right side. An injury to the right half of the brain will cause some paralysis of a muscle on the left side and vice versa.

THE MIND AND THE BRAIN

Understanding the relationship between the physical brain and the functional mind is not a difficult one. I have just given you some basic information that I am sure you already knew regarding the function of the brain. This information was presented as an introduction to understanding the role that your mind plays in relation to your brain. The first thing you should know is that the mind is not produced by the brain. The mind enhances the brain through thought instead of the brain making thought. The brain is merely the instrument of the one who thinks, just as a piano is the instrument of the one who plays. Without being used, it is useless and can do nothing. In a nutshell, the brain is only a recording instrument for the mind and personality behind it. When you were born, the record in your brain was blank. There was no impression made on any part as yet. No-one knew what you were to become or grow into. You could have been a doctor, lawyer, teacher, politician, mechanic, vagabond, con-artist, or murderer. No one knew. It was all dependent upon the seed that was concealed within your mind, which would eventually shape your personality. Your environment played a vital role in what you evolved into as well as the experiences and exposure you had, but it was your mind that determined how your environment was to affect you. There were already certain genetic tendencies in your make-up inherited from your ancestors, but those are easy to overcome by placing opposing habits in place of the unfavorable ones. You can imprint whatever you want upon your brain, but it is your mind that determines how you shall respond to those things.

The brain is like a tape recorder which records things on a particular brain locality and retrieves those things upon request. Brain-building requires mental labor, concentration and self-discipline, but the reward is great for the person who makes the sacrifice. If your mind gives you the desire for a noble personality, you must imprint upon your brain the desire for this noble change. You can not show forth an honest, noble, and humble personality until your mind gives you the desire for it. It is commonly understood that the consistent use of certain faculties is dependent upon certain localities in the brain. There is a locality for speaking, reading, computing mathematical figures, singing, dancing, and playing musical instruments. According to the tools you give it, so will the expression of your soul be. Desires originate in the mind first, then are written upon the brain. The mental or physical exercise needed is then executed. What really matters is the desire in the mind to progress in positive ways. That is what makes your personality. The mind simply makes the expression through the brain. We often make two mistakes as it pertains to brain-power. We underestimate our own brain-power and overestimate the brain-power of others. The people that we perceive as ingenious are only those who have exercised the self-discipline that it takes to expand their brain-power, but it is not brain power that we should seek. It is actually "mind" power. The thing to do is to stop seeking to become smarter through brain-building, but actually strive to become wiser through mind development.

YOUR PERCEPTIONS AND BELIEF SYSTEM

Now that we have an understanding of the fact that it is your mind that makes your brain, then the question arises: Where does the mind come from? The mind is spiritual, which came from God. He gave you your mind, your spirit and your soul. He also gave you free-will and self-choice to shape your mind the way you would have it to be once you entered the age of understanding. The mind is totally independent of the brain, but it molds the brain as a potter molds clay. Mind cannot be located anywhere in the body. It is spiritual. When you were born, your mind connected to your body, although the mind had not yet been developed. Within your mind was your personality, a particular formula, and a seed that was to make you into the unique person that you are. All that you are and every experience that you have had contributes to how you see things in the world around you. Your personality is the result of experiences and environment which has been shaped by what you have been taught and what you have seen and heard throughout your lifetime. If you have been taught that miracles happen and can occur in your life, then your mind is open to miracles and they can manifest in your life easily. If you are around people who are constantly manifesting their desires and achieving success to a noteworthy degree, then you will believe that you can do the same. Your mind plays a very important role in the belief system that you hold. Some people have put up a wall against change and hold on ever so tightly to their superstitions and hand-me-down tradition that they are against anything contrary to their beliefs. They do this simply because it's been carried down from generation to generation, most often without any careful analysis or scrutiny. Is it likely that a negative, pessimistic, complaining person will experience miracles in their life? You must be positive in order to allow the operation of miracles into your life. When you are positive, you see that your life will change for the better. Analyze your thoughts on a daily basis. Determine whether the nature of your predominating thoughts is positive or negative. Recognize any hindering thoughts and/or beliefs and replace them with constructive thoughts of faith and courage.

JUST BELIEVE

Belief is the key that will unlock the door to your greatest desires. When I think of a person who had a belief that was strong, unshakable, and unwavering, I think of the woman with the issue of blood from Mathew Chapter 9 in the Bible. This woman knew beyond a shadow of a doubt that if she could just touch the hem of Jesus' garment, she would be healed. She did not doubt by saying to herself, "What if it doesn't work?" Had she doubted in her heart, one could certainly have understood. After all, she had seen many doctors and none could cure her. She had been bleeding for 12 years, had undergone many treatments, and yet she still suffered. She was dying. Blood represents life. She was losing blood each day from a slow hemorrhage, therefore she was losing life with each passing day. However, in spite of the many years, the many tears, the disappointments and wasted money, she never gave up. She had only heard about Jesus and His miracles, believed in her heart that He could heal her, and decided to find Him. She had faith in His miracle-working power. This woman was bold, but unassuming. Her persistence indicated that she was an unusual person, but a determined one. Desperate times call for desperate measures and this woman was desperate to be healed. She did not let discouragement, frustration or distress keep her from finding a healing that she knew in her heart was out there. When she heard of Jesus, she got right up and sought to find Him. That is a rare confidence for a woman living back in those times. It is actually a rare confidence for today's times. We tend to accept the prognosis given to us as our final analysis. By many standards, most would have given up and given in to their affliction, but not this woman! She refused to let that sickness be the death of her. Her strategic plan to press her way to Jesus was a decision of real courage, and her persistence, boldness, and determination paid off. The same principle applies to your life and the miracle that you are seeking. As she was, so must you be persistent, bold, determined and expectant!

A miracle is never a coincidence regardless of how extraordinary or momentous it may be. A miracle is a supernatural intervention from the normal course of events. It is a divine overriding of, or interference with, natural order. It is something other than a coincidence. Dr. Eric Mascall, Oxford lecturer in the philosophy of religion asserts that the word miracle signifies in Christian Theology, *"a striking interposition of divine power by which the operations of the ordinary course of nature are overruled, suspended, or modified."* Do you believe that God can override the normal course of things just to bring you a miracle? He certainly can, if you just believe. In order to open your mind to receive miracles, your mind has to believe that miracles do happen. Everything is done unto you to the degree that you believe. When Jesus was working miracles, He assured us that we have the same power to do even as He did, but to a greater degree. Why then do we not perform these miracles? The answer is that we doubt our power. There is great power in believing. Belief determines what you accomplish in life and how far you will go. Others see in you what you see in yourself. If you believe that you are a miracle and you believe that miracles can operate in your life, then others will think that same thing about you too. Your mind must always be in a state of receptivity. Expect that a supernatural intervention can and will happen in your life at any given moment. It is when you are open to God working through you that you receive miracles, signs, and wonders. Be always in an expectancy state of mind. God performs miracles in you, through you, and around you, but you must be open to receiving. Your receptivity has to be wide enough for God's expression to be performed in your life unhindered. Open your mind to the influx of all that God has for you.

A WALKING MIRACLE

Yes, you are a walking miracle, and you are *"fearfully and wonderfully made." (Psalm 139:14).* You are valuable in God's sight and He loves you deeply and cares about every aspect of your life. There is a reason that you have the personality that you do, the desires that you do, the eccentricities that you do. There is a reason that you are different from everybody else. He made you unique for His own purpose. One of my favorite quotes written by Marianne Williamson is the following: *"A tulip doesn't strive to impress anyone. It doesn't struggle to be different than a rose. It doesn't have to. It is different. And there's room in the garden for every flower."* If you are not content with the person that God has made you to be inside and out, then you will never truly be content or able to accept anyone else and their flaws because you do not deeply accept yourself and the person you are. We see in others what we see in ourselves. We often tend to size up everybody we encounter but ourselves. The way you see others is a reflection of how you see yourself. If you are a trusting person, then you see others as trusting. If you are a critical person, then you see others as critical. If you are a compassionate person, then you see others as caring. If you can see God in everything, God will look back at you through everything. Until you are able to accept who you are, the color of your skin, how you look, and how God created you to be, you will always find fault in others. If you are not comfortable with yourself, you will never be comfortable with anyone else. T.D. Jakes wrote in his book, 'The Lady, Her Lover, and Her Lord' *"When we don't value ourselves, we tend to attract people who support that devalued image."* Love and respect yourself for your uniqueness and individuality. Have a healthy love and respect for who you are, and when you do, you will be able to love others for who they are and all that God created them to be. Self-approval is essential to healthy living. It is the catalyst from which your goals are emanated, pursued, and accomplished. A negative self image will keep you from being successful. Self-hatred, fear, guilt, shame, and unforgiveness block your growth. It is time for us to forgive ourselves, love ourselves, and move forward with confidence in ourselves. Watch how your new self-perception carries over into every aspect of your life including your relationships, your professional interactions, and ultimately the world around you. By loving yourself, you open up the possibility for others to love you too. Having confidence in yourself is not being arrogant. It is being self-assured, which is very necessary in order to maintain healthy relationships with others. Walk in this world with humility and grace, yet be confident and fearless!

You are who you are for a reason.
You're part of an intricate plan.
You're a precious and perfect unique design.
Called God's special woman or man.

You look like you do for a reason.
Our God made no mistake.
He knit you together within the womb.
You're just what He wanted to make.

The parents you had were the ones He chose,
And no matter how you may feel,
They were custom-designed with God's plan in mind,
And they bear the master's seal.

No, the trauma you faced was not easy.
And God wept that it hurt you so,
But it was allowed to shape your heart
So that into His likeness you'd grow.

You are who you are for a reason,
You've been formed by the Master's rod.
You are who you are beloved,
Because there is a wonderful God.

Russell Kelfer

USING YOUR GOD-GIVEN AUTHORITY

You walk with power and authority within you. Do you know how pervasive that power is? If you knew the amount of supernatural supremacy that you have within, you would never be deceived by the natural appearances of things again. What a shame it would be for all of your power to be untapped and unused, but revealed to you on judgment day when you meet your Maker face to face. What if you were to ask the Lord why He allowed you to be sick and He showed you the healing power inside of you that you did not use to heal yourself. What if you were to ask Him why you lived in poverty and He showed you all the wealth and abundance that surrounded you on a daily basis that you never took hold of? What if you were to ask Him why you never seemed to have any opportunities, and He showed you the many doors that were opened just for you to walk though, but you kept going through the wrong doors? What if you asked God why this and why that, and He showed you the solutions that resided within you to solve every problem that you ever faced? What a shame that would be for all your power to have been wasted. Do not wait until that day, but find the channel now whereby you may tap into the power within you to solve every problem, difficulty, or predicament in your life. You have all the tools needed right now to solve any problem you face. Those tools are your mind, body, and spirit. Your mind is the source from which your thoughts originate and are manifested into your reality. Your body is the instrument by which God expresses Himself through you by means of seeing, hearing, touching, tasting, smelling, and moving. Your spirit is where God resides, and through it, He communicates with you. When you walk in authority, external circumstances no longer dictate your actions, but you control your circumstances exactly the way you want them to be.

The Lord Jesus Christ left this authority for you after His ascension to heaven, but you have to make the choice to accept it and use it. The earth is ours to rule and this authority has never been taken back from us. You have total power and authority over your environment and ultimately your destiny. Through this authority, you can improve yourself, change yourself, recreate yourself, control your environment and master your destiny. All things are in subjection to you and are under your feet. You are not subjected to any forces of evil. On the contrary, they are supposed to be subjected to you, but when you do not use the power and authority you have, the enemy wreaks havoc in your life and causes chaos, disharmony, and all sorts of confusion and disorder. Those evil forces, opposing the will of God have free reign over all that is yours. You must use the power that is within you, which was given to you by the Lord, the Maker and Creator of the universe. God has given you free-will and self-choice. He is not going to force you to use your power. He will not compel you to exercise your authority. He has told you in His Word that the power is within you. When you are ready to use your power, it is ready, available, and will emerge in you. Recognize it. Take hold of it. Use it! It is this truth that you need to know, because it will make you free.

YOUR GOD-GIVEN AUTHORITY

You walk with God-given authority and when you begin fully knowing and recognizing that truth, you will begin to exude a confidence that all will see and feel. Demons will flee from you because of the authority and power that you walk with. You cannot exhibit a demonstration of God's power if you do not believe you have it. Without authority you cannot have any kind of rulership over anything. With authority, you will be recognized in the spirit and also in the natural as a powerful being. In the natural, the power and authority may not easily be identified by a name, but people will know that there is something mystical that you walk with. If you went to the nearest intersection and began directing traffic with ordinary clothes on, not many would regard you as having authority to direct traffic. You may even get run over if you are not careful. But if you were to begin directing traffic with a police officer's uniform on, you could step into that intersection, hold your hand up, and traffic would come to a halt. Cars would stop because you would be recognized as having designated authority. You should be recognized in the spirit world as a person with designated authority as well. You also should be identified in the natural as a person who walks with supernatural authority. Man has ignorantly given his authority to the enemy, but the enemy can only use that power through man. Evil Forces can only influence the world to the degree that people choose to sin and live in disobedience to God. When they do this, they contaminate and eventually relinquish any true authority they have. Those who exercise authority with selfish motives are corrupt, regardless of their pretentious piety. It is important to realize that when we are truly surrendered to Christ, we are to handle authority with the greatest care, knowing that we are His servants. No one is established authoritatively unless God allows it. God does share His authority with His people, and used in humility and wisdom, authority is a powerful tool. But when that power is used for self-exaltation, then leadership, effectiveness, and credibility is weakened, and we do those under our leadership a great disservice. Use the power of authority that is within you and use it for your highest good and the highest good of others. That is the will of God for your life.

CHAPTER 3 KEY POINTS:

- ❖ If you want a noble personality, you must imprint upon your brain the desire for this noble change. You can not show forth an honest, noble, and humble personality until you have written honest and noble desires upon your brain.

- ❖ A miracle is never a coincidence regardless of how extraordinary or momentous it may be.

- ❖ If you are not content with the person that God has made you to be inside and out, then you will never truly be content or able to accept anyone else and their flaws.

- ❖ The Lord Jesus Christ left this authority for you after His ascension to heaven, but you have to make the choice to accept it and use it.

- ❖ If you knew the amount of supernatural power that you have within, you would never be deceived by the natural appearances of things again.

4

SHARE YOUR GIFTS WITH THE WORLD

> *When I stand before God at the end of my life, I would hope that I would not have a single bit of talent left, and could say, "I used everything you gave me."*
> *Erma Bombeck*

When you were born, you had a gift that God placed inside you to be used for His glory. This gift has been tailor-made exclusively for you, and no one can bring forth the gift inside you but you. Many people know what their gift is, and in knowing what your gift is and using it, you are walking in your divine purpose. It is a liberating feeling to know that you are fulfilling the assignment that God placed you on this earth to complete. There is satisfaction and gratification, a sense of fulfillment each time you do something in connection with it, and total pleasure in doing it. Unfortunately, there are many people who do not know what their gift is, and in not knowing, they are unfulfilled and dissatisfied with life. In some people the gifts are easy to recognize and with others, the gifts appear to be hidden. God created you for His purpose and when you seek Him for answers, He provides those answers concerning your life. You did not create yourself, therefore you can not know what you were created for until He reveals it to you. Many people in this world are living their lives unfulfilled. There is nothing more frustrating in life than being unfulfilled in your purpose. God has individually given each of us an assignment. Before you were born, He wrote in the Lamb's Book of Life what your assignment was to be on earth. Your purpose in this life is in direct proportion with the gifts that God has placed inside you. It could be something that you view as insignificant. We tend to call things insignificant if those things are not glamorous or in the spotlight. Your gifts may be something as modest and humble as sewing clothes or fixing appliances. It could be that you are gifted in mechanics. You may be able to sing or dance. You may be a creative writer or a meticulous painter or carpenter. Some people can play an instrument by ear, but cannot read music. That is a gift. You could be brilliant with numbers, great with encouraging other people, an outstanding artist, or a first-rate cook. You may have a gift for cleaning, building things or writing poetry. God has given each of us at least one gift to be used for His glory, but whatever your gift is, no one can do it the unique way you can. Although there may be others with skill in the same area as your gift, there is something about the way *you* do it. That "something" is the anointing that God has placed upon you for your particular gift and when you do it, there is a power that goes forth from you that no one else has, unless they are using their God-anointed gift.

God seeks expression through us each and every day and He expresses Himself through men, women, and children. The variation of gifts we have are all for God. He wants mouth pieces to sing beautiful songs for Him and to speak His truths. He wants hands to play harmonious music, draw beautiful pictures, and build magnificent skyscrapers for Him. He wants eyes to behold His beautiful creations and to experience His miracles. He wants feet to dance for Him and run His errands. He wants to express Himself through us because it is Him that enjoys all these things. Ernest Holmes said in his book, *This Thing Called You* that, "*An unexpressed person is incomplete.*" Life is an unfoldment from the cradle to the grave. Most of us have many gifts, but we all have at least one. Those many gifts that some of us have are usually developed from opening the channel to the use of the one main gift. The others emerge as outgrowths. Once you start using your God-given talent, a domino effect begins to follow and you begin expressing other talents you never knew you had. Once the one main faculty is opened and developed, it leads to other faculties being opened and there is no limit to how far and how high you can go.

Only as high as I reach can I grow.
Only as far as I seek can I go.
Only as deep as I look can I see.
Only as much as I dream can I be.

Karen Raven

The key is to take your particular talent to a level where it has never been taken before. With the gifts you have been imparted with, comes the responsibility to use and develop them. Keep your effort on the areas where you shine. Some of the things other people find uninteresting can actually energize and enrich you if it's your gift.

AN UNOPENED GIFT

In the Bible parable of the talents, the master prepared to go on a long journey, but before leaving, he gave each of his servants different amounts of talents. When he returned back from his journey, he approached each of his servants expecting a profit from the talents that he had left them with. One servant in particular did absolutely nothing with the talent that he was given. The other servants worked and multiplied their talents, but the one servant hid his in a napkin. He thought he was actually doing something commendable by returning the master's talent back to him unused and untouched, but that infuriated the master. The master was expecting a profit from him just as the other servants had made a profit with their talents. As a result of doing nothing with the talent, the one he had was taken from him and he was called *wicked*. The Parable of the Talents is one of the stories Jesus told to teach a moral lesson. Although the word "talents" in the story refers to money, you can obviously extend the meaning to the spiritual talents that God has placed inside of you. This simple story makes some interesting points that are applicable to the pursuit of personal development. First, we are all given a different starting position. Some of us are born into abundance (five talents). Others are born into scarcity (one talent). But what matters is not what we are given, but what we do with it. Jesus acknowledges the inequities of life, but He also suggests that our starting conditions are irrelevant. The person with five talents earned five more, and the one with two talents earned two more, but both were rewarded evenly because both earned a 100% gain. What can we learn from this story? We need to use whatever "talent" God has given to us. It might be money or ability. Whatever it is, if we use it wisely, He will increase it, but if we don't use it, we will lose it. Make a list of the things you do well. Use those talents for God. You may discover that after using your talent, He has doubled it. Find a way to use all your talents for His Honor.

Prosperity is Your Birthright!

RECOGNITION OF YOUR GIFTS

Once you have recognized what your unique gift is, you must then exercise it. It is not always easy for people to recognize what their gift is and this can be frustrating. I see this in many people who are happily married with children. I also see that people who are content with mediocrity have a hard time recognizing what their gift is. It has often occurred that when individuals are content with family life (their spouses and children), they tend to live the majority of their lives for them, oftentimes neglecting their own personal goals. Their goals typically are put on the backburner, and their focus is on their children and/or their spouse. Their happiness comes from making their children and/or spouse happy. In most cases, these individuals are fairly pleased with life because family indeed is fulfilling and rewarding. It is a blessing to be able to come home to a loving family, to be needed and relied upon, to love and care for them and have them love you in return. It is equally satisfying to be able to emotionally support one's spouse and assist in fulfilling his or her dreams. It is sometimes not until the spouse has achieved all of his or her goals and the children are all grown up that one realizes that they have not really done much for themselves. Their spouse has a gratifying sense of personal achievement, the children are off and doing well with the guidance and support that was provided for them and everybody else is doing well and feeling fulfilled except them. When it's all said and done, "What have I accomplished for myself?" is the question that one asks. What personal fulfillment (unrelated to family) have I experienced? They've spent so much time giving to everyone else that they never really took the time to find out what they really wanted to achieve out of life for themselves. This is usually when individuals sit back and ponder as to where all the time went. During this deep reflection, individuals actually ask themselves what their real purpose in life is. You must ensure that your life has balance. Nurturing your family is admirable and essentially your reasonable duty as a mother, father, son or daughter, but you must take the time for yourself to discover what extraordinary and unique gift is inside you. You must then take the time to utilize your gift. If the gift inside is not easily recognizable, then God is always ready to answer prayers. In fact, He says in Jeremiah 29:11, *"For I know the thoughts that I think toward you, says the Lord, thoughts of peace, and not of evil, to give you an expected end"*. In His Word, it is also written that if you seek, you shall find. *Ask, and it shall be given you; seek, and ye shall find;*

knock, and it shall be opened unto you. (Mathew 7:7). Only He knows why He created you and He desires that you know too. You were made by God for God. It is only in Him that you discover your purpose, your meaning, your destiny. Before you were even conceived, He had plans for you and designed an assignment specifically for you.

Your gift is given to you to be exercised to the greatest potential. If you have a gift for encouraging people and lifting their spirits, then you need to do this every opportunity you get. If someone calls you at two o'clock in the morning, you need to wake up and use your gift of encouragement to make them feel better. With practice, every talent gets better and grows stronger. You must not hide your gift. It must come into fruition and by your constant use of it, other gifts will be discovered. As you use your God-given talent, you are actually walking in the unfolding of your destiny, because your gifts correspond with your destiny. Know that you are on the right road when you are using your gifts, especially for His glory and honor. Can't you feel it inside? Don't you feel the power rising in you when you do the thing that you absolutely love? Recognize it! Claim it! Unify yourself with it! Become acquainted with it! It is already inside you waiting to come forth. Let it come forth in a powerful way!

SELF-EDUCATION

We have all heard that education is the key to success, but a more accurate statement is that, "The *application* of education is the key to success". If knowledge is applied and guided strategically, it leads one to success. Education or knowledge is only latent power if not used. In the world we live in today, a college education is highly valued and respected. The more college degrees a person has, the more "intelligent" that person is viewed in society's eye. More often than not, people without a formal education are looked down upon and regarded as failures unless they have become extremely successful in a massive way in spite of their lack of education; but unfortunately there are many people who go through life with inferiority complexes because they are not educated in the formal sense of the word. It is also unfortunate that although American public schools are free, they are not taken advantage of to the extent that they should or could be. Perhaps the fact that it is free may be the reason that it is not taken advantage of. We seem to value only things with a high price tag. The textbooks, classroom instruction, certified teachers, and hot meals are free for most children in public schools. Tax payers pay for it, but despite its accessibility, public education is still taken for granted. In American public schools, a high-school diploma is available to any student who attends classes and completes assignments accurately. At any rate, the majority of schoolwork in grades K-12 is mostly memorization. In this country, if one has a good memory, that person is considered intelligent. If a student can retain and reiterate information taught to him or her and spit out that information in words or on paper accurately, he or she is in very good shape because that is basically what elementary, middle, and high school is about, memorization. In my opinion, the American government is extremely generous in allowing our children to attend public schools at no cost. There are some countries where an education must be paid for, and if a family is economically disadvantaged, the children do not receive the benefit of an education. In America, financial arrangements for higher learning after high school must be made, but the opportunity for a high-school diploma is available to all America's children.

    I certainly agree that a college education is needed in America today and should be sought in as many ways as possible, but the traditional form of education behind four walls in a classroom is not the only method of education and does not work for everybody. Self-teaching is another form of education. We are all self-taught to a certain extent. Self-education is a beneficial and valuable form of education that anyone can acquire because this kind of information is initiated by the individual with the intention to truly learn. This form of education is retained easier because the person who seeks the knowledge has a personal interest, and when there is a vested interest in anything, there is concentration and attention there. Dependency on self to find and apply information is a powerful skill, but the knowledge acquired must be used for personal growth and development. This is a valuable asset used by great achievers. When the art of self-education is mastered, a person may travel the world without walking out of their front door. Opportunities to acquire success beyond one's wildest dreams are discovered through self-knowledge if the information is rightly applied. Self-educated people are not dependent upon others for knowledge. If a specialized skill is needed, that person knows how to acquire it without dependence on teachers, professors, or others. Of course it is always wise to seek the assistance of experts in the field, but when that is not always feasible, a person should know where to get the information for themselves. A person who knows where and how to find information for anything they desire to know and then knows how to take that information and organize it into plans for a specific purpose, is already educated, regardless of whether they have formal schooling or not. In fact, Dale Carnegie stated in his book, 'How to Win Friends and Influence People' that, *"The person who has technical knowledge, plus the ability to express ideas, to assume leadership and to arouse enthusiasm among people... is headed for higher earning power."* He did not say one word about having a formal education. Any person whose brain is developed normally can learn anything that is to be learned or become anything that is possible to become. It is all a matter of will. Make it your business to always be expanding and enlarging your capacity to know and experience. Ideally, self-education should supplement formal education, but when there is the absence of a formal education a person may educate themselves. When a person uses self-knowledge to acquire anything they want or its equivalent, that person is truly educated.

In the business world, people are promoted because of their abilities to learn new skills fast. Supervisors may not recognize an individual's learning style, but they do recognize results, and in corporate America, that is all that counts. People who know how to educate themselves have the ability to advance in any endeavor. Classroom education was designed by intellectuals for intellectuals, and in the academic setting, anyone who does not have the ability to put clear thoughts on paper is labeled a failure. Natural skills, talents, and abilities including mechanical skills do not count unfortunately. Non-academic skills are typically ignored. This is because the curriculum usually only recognizes academic and cognitive skills. A person who has the gift of potentially becoming a great welder or mechanic is labeled a failure in a pure academic setting. However, great achievers in life use creativity and intestinal fortitude to overcome barriers such as the ones they may have encountered in the classroom. Teaching to a test does not inspire a love for learning nor does it motivate anyone to want to further enhance their knowledge. The goal of formal education should be to develop a love to learn that stays with a person throughout a lifetime. Education is a lifetime experience.

When it comes to your natural gifts, talents, and abilities, it should be your priority to learn everything about this skill as you possibly can. If

Prosperity is Your Birthright!

you were born with the innate ability to do something that most people can not do, then educate yourself on the intricacies that go with the gift. Expand your knowledge of the skill so that it will be the source by which wealth comes into your life. Study the person who is the best in his or her field. Research them, learn from them, but do not worship them. Your goal is to become better than them. You will not be ill-prepared and you will not be mediocre if you take the time to learn, study, and research your skill. You will be the best in the game if you do this. Robert Collier says in his book 'Secret of the Ages', the following as it pertains to being well-equipped: *"Only as you are equipped for service can you serve; only as you serve are you of value to others; only as you are of value to others are you paid."* There are many people who have achieved great success and prosperity without a college education. What they did have was a gift not recognized in the classroom, but one they harnessed in ways that made them prosperous beyond their wildest dreams. Success is not the result of making money, however. Making money is the result of success.

You only earn money *after* you are successful. When you focus on serving people, the money will come. Your objective should be on servicing more people in a useful way that will bring meaning, joy, and a contribution to the world. When you focus on this, the money will come. Money comes as a result of the degree of service you render. The amount of money that comes to you is a measuring stick for the amount and quality of service you have given. The following people were self-educated and used that education to serve people in an impactful way using projects as their education tools. Academic achievement was a by-product. Some never went to school while others received very little schooling. The ideas of these people changed the way we still live today:

Abraham Lincoln (1809-1865)
Sixteenth president of the United States, responsible for the abolition of slavery; led the country through its greatest internal crisis, the American Civil War; noted for making the following statement regarding slavery: *"If slavery is not wrong, then nothing is*

wrong." In his famous Emancipation Proclamation, he announced that all slaves in the Confederate States would be freed on January 1, 1863.

Formal Education: About 1 year

Thomas Edison (1847-1931)
Inventor of the electric light, microphone, telephone receiver; received over 1,093 patents

Formal Education: None, educated at home by his mother

Henry Ford (1863-1947)
Was the American founder of the Ford Motor Company and father of modern assembly lines used in mass production; was awarded 161 U.S. patents; became one of the richest and best-known people in the world. Millions of people drive "Ford" cars today.

Formal Education: Attended school until he was 15 then dropped out

Walt Disney (1901-1966)
Co-founded "The Walt Disney Company", which today has annual revenues of approximately $35 billion; he created many of the world's most famous fictional characters including Mickey Mouse and Donald Duck

Formal Education: 1 year of high school

Alexander Graham Bell (1847-1922)
Invented the telephone; formed Bell Telephone Company; founded a school for deaf mutes

Formal Education: Schooled by his mother at home

Wright Brothers: Wilber Wright (1867-1912) Orville Wright (1871-1948)
Inventors of the first airplane

> Formal Education: None. Were both home schooled by their mother.

Frederick Douglass (1817-1895)
Black Abolitionist and Orator; born a slave; published three autobiographies; was taught the letters of the alphabet by his master's wife; taught himself to write by tracing the letters on the prows of ships.

> Formal Education: None

The point here is that an educated person is not particularly one with college degrees. You may educate yourself and not have one college degree or diploma under your belt, yet you could be the one to change the world through the use of your mind through self-education. Self-education is your gift to yourself and this you can share with the world. College teaches a person in a specific field of study only. That's why there are so many degrees and certificates out there because there are so many different fields of study. You may not have one college degree, yet you may be able to educate a person with a degree on a particular area they know absolutely nothing about because their education was directed in a designated field of study only. The key is to educate yourself. It does not matter whether you do it by way of the classroom or by way of self-knowledge. A formal education is definitely an asset and

advantage, but not having one should never be used as an excuse for a person's lot in life or justification for poverty or lack. People who make excuses don't make money and people who make money don't make excuses. If you really want to do something you'll find a way. If you don't, you'll find an excuse. The key is to continue learning, especially in the areas where you are talented and use the information to help you grow and prosper. Education for you should only end after your spirit has returned back to God. Other than that, you should be continuously learning each and every day. As I close, I will leave you with this quote from Dr. Martin Luther King, Jr. which says, *"Everybody can be great because everybody can serve. You don't have to have a college degree to serve. You don't have to make your subject and verb agree to serve... You only need a heart full of grace. A soul generated by love.*

MAKE ROOM FOR YOUR GIFTS

You were put on this earth to make a contribution to the world. That is why you exist – to contribute, to serve, to give of yourself, to reach towards your highest good, and to make a difference in the world. Making the world a better place to live is the duty of all mankind. When you share your gifts with the world, you are contributing to mankind in a positive way. Those gifts were placed in you so that God can express Himself in the world through you. If you do not accomplish what God has called you to do through your gifts, it will never get done. You have an assignment that must be completed before you leave this earth. No-one can complete your assignment but you, just as no one can breathe your air for you. You must express yourself with the confidence and assurance that you will complete your assignment by using your gifts, and you will complete this assignment with excellence. There is room for you and your talents, but you must compel that room. The world is only harsh to individuals who do not compel room for their gifts. Whatever your action will be concerning the strengthening of your gifts, that action is to be done right now, not sometime in the future, but right now. You can not act in the future because the future is not here. Although you should prepare for it, it is not promised. You can not act in the past because the past is gone forever. You can only act now. Do not wait for a change of environment before you begin expressing your gifts, but make a change of environment by using your gifts now. Hold to the vision of what you want and begin acting right now today. Use your gifts to make a better life for yourself. Capitalize on your gifts. They are yours to use in any way you choose, but always for good. You may use your particular gifts to bring money, abundance, and prosperity to yourself. Your life will be empty if you are not useful and there will be a void that will remain until you become a meaningful contributor to the world. Rewards will follow service, receiving will follow giving, and leaving an impression will follow making a difference. You will perform your best when contributing your talents to something that you believe in. Contrary to what you may think, you do make a difference in this

Prosperity is Your Birthright!

world. Life is to be enjoyed and you will enjoy it most when you are doing the things that make you feel the most gratified. When you begin to share your gifts with the world with the intention to serve, you will receive far in excess to what you give.

> Yesterday is but a dream.
> Tomorrow is only a vision,
> But today well lived
> makes every yesterday
> a dream of happiness,
> and every tomorrow
> a vision of hope.
> Look well therefore to this day!

CHAPTER 4 KEY POINTS:

- ❖ God seeks expression through us each and every day and He expresses Himself through men, women, and children. The variation of gifts we have are all for God.

- ❖ Jesus acknowledges the inequities of life, but He also suggests that our starting conditions are irrelevant.

- ❖ You were made by God for God. It is only in Him that you discover your purpose, your meaning, your destiny.

- ❖ A person who knows where and how to find information for anything they desire to know and then knows how to take that information and organize it into plans for a specific purpose, is already educated.

- ❖ Life is to be enjoyed and you will enjoy it most when you are doing the things that make you feel the most gratified.

5
PREPARE TO RECEIVE WHAT YOU BELIEVE

> *All men dream, but not equally. Those who dream by night in the dusty recesses of their minds, wake in the day to find that it was vanity, but the dreamers of the day are powerful men, for they act on their dreams with open eyes, to make them possible.*
>
> *Thomas E. Lawrence*

Believing is the key to acquiring what you want. Once your consciousness has been expanded to a level where all your aspirations are becoming evident in your life, you must then make the preparation for them so that when they arrive, you may properly receive them. If you ask for, pray for, and mediate for success, but you subconsciously prepare for failure, you will get what you *"prepare"* for. You must prepare for the thing that you have envisioned when there isn't even the slightest sign of it in sight. Desiring, planning, speaking about and visualizing what you want is great. These are the preliminary steps that you must take in order to achieve the object of your desires, but your subconscious mind must accept everything that you do and say about your desires as existent facts. This is why when you speak of your ideal, you speak with conviction, assurance, confidence, feeling and great expectancy. Things come to you through your subconscious mind, which is your inner world. It is what does the manifesting. When your subconscious mind has taken your conscious desire as an existent fact with no doubt or fears, but absolute faith, you then have what you want. It is only a matter of time before your desires manifest. It is of the greatest importance that you know this. For this reason you repeat your affirmation, review your goals, develop timelines for yourself, visualize your ideals, and speak of things in the present tense. When you do these things, you are impressing upon your subconscious mind that you already have these things, and the subconscious mind will create the physical environment that embodies those

Prosperity is Your Birthright!

things. When your concept is big and your belief is unwavering, you will get the biggest flow into your life. You can only receive what you "see" yourself receiving. There are no big things or little things in God. What you perceive as big, you often think is hard to acquire; whereas, something that you perceive as small may be simple to acquire in your mind. There is no big or little in God. If you think you can experience only a little good, then you will experience only a little good. The things that we view as big are limits that we have given to ourselves as it relates to acquiring them. Our belief sets the limit on everything. To a millionaire who never had to worry about monetary things as an issue, one million dollars may be viewed as a relatively small amount of money. Millions of dollars may flow in and out of his or her life easily with no contemplation on where it comes from or where it goes. On the contrary, to an economically deprived person, one million dollars may appear to be a humungous amount of money. To that person, a million dollars may seem impossible to obtain. Having this erroneous belief of a million dollars being impossible to obtain, it will be for the person who actually believes that. When you believe that things are hard to acquire, then they will be. As high as you make your mark in your mind and spirit, that is how big your outward manifestation will be. It is the nature of God to give us only what we are able to take. It is unto you as you believe. For the record, I would like to declare that, *"I know a million dollars will come to me and you, (the reader of this book) easily and quickly with no strain on our part. I speak this, decree it, declare it, claim it and unify with it for both you and I!"* The question is, *Are you ready to receive a million dollars when it comes to you?* If you are consciously in a state of receptivity and expecting big things to come to you, they will surely come, including money. Your consciousness must be widened in order to receive big projects, large amounts of money and prominent people into your life. Stop pursuing small things. Stop setting small goals. Unify yourself in your consciousness with bigger things than you normally would. If you want a higher position on your job, do not go after the position right above you, go after the one above that one. If you do not yet have the credentials for that one, then get the credentials. One thing that limits our progress is the fact that we are so used to "ordering medium" meaning to settle for less than the best or highest. God made us "extra large", not medium, so start ordering and expecting extra large. Make a realistic estimate of your skills and abilities, then raise it ten percent. Stop hanging around people with no goals, no ambition, petty conversation, and a negative outlook on life. Attract extraordinary people to you by sending out the vibration that you are an extraordinary, influential, and great person. Great people hang around great people, attract great things, and exude great confidence. Show me the kind of people you hang out with and I can tell you the kind of person you really are. It is better to be alone than in the wrong company. If you hang with snakes, you will learn how to crawl, but if you associate with eagles, you will learn how to fly high. You become like those with whom you closely associate. Those who don't increase you will eventually decrease you. Wise is the person who fortifies his life with the right friendships.

FEEL THE PRESENCE OF THE THINGS DESIRED

After I left my husband, I had no place to go. I lived with a friend for a while, and then moved into an apartment. Knowing that this journey in the wilderness was temporary, I kept my eyes on my new goal, which was purchasing a home for my son and me. I had a plan. Every time I received my paycheck, I bought things for my soon-to-be new house. I had purchased so many new things for the home that I was at a point where I could feel the embodiment of the house all around me. When I finally did move into my new home, I had all the things needed for it including things for the kitchen, living room, bedrooms and bathrooms. I had been preparing for what I was expecting, therefore I had room in my consciousness to receive it. There was no doubt in me at all that I would soon be moving into my own home. My subconsciousness knew that I was convinced about my new home and it manifested into my life as I believed. There should be no room for doubt in your consciousness. When your expectations are carried to your subconscious mind, there must be no doubt at all there, only firm conviction and calm assurance that the things you desire are forthcoming.

Many people expect so much of the worse to happen and the worse does happen. They then say, *"I knew it was going to happen."* Well of course, it happened as they believed it would. Everything is done unto you according to your belief. Some people often attract things to them which they do not consciously desire, but which they have become identified with in their subconsciousness. Have you ever known someone who said, *"Every person I get involved with always ends up cheating on me."* Why is that? It is because deep within, they believe in their subconscious mind that every person they connect with will cheat on them, so they attract what they believe. We all attract particular kinds of situations and people to us. Therefore, we must always be consciously aware of the mental attitude we are exuding. We must be sure to stay on the positive current that attracts good into our lives. Take an inventory of the caliber of friends you have, the situations you find yourself in, the nature of conversations you engage in, the things that you encounter. This will give you a good indication as to the kind of person you are. Who and what you attract tells you what you are drawing and the nature of what you are sending out. What you think, do, or feel is an indication of what you are. I have heard of women who frequently attract men into their lives who physically abuse them. Others attract people who steal from them, use them, lie to them, etc. And yet, there are people who attract wonderful, honest, kind-hearted people who enhance their lives. Why is that so? Why do you think that some people attract good and others attract bad into their lives? There are many answers to this question, so I shall elaborate on two. My favorite is 1.) It is done unto you as you "believe". If a person does not believe he or she deserves better, he or she will never get better. There are those who do not value themselves and in not valuing oneself, you attract individuals who will support that devalued opinion by mistreating you. This oftentimes comes from having a low self-esteem. 2.) Whatever is emanating from your thought world is what attracts things, people and situations to you. When there is doubt and fear, you attract people who will do things to cause you to continue doubting people and fearing the worse. Fear and worry are poisons. Through distorted mental pictures, they bring to pass the things feared. Sorrow looks back. Worry looks around, but faith looks up. Where there is confidence and great expectation, there is peace all around.

DIRECT YOUR OWN PATHS

You had no control over the lot that you were born into. You had no control over who your parents were or the environment in which you were raised. You came into this world naked and helpless. Someone cared for you, nurtured you, fed you, clothed you, and guided you unto the point of adulthood. When you became an adult, responsibility rested upon you to direct yourself into areas leading to continued education, employment, attainment of property and acquiring a family. Your accumulated experiences, surroundings, education, and guidance all contributed to making you the individual you are now. You were to take those accumulated experiences of your life and decide what you wanted your life to be, what role you wanted to play, what you wanted to contribute to the world, how much money you wanted to make, and the type of lifestyle you wanted to live. Once you became an adult, it was no one else's responsibility for how your life was to turn out. That rested exclusively with you. You had seen enough, heard enough, experienced enough, and discovered enough to know the road that you wanted to travel. You were to direct your own paths because you are the navigator, the captain, the master of your life. No one can live your life for you and no one else can acquire success and prosperity for you. Nobody else can learn a lesson for you. To be honest, no one really cares whether you decide to become prosperous, remain mediocre, or become a failure. Of course, parents always want what is best for their children regardless of how old they are, and spouses want their counterpart to be successful because it benefits him or her; but if you were to give up on life and become a bum, your closest family and friends would shake their heads and say, "What a shame." They would probably comment on the fact that you had so much potential and then go home to their immediate families. There are a faithful few in one's life (if they are lucky) who would genuinely care what you did with yourself and would try and help you get back on your feet, but the point is that you only have one life, and it should be your ultimate goal to live it to the fullest. If you do, the world will be a better place because of your contribution, but if you don't, the world will still go on. No one is so loyal to you that they will join you in your endeavor to become a vagrant simply because that is what you decided to become. With or without you, life goes on, so why not let it progress with you on board making it better?

    You have to fill your place in society. You must compel room for your skills. You have to stand out above the rest. You have to demand respect by becoming successful in a massive way. You are only given one life. You control your destiny, your joy, your inner peace, your fortune to the exact extent that you can think them completely out, visualize them, believe in them. This life is meant to be lived. Your talents are meant to be used. Your gifts are to be shared. Living haphazardly day to day is not real living. Going to work every day, coming home, cooking dinner, caring for the family and getting prepared to do the same thing the next day is not real living. Real living consists in achieving your personal goals, contributing to the world in a meaningful way, making a career doing something that you absolutely love, spending quality time with family and friends, utilizing the gifts and talents that God has placed inside you, traveling to different places of God's universe, eating and drinking in a good way, and honoring and worshipping your Maker and Creator.

Every single day of your life should be lived to the fullest. What you do each day should contribute to you becoming a more fulfilled human being. At the end of each day before you prepare to rest, an inventory of the day's events should be done and the review of the day should be pleasant and productive. When there is joy in your heart from having lived a full day where you have put a smile on someone's face, worked at your best, eaten good, hearty meals, and enjoyed laughter and good company, then you have lived that day to the fullest. All days will not be pleasant days, but when you know that you have handled a difficult situation with integrity, dignity, good judgment and wise decision making, then you have had a productive day. Directing your own path means that you know where you want to go in life and you are making plans to get there. You know the path that you need to take and you are allowing nothing and no one to deter you from that path. This you must do my friend. Life is about progression.

Everybody and everything is always moving and changing. Nothing remains the same. The goal is to move forward, not backward. You will not remain where you are forever, that's for sure. When you look back over your life a year from now, you should be more successful than you are today. You will either go forward or backward, but you will move, or be moved out of the way.

MAXIMIZING THE DAY

It is the successful days that get you where you want to go. If everyday is a failure, you will never achieve what you desire; but if everyday is a success, then you can not fail to achieve what you desire. You should be doing something everyday with your God-given gift that will bring you closer to the accomplishment of your goals. Time waits for no one and time will continue to pass whether you make sufficient use of it or not. We are all given the same 24 hours in a day. Continuous development and meaningful growth happens when you make the proper use of time, that 24 hours that you are given each day. If you are a failure today, it is because of your inappropriate use of past time. If you are somewhat of a success today, it is because of your effective use of past time. If a person can and will make the right use of time, he or she is sure to become a success. For instance, as I write this sentence, I could be at a party to which I was invited tonight. Enjoying life is indeed a gift and there should definitely be a balanced amount of work and play, but I chose not to attend the party. I chose to use my time to work on this book. There would be nothing wrong with me attending the party, but my use of time right now is being spent doing something that will bring me closer to achieving my current goal of completing this book. My sacrifice in order to obtain future success is giving up some (much needed) fun. Sometimes it takes a sacrifice of sleep and play in order to get you where you want to be in the near future. It is true that all work and no play makes Jack a dull boy, but all play and no work makes Jack a poor boy. Jack needs a balanced amount of both.

Although doing all that one can do in a day is essential, it is more vital that the things being performed are being done in an efficient and precise manner. Not many things indifferently, but one thing supremely is the demand of this world. If you scatter your efforts, you will never succeed; and if you do things in a half-finished, insufficient manner you will not succeed. Wallace Wattles in his book, *The Science of Getting Rich* states that, *"The cause of failure is doing too many things in an inefficient manner. You will see that it is a self-evident proposition that if you do not do any inefficient acts, and if you do a sufficient number of efficient acts, you will become rich."*

A MANNER OF SPEAKING

Death and life are in the power of the tongue. (Proverbs 18:21). I had always heard that phrase from the Bible, but it was only until about ten years ago that I really understood what that proverb actually meant. To me, it means that we can speak words of death into a situation or we can speak words of life into a situation, and according to the words that we have spoken, the situation will change for better or worse. Over the course of years, I came to understand the significance of the power that our words contain when we release them into the atmosphere. The word that you release from your mouth determines your successes or failures. You are to speak only what you choose to see manifested. To change the reality of your life, you must change the speech that you use on a daily basis, which makes your reality what it is. Your words contain the power to kill or heal, bless or curse, tear down or build up, create or destroy. Your language will expand as your consciousness expands. Your consciousness will expand as your language expands. Your everyday conversation reveals exactly what is in your mind, discloses what you are agreeing with, divulges what you believe in, and is therefore creating your reality. You must take control of your mind and mouth. Who you are and what you think or feel is always revealed when you speak. Your life is shaped by the predominant thoughts you entertain and the words you speak. Your own words shape your world and everything in it. Since you were created in the image of God and His Spirit lives within you, then your words are of the same creative force as God's word. There is a power, intelligence and a law which operates upon your word.

Your words are self-fulfilling prophecy. Be careful of what you think and talk because thoughts run in currents and what you think or say will attract back to you the physical equivalent containing the elements that made up the words you spoke. If thoughts were visible to the natural eye, we would see currents running to and from people that their words and attitudes have placed them on. Everyone with the same nature of thought would be on the same current. Those with a high level of motivation and joy would be on the same current. Those with similar temperament and character would be on the same current. Those depressed and unhappy would be on the same current, those whose motives are to commit crimes would be on the same current. We would be able to see forces connecting those together with like mental states. Prentice Mulford, in his book 'Thoughts are Things' states, *"When you are in low spirits, you have acting on you the thought current coming from all others in low spirits. You are in oneness with the depressive order of thought"*. When you speak of the attainment of your goals, you attract all the elements needed to help you accomplish those goals. When people talk of business or entrepreneurship, they attract a business current of idea, initiative, and plans. You attract what you speak about. When you change your belief system in thought, words, and emotional pattern, you change your whole body, you change your situations, and you change your reality. The more specific you are when speaking positive, the quicker the manifestation, the greater you feel, the more powerful the materialization.

We decree our realities one word at a time. Definite statements produce definite results.

Feeling is essential in order for words to manifest. Emotions play a vital role when it comes to manifestation. The four major emotions are happiness, anger, fear, and sadness. These emotions are very strong and when we speak through them, our words are the most powerful and they manifest quickly because of the strength, vitality, and conviction carried with the words as they are released. For this reason, we must be very careful of what we say when experiencing these strong feelings. The manifestation could be instantaneous. Whenever you speak with feeling and conviction, you strengthen the magnet within you by attracting the things, people and situations that correspond with your words and emotions. Sometimes it's too late to take the words back because they may already be in the process of manifesting if they were spoken with great power and conviction. You must guard your mouth! Speaking positive affirmations into your life is a productive habit. Speaking negatively is a bad one.

SPEAK YOUR BLESSINGS

Affirmations are words of life that begin to shape our thoughts and ultimately the consciousness of the person speaking. As one begins to use affirmations, he or she may say them robotically at first, not really feeling the power behind the words, but as the words are constantly spoken, they sink into the subconsciousness and we know that it is the subconscious mind that creates the realities of everyone's life. You absolutely must begin to speak a straight affirmative language. The universe gives *to* you *through* you. It is a known fact that words often repeated form patterns in the mind which automatically reproduce themselves. Your entire life can be changed for good just by the words that you speak on a daily basis. Your words can magnetize prosperity, harmony, peace, and good toward you, or your words can draw poverty, discord, frustration and evil toward you. You are always attracting or repelling. How? because your mental attitude is the magnet. The thoughts that you entertain determines your mental attitude. If your thoughts are negative, you will exude a negative disposition and the words that you speak will be negative, thus attracting negativity to you. If your thoughts are positive, then your conversation will be of a positive nature, thus attracting good to you. Your mental attitude is a mirror of your mind reflecting your thinking. When your mental attitude is positive, your abilities reach a maximum of effectiveness and good results inevitably follow. The quality of your thought is the measure of your power. Your thoughts and attitude influence people for or against your interests and it is people that you need in this world to get you where you want and need to go, so why not use the power of thought to influence people for your interests. All people need people. Never forget that. Every one of your daily secret thoughts are real things, which are acting on the minds of other people. A positive attitude is your lottery ticket that will win for you in every situation!

CAUSE AND EFFECT

In the world we live in, there are man-made laws that everyone must abide by. When we choose to break the laws, there are penalties and consequences that we must pay. Not only must we obey the laws of the land, but we must also obey the laws of nature. There are many, many universal laws and when we learn them and govern ourselves in harmony with them, life is a beautiful thing. The laws are really simple to keep. Universal Laws also referred to as Spiritual Laws or Laws of Nature are the unwavering and unchanging principles that rule our entire universe and are the means by which our world and the entire cosmos exist. These laws are universal, meaning they exist everywhere you are and at all times. There is one specific law that is always acting upon us each and every day, in every way, and through everything we think and say. That is the law of cause and effect which automatically compels us to reap as we sow. Ralph Waldo Emerson called this law the "Law of Laws." Nothing rewards or punishes us but this, which is the law of cause and effect. This law works at all times with absolute justice. It is unchanging, unwavering, deliberate, and precise in its application and delivery. Ignorance of the law excuses no one from its effects. The law dictates that any action that is initiated produces or returns a result or outcome in exact proportion to the action or causes which initiated it. Every time you speak, a law is in effect. When you act, you are initiating a cause. The law will bring the effect. The law has no motive. It is a blind, powerful force, which simply acts. This can also be referred to as sowing and reaping or "Karma".

There is never a cause without an effect nor an effect without a cause. There will never be one without the other, just as there is no light without darkness no top without a bottom, or no inside without an outside. Effect follows cause as night follows the day. Health, happiness and prosperity are effects, not causes. Sickness, misery and poverty are effects as well. This law can and is used to bring happiness and goodness as well as wretchedness and evil. This law can heal just as certain as it can kill. This law can convert loss into gain, failure into success and fear into faith. The power which appears to bind is the same power that can set us free! You must subject yourself to the law if you wish the law to subject itself to you. If there is destruction in the cause, the law must destroy. If there is good in the cause, it will execute goodness and healing. When your will and purpose are in line with God's will and purpose for your life, you cannot and will not use the law destructively. The misuse of this power has brought upon mankind every suffering condition. You have a perfect right to the law of cause and effect for personal advancement and to bring prosperity and happiness into your life. You do the choosing. Needless-to-say, the law must be consciously and constructively used. The law is one of freedom and not bondage. Freedom and bondage, good and evil, peace and discord are all different ways of using this one power. As you come into knowledge of this law, you must deliberately begin to use it for good, although you may have in times past used it ignorantly for evil. Every time you think and speak, you use this law. You are a law unto yourself. Create the laws of your life. Let your life be centered around your words and thoughts in a powerful, positive way. In order to live a life of harmonious, prosperous, peaceful effect, ensure that the causes are of the same nature. The effect corresponds with its cause and will execute with precise exactitude.

When you look at the life of someone who seems to be successful and powerful, just know that the effects you see in that person's life are the result of specific causes initiated by that person. Causes are the result of decisions and decisions are the result of thoughts acted upon. When we see powerful manifestations in a person's life, never forget that no big achievement came easy. There is always hard work, labor, some sleepless nights, a few failures, some disappointments, hurts, and obstacles, but with persistence comes success. Success usually comes right after some major defeat. Do not be deceived into thinking that success just dropped into a person's lap, or that a person was just "lucky". There is no such thing as "luck". Success is an effect and if you investigate back far enough, you will find that the cause of success goes back to a person's mental attitude.

If someone has a college degree, it is because that person had a *thought* to enroll in college (or their parents had the thought). Nevertheless, he or she acted on that thought and went to college. The graduation ceremony was the ultimate *effect* of enrolling, and enrolling was the ultimate *cause*. We tend to look at people and sometimes wonder what "breaks" they had in life. We often fail to realize that people make their own breaks when they place themselves in positions to receive breaks. Breaks often come after you take hold of opportunity quickly. Yes, it is true that some people are promoted because of who they are connected or related to, but if those who are promoted for reasons other than their qualifications or competence can not produce the desired results, they will eventually eliminate themselves. Those people should not be your concern, nor is it your business to worry about. We certainly don't complain when we are on the receiving end of favoritism. Many times "breaks" come as a reward from God for the hard work and labor that one has put into their own personal development. The one giving the "break" is usually a messenger being used to deliver the blessing. We must learn to stop judging by outward appearances of things and sow our own seeds of goodness, hard work and labor so that when the time arrives, our "breaks" will come. Everything happens when and how it is supposed to happen. There are never any mistakes. Let the law of cause and effect operate in your life in a positive way. A life without cause is a life without effect. Make sure you have a life with great cause. Remember, there is never an effect without an adequate cause. Your mental attitude determines the cause.

CHAPTER 5 KEY POINTS:

- ❖ When your concept is big and your belief is unwavering, you will get the biggest flow into your life. You can only receive what you "see" yourself receiving. There are no big things or little things in God.

- ❖ Take an inventory of the caliber of friends you have, the situations you find yourself in, the nature of conversations you engage in, the things that you encounter. This will give you a good indication as to the kind of person you are. Who and what you attract tells you what you are drawing and the nature of what you are sending out.

- ❖ No one can live your life for you and no one else can acquire success and prosperity for you. Nobody else can learn a lesson for you.

- ❖ It is the successful days that get you where you want to go. If everyday is a failure, you will never receive what you desire; but if everyday is a success, then you can not fail to achieve what you desire.

- ❖ Let the law of cause and effect operate in your life in a positive way. A life without cause is a life without effect. Make sure you have a life with great cause.

6

EXPANDING YOUR CONSCIOUSNESS

> *You have to move up to another level of thinking, which is true for me and everybody else. Everybody has to learn to think differently, bigger to be open to possibilities.*
>
> Oprah Winfrey

There are many ways you can expand your consciousness, but in order for the consciousness to be expanded, you must be open-minded enough to analyze your belief system. As you know, it is done unto you as you believe. The beliefs you carry around inside your mind can either enrich your life or limit it. For many people, their life is limited because they carry around self-defeating beliefs which cause them to have low self-esteem and low self-confidence. Confidence depends on the type of thoughts you habitually allow to occupy your mind. Think defeat and you are bound to feel defeated. Therefore, the degree to which you reprogram yourself from false beliefs will be in direct proportion to the amount of truth that you are willing to accept about yourself. You must gain self-confidence through self-reliance. When you begin to open your mind to greater possibilities for yourself, your consciousness begins to expand and you are then opened to seeing the truth of who you deeply are. False beliefs are automatically removed and replaced with true beliefs that you know to be real and are willing to accept as truth.

Albert Einstein once stated, *"No problem can be solved from the same level of consciousness that created it."* What Mr. Einstein seemed to understand when he made this statement is that when one develops a higher level of thinking, he or she has access to a power that exists beyond ordinary awareness or understanding. When the consciousness is widened, solutions to problems become evident and answers to difficult circumstances are made clear. When your consciousness is expanded, your world is also expanded because as you are aware of more, you experience more. Accessing a higher level of consciousness is awakening to a new reality, an expanded reality which imposes no boundaries on what you can be or do. Your mind has the power to direct your consciousness by choosing what you think about. Expanding your consciousness means being aware of everything that may have an influence on your actions, behavior, values, goals, and daily decisions. Living with an expanded consciousness means more than just seeing and knowing, but acting on what you see and know. It is futile to have developed an expanded consciousness and then doing nothing to bring more into it. The purpose of expanding anything is to make room for more coming in. Once your consciousness is widened, something must be brought into it. The space could be made for receiving more money, greater wisdom, ingenuity, intuition, creativity, marvelous opportunities, a higher degree of learning, a promotion, an influx of new friends, etc. Something has to be brought into your new conscious place, which has been made available through a higher level of thinking. In order to do that, it takes work on your part. The following are some things that you can do to expand your consciousness:

- **Pray**. Keep the lines of communication between you and God open. Listen as He speaks to you, leads you and guides you. Expect Him to answer.

- **Read and study** with an open mind. Reading expands your knowledge and strengthens your mind. Keep your mind stimulated with new information.

- **Be open** to the possibility that what you currently believe to be true about certain things may in fact be false. Be prepared to release those hindering beliefs if you have to.

- **Think** about the person you are and ask yourself, What do I stand for? What do I believe? What do I want out of life? Then compare your answers with the person that you are today and see if they match.

- **Keep an open mind** when you are presented with new information. Do not accept it as truth or reject it as false right away. You can still listen to something without having to immediately accept or reject it.

- **Pay attention** to the things you strongly defend. These are sometimes deeply ingrained beliefs that you are holding onto tightly. Most likely they were implanted during your childhood.

- **Find your motivation,** the thing that makes you feel alive and begin doing that thing more and more.

- **Follow your intuition.** It can lead to great opportunities.

- **See your mistakes** as valuable learning experiences from which you can grow.

THE CONFIDENCE TO BE YOURSELF

A major characteristic contributing to the quality of your life is confidence. With confidence, you pursue your goals and dreams with boldness. With confidence, you tackle life's challenges with the faith that you will overcome each one. Confident people "believe" that they are important and they know that their lives matter. They make a difference in this world. They are fully aware both of their strengths and weaknesses and they tackle their weaknesses in order to strengthen them. Without a doubt, people who develop goals and diligently work towards accomplishing them, get more achieved with self-confidence than without it. They walk in this world with assurance in the things they know how to do and with the openness to learn the things they need to learn. These are the leaders of our world, the movers and shakers, the doers. Self-confidence is a hot commodity, in that everybody wants it, and yet people envy those who have it. It compels people to you. People have always been drawn to those who do their own thing without worrying about who is scrutinizing them, talking about them, or who likes or dislikes them. Their confident demeanor draws others to them. This is because self-confident people have qualities that everyone admires. The confidence is in their walk, their talk, their conversation, and their behaviors.

Prosperity is Your Birthright!

I have noticed that when it comes to confidence, one's appearance often does not matter because their confidence supersedes everything else about them. I recently had this conversation about confidence with a friend of mine who spent her childhood, teenage years, and early adolescent years struggling with low self-esteem and she talks about it often. My friend is very attractive and talented. People often comment on her beauty, but according to her, she was not always pretty. She says that she was in fact so unattractive that as a little girl, she was often mistaken for a boy. She states that in middle and high school she was tall, thin, and had very short hair, which made her very self-conscious. She claims that she never received any attention from boys and did not have very many friends. Although she has transformed into a beautiful swan, the deeply ingrained, long-held beliefs about not being pretty, feeling insecure, and not being worthy of a quality man are still with her. Hence, she continues to attract men who at some point will do something to cause her to reflect back on those feelings of insecurity. Her confidence level has significantly risen since childhood and teenage years, but in my opinion, she has to completely eradiate those deeply ingrained beliefs about not being worthy so that her self-assurance can rise mightily to the surface and radiate powerfully. If she had the confidence right now to match the beauty she has right now, she would never be insecure again.

On the other hand, I had another friend who had so much confidence that it projected everywhere she went. We had been friends since elementary school and we also attended college together. After college she moved away and I lost contact with her, but I recall during our college years that she exuded so much confidence that she was never afraid to do anything she wanted to do, wear anything she wanted to wear, or approach any man that she wanted to approach. Her confidence did not cross over to arrogance either, as that sometimes does happen, but was just enough to accomplish what she set out to achieve. Her boyfriends were always very nice-looking and the man she ended up marrying is very handsome as well. The kicker was that physically, she was not the most attractive woman to the average eye, but she believed that she was just as pretty as any other pretty woman. She had a very high self-esteem. Several of my other friends at that time (being as vain as they were), would often ask me why I hung out with her because she was "so ugly" according to them. As I look back, I realize that I hung out with her because not only was she a great friend, but I wanted some of her confidence to rub off on me. Self-confident people inspire confidence in others. Before she moved away, she had a party to which I was invited. I went to the party with my other friend who had the self-esteem issue. After the party was over and we were driving home, I asked my friend the following while we were in the car, *"What do you think of my friend so-in-so?"* She said, *"I think she is very nice and she seems to be a lot of fun"*. I then said, *"Do you think that she's attractive?"* She paused for a second, so I said, *"Just be honest."* Then she said, *"No, I don't think she is attractive at all"*. I proceeded to tell her that so-in-so has always bubbled over with self-confidence. Next, I asked if she saw my friend's husband and she replied, *"yes"*.

She then said, *"I was shocked when I saw her husband because he is so handsome and they don't look like they belong together."* I knew she meant that a handsome man would conceivably be with an attractive lady and a not-so-attractive man would be with a not-so-attractive lady, but that is not the case when it comes to self-confident people. In the eye of a person with confidence, they are just as nice looking as their partner and others see in them what they see in themselves. At that point, I told her how my friend had always had nice-looking boyfriends in college because of the confidence that she exuded.

People are drawn to people who have confidence because they want it too. No normal person is drawn to a person with low self-esteem regardless of how beautiful or handsome they may be. When a person is drawn to someone with low self-esteem, it is because of one of two reasons: either to help the person realize the greatness inside them in order to raise their confidence level, or because the controlling, dominating personality the other person possesses, seeks a victim to control in order to feed their distorted ego. Mistreating, abusing and overpowering other people is the mode of operation for another insecure person or control freak. One with a low self-esteem is the perfect person to control and abuse. With low self-esteem, you can not positively contribute to anyone's life because that which you do, comes from wanting acceptance and validation from others. People with low self-esteem constantly withdraw from other people to the point that it sometimes becomes draining because they are so needy. You don't need to seek approval from others. The only approval you need is God's approval. Be the type of person who pours into the lives of others in a positive way. True confidence comes from knowing that you are worthy and deserving of the

Prosperity is Your Birthright!

things you seek and through self-reliance, you pursue those things. Adopt an attitude that anything is possible and recognize that it is possible because you deserve it and are worthy of it. You must believe and know that the whole universe is on your side. Everything goes back to beliefs, thoughts, and words. One of the biggest causes of low self-confidence is the thoughts you have on a daily basis that support the low self-esteem. Make sure that the thoughts you entertain are not negative and self-defeating, which minimizes your self-worth. Practice self-confidence on a daily basis. The following are some things that you can do to practice being confident:

- Be assured in your conversations and give eye contact.

- Be assured and certain when speaking to others. Know what you are talking about and convey that knowledge in a self-assured way.

- Walk with your back straight and your head held high. Typically, people with low self-esteem walk a little slower than most people and often keep their head looking down at the ground. A head that is held high is a sign of a person who has self confidence.

- Initiate conversations when it is appropriate to do so. Introduce yourself to people and engage in positive discussions.

- Dress in a manner that says you are important. Stay well-groomed.

- Speak out when it is necessary to do so (only when it's necessary).

- Never let anyone mistreat you. Stand up for yourself.

- Do not compromise your integrity. Hold on to your morals. Always be ethical and remain honest.

Expanding Your Consciousness

With self-confidence, you draw a different caliber of people to you. You begin to feel good about yourself and your thinking process changes for the better. Practice confidence and your fears and insecurities will soon vanish.

YOUR MASTERMIND ALLIANCE

A Mastermind alliance consists of a group of individuals with like minds and spirits. All individuals in a Mastermind Group develop goals and objectives for themselves for the current year and sometimes for five and ten years down the line. There are also goals and objectives for the Mastermind Group as a whole. Meetings are held on a frequent and consistent basis and in the meetings, individual reports are read on the progress of goals that members in the group have made for themselves.

A report is given from each person in nine areas, which are spiritual, financial, educational, family, recreational, personal, health, business/career, and civic. It is vital that everyone in the group is in harmony with one another because in the meetings, dreams and personal goals are divulged, plans for accomplishing them are delineated, and guidance from members in the group is sought and given. Aspirations are discussed in detail and direction and advice is also given. The Mastermind Meetings must be significantly beneficial, encouraging, inspiring, and serious in nature. In my first book '*Destined for Great Things'*, I talked about how I became a member of *The Mastermind Women's Group*, now called, *The International Mastermind Association.* As I stated in that book, the group changed my life. I am a firm believer that when the student is ready, the teacher will appear. It was at that time in my life that I needed balance, and learning how to develop, organize, and plan out my life was and still is very beneficial for me. The accountability component of having a Mastermind Group is the piece that is essential because when you are held responsible for doing the things that you say you are going to do, you are more inclined to get those things done. In an effective Mastermind Group, everyone benefits from the knowledge, education, and experience of everyone else. Your aspirations are not to be broadcasted to the world before they come into fruition. They are to be revealed to your closest loved ones and your Mastermind Group only. The

Prosperity is Your Birthright!

Mastermind principle holds the secret to power. This principle is exercised by people who surround themselves with other people with great minds. No one person has sufficient experience, education, and knowledge to make it in this world without the cooperation of other people. Every plan you adopt in your endeavor to accomplish your goals to a notable degree should be the joint effort of yourself and other members of your Mastermind Group. A group of minds allied together in a spirit of harmony will provide more thought energy than a single brain alone. The best way to show the world what you are going to do is by showing the world what you have already done. You must illustrate. Talk is cheap. You must demonstrate. You only know as much as you can prove by manifestation. The credibility of your word is in your accomplishments.

    Anyone can say they are going to do something and never do it. It is not those who broadcast, but those who actually accomplish who are respected in this world. The wisest thing to do when you make up in your mind to do something is to keep it to yourself or your Mastermind Group only. Mistakes are repeatedly made when people broadcast their intentions to the world to soon. The world is then waiting for your demonstration or your downfall. As negative as it may sound, it is true that not everybody wants you to succeed. When I make a decision to do something meaningful, I rarely tell anyone. When I wrote my first book, *Destined for Great Things,* I told not one soul. My close friends and family members found out about the book when I placed a copy in their hands. You take the chance of having to fight with hindering spiritual forces being sent to you when you announce your intentions prematurely. Where those forces come from does not matter. What matters is that you do not do and say things that will open the door allowing those negative forces in. Learn to keep a tight lip until the time comes to announce your accomplishments on the rooftops!

    A study of rich and powerful men and women through the ages would reveal their frequent association with their Mastermind Alliance. Jesus surrounded Himself with His disciples, which was His Mastermind Group. During His private time alone with them, away from the multitude of people, He revealed His purpose, His objective, and imparted into them spiritual wisdom that carried them through the adversities they encountered long after His death. He had intimate conversations with them that the ordinary public was not privy to. Records reveal that Andrew Carnegie, Henry Ford, Oprah Winfrey, Barack Obama, Warren Buffett, Donald Trump, and many other prominent and powerful individuals had or continue to have a Mastermind Group that they meet with on a frequent basis. Powerful organizations, corporations and all types of companies have Board of Directors or Executive Teams, which is nothing but a Mastermind Group that meets to discuss the progress and development of the entity. No man is an island. You need people in order to help get you where you desire to go. The key is to be able to identify trustworthy, reliable people who share similar ideologies and who are as serious about making an impact in this world as you are. If you are not a part of a Mastermind Group, then form one. You may contact The International Mastermind Association at www. Internationalmasterminders.com for membership information and for a step by step guide on how to form a successful Mastermind Alliance.

A STRONG SUCCESS FOUNDATION

It takes commitment to accomplish anything worth its weight in salt. Obtaining prosperity through accomplishing meaningful goals will take total commitment on your part. Commitment to your goals, your vision, and to yourself means that you will perform every right action towards producing the desired outcome in the areas where you are committed. When your heart and soul is truly in something meaningful, you commit yourself to it in mind, body, and spirit. When you are committed to a person, you do what you can to maintain harmony, peace, and a healthy interaction between you and that person. When you are committed to a job, you focus diligently in a spirit of excellence to ensure that the end result is to your satisfaction or the approval of your immediate supervisor. When you are committed to yourself, you awaken each day with a sense of purpose, pride, and determination to effectively carry things through. All life is an unfoldment from the cradle to the grave and the way in which your life unfolds depends only on you. You must have the will to do, the determination to be, and the joy in becoming. With commitment, determination, and faith, you can become anything you desire to be. There are certain attributes that distinguishes powerful, successful and prosperous people from the average, mediocre, and common people. These attributes are not hidden. In fact, they stick out like a sore thumb. Yet, even in knowing what they are, people still do not practice them because of the hard work and exertion that goes into doing them. They feel they can obtain wealth and success without having to exercise these

Prosperity is Your Birthright!

attributes. These attributes are: decision, commitment, self-discipline, perseverance, follow-through, and faith. If your success builds from a foundation with these attributes, then when the winds and rains come, you will remain strong because of the foundation upon which your success is being built. Lets take a look at why these attributes are so important.

- **Decision**. This is the starting point. When you decide that you are going to do something worthy and meaningful, all the elements needed to carry out this decision come to you. After you have made your initial decision to pursue a worthy goal, there will be more decisions to be made along the way. Make them quickly and promptly. Do not let too much time go by before reaching your definite decision.

- **Commitment**. In order to ensure that your goal will be carried out in the most effective and precise manner,
  you must be committed to the process from beginning to end. You can not let your commitment to your goal diminish. Commitment means being faithful to your goal and watchful in every aspect of the progression. With commitment, you can foresee any challenges that may arise, and take steps to prevent or diminish any hindrances.

- **Self-discipline**. This is an area that many people lack because it requires mental and physical exertion. Self-discipline means sacrifice. It means giving up one thing to accomplish another. Most people do not like to give up the comforts of their daily regiment in order to pray, run, write goals, recite personal affirmations, staying after work late or lose sleep. The reward however is great for the person who can discipline himself or herself in order to gain power, authority and prosperity by doing those things.

- **Perseverance**. Think of a person running a marathon. Imagine the person starting out with great strength and enthusiasm, but then it starts raining. He continues running although the rain comes down harder. The rain has slowed him down, but he continues to run. Next, it begins snowing, but he continues to run in the snow. He has been forced to slow down again because the slippery snow could cause him to fall, so he is very careful. The snow melts away, but then thick

fog begins to form dimming his vision. He continues to run, although his vision and motivation has decreased somewhat, but way in the distance, he sees the finish line, so he continues to run as his vision clears up. Although his motivation is returning, he comes to a roadblock and so he makes a detour, but continues towards the finish line. Coming from another direction, he continues running never doubting that he will reach the finish line. He hears people shouting at him to just give up because they see that he is weary and tired, but
he continues running and finally reaches the finish line and realizes that the prize is greater than he even imagined it would be! He has overcome the rain, the snow, the fog, the detours, and the negative, although well-meaning suggestions of others to give up. He kept his eyes on his goal and made it to the finish line. His character is now stronger, his perseverance is enhanced, and his commitment has increased. This is what perseverance is. No matter what obstacles may present themselves to you on your journey to fulfilling your dreams, you continue moving forward with your eyes on the prize. Perseverance and commitment go hand-in-hand. They are twin brothers.

- **Follow-through**. Without follow-through, you will never accomplish anything. This is another common area that people struggle in. They start many worthy things but do not finish any of them. When you start something and do not follow through until it's completed, you have formed the habit of failure and your subconscious mind gets into the habit of never allowing you to complete anything. How many people do you know who attended some college, quit and say they only need three or four more classes towards their degree? I know a few. Nobody cares about that. All people know is that you do not have a college degree. How many people do you know that started reading a book and never finished it? There is nothing worse than starting multiple tasks and not finishing any of them. At the end of the day, what have you really accomplished? All you have to show for your efforts are a bunch of incomplete projects. Make sure that you follow-through on every task you start until each task is completed.

- **Faith**. Without faith it is impossible to please God or accomplish anything. It is done unto you as you believe. If you do not believe you will succeed, then why start at all? Faith is the unwavering belief that you will have whatever you are setting out to achieve. There is a power greater than yourself that operates upon your faith. The positive thoughts and convictions you have about your desires mixed with faith creates the formula that will bring the manifestation speedily. Faith is knowing regardless of what the outward conditions look like. Faith is trusting. Faith is acting. Faith is the evidence of things not seen with the natural eye, but knowing those things will manifest in the natural world.

With the consistent implementation of the above attributes in your life, you are sure on your way to success built upon a strong foundation. Anything a person desires to enhance gets stronger through practice. As you implement these attributes into your life, the sacrifice will feel like a struggle in the beginning, but with each added effort, they become less difficult to do, and will eventually become automatic. You will reap the fruit of your efforts if you persist. You will become a person of great power. You will stand out among the rest because of the time, effort, and sacrifice that you put into the achievement of your goals. It is the one march more that wins the campaign, the half a neck nearer that wins the race, and the five minutes more that wins the fight. The reward is worth the sacrifice.

DISCERNMENT

As prosperity and success become evident in your life, you become influential and powerful. People will flock to you. They want to be in your inner circle. They want access to you. They want access to your ear because if they have your ear, they are in a better position to influence you. Most people have motives and the more powerful, influential, prominent, or wealthy you become, the more subjected you are to becoming a target for people who mean you no good. I've always taken heed to the following: *"Don't be afraid of enemies who attack you, be afraid of friends who flatter you"* (too much). I parenthetically added the last two words because everyone likes to be given an honest compliment every now and then.

As I speak on this subject, I find it fitting to use two celebrity figures to elaborate on my point. Sadly, I learned earlier this evening that Michael Jackson died. As I sat in shock watching CNN, I listened to the various people who knew him speak of specific things that were happening in his life. Glued to the television listening to so many commentaries, there were a few statements that really stuck out in my head. One person said that Michael had many vultures around him whose motives were not in his best interest. Another person substantiating this, mentioned that Michael's mother had once said that he was a target and was going to have to learn lessons about people for himself. Yet another person said that Michael had been hurt by so many people who he thought were his true friends, but betrayed him. Similarly, when Brittney Spears was in the media for her shortcomings, a comparable statement was made about her. It was said that she had enablers around her promoting her destructive behaviors and shielded her from others. Just in observing the lives of these two individuals, it seems appropriate to state that when a person is in their most vulnerable state, they are more inclined to attract enablers, because these enablers appear to fill their void momentarily by telling them what they want to hear and approving of their distorted decisions and outlandish behaviors. You can count on the enemy to show up at your most vulnerable moment.

There is a difference between shielding a person and protecting them. In the cases of Michael and Brittney, it appears that the shielding by unknown "outside folks" was to keep well-meaning people away, not to protect them. A family member or true friend will not allow a loved one to continue abusing themselves to the point of self-destruction. When these behaviors are enabled, it is usually because the enabling individual is afraid they will be rejected by the victim if they bring up the issues and so they sit back and let the person abuse themselves. It is usually a concerned family member or close friend (with no ulterior motives) who speaks out when they see the person headed for destruction. For a season, the victim gets angry and shuts the friend or family member out of their lives, but when (and if) they clean up their act, they come back and thank those who stood up to help them. My point in bringing up these two individuals is to underscore the need for discernment when it comes to people that you allow into your inner circle of friends. Genuine friends are very rare and you must use discernment to know who is truly sincere with no motives. Acquaintances and associates come a dime a dozen, but true friends will be there when you are up and also down. Always remember that the world kicks you when you're down and loves you when you are up. True friends are there no matter what. Those who were your friends before your prosperity will remain your friends through thick and thin. God will give discernment to those who ask for it.

My heart reaches out to Michael Jackson's family. His death was a shocker that touched me as a child growing up listening to his music. In listening to different people speak of him, there were some great qualities that were mentioned, which supports some things that have been written in this chapter. Donna Summer said that, *"Michael occupied a large space."* This brings to mind what happens when a person's consciousness has been widened. Without a doubt, Michael had an expanded consciousness, which allowed massive wealth, ingenuity, originality, creativity, humongous projects, and so much more to flow into his life through his consciousness. Many years ago, I saw an interview where Michael stated that he goes off alone to allow his imagination to soar. He stated that when he did this, his creative juices flowed and he came back and created masterpieces. Without a doubt, we know that Michael created masterpieces. His creative ideas came to him during meditation, substantiating yet another point. Donna Summer also said, *"His greatness was his perfection"*. This brings to mind a spirit of follow-through that we talked about. Michael Jackson took great pride and precision in his projects and worked them until they were fully completed. He had a follow-through spirit. It was said that he demanded perfection. This is indeed a good attribute to have, but one must be very careful, because a perfectionist is usually prone to lots of stress. Coincidentally, stress was said to be a contributor to Michael Jackson's death. Striving for perfection goes hand in hand with working in a spirit of excellence, but one must not be so rigid that mistakes cause their stress level to increase. It was also mentioned by many people that Michael was a trailblazer. This goes back to ingenuity. He did what he set out to do using ingenuity that operated in his subconscious mind and as a result, closed doors that had been shut were opened, which benefited not only him, but those who came behind him.

The King of Pop was in the process of making a 50 concert come-back starting in London when he suddenly passed away. The concert will never be performed, but some doubted whether he was going to be able to make a comeback. After his death, many asked if he would have been able to do it,

Expanding Your Consciousness

calling him a "has been". Each time I heard the question asked, it brought to mind a poem written by Walt Mason called '*Has-beens do Come Back*':

> I've just been reading of a man
> who joined the has-been ranks,
> at fifty years without a cent,
> or credit at the banks.
>
> But undismayed he buckled down,
> refusing to be beat,
> and captured fortune and renown;
> he's now on Easy Street.
>
> Men say that fellows down and out
> never leave the rocky track,
> but facts will show, beyond a doubt,
> that has-beens do come back.
>
> I know, for I who write this rhyme,
> when forty-odd years old,
> was down and out, without a dime,
> my whiskers full of mold.
>
> By black disaster I was trounced
> until it jarred my spine;
> I was a failure so pronounced
> I didn't need a sign.
>
> And after I had soaked my coat,
> I said at forty-three,
> I'll see if I can catch the goat
> that has escaped from me.
>
> I labored hard; I strained my dome,
> to do my daily grind,
> until in triumph I came home,

> my Billy-goat behind.
>
> And any man who still has health
> may with the winners stack,
> and have a chance at fame and wealth
> for has-beens do come back!

In my humble opinion, I say "yes", Michael Jackson could have made a major come-back. Unfortunately, the poem reads that, "*any man who still has health...*" can come back. I am not so sure that our dear Michael had the necessary health. However, he left a powerful legacy and that legacy will live on forever through his music. His vision and creativity revolutionized the music industry and we will be forever thankful for what he contributed to the world. Michael Jackson once quoted a saying from Michael Angelo that fits himself ever so perfectly: "*I know the creator will go, but his work survives.*" There was never any one like Michael Jackson on this planet and never ever will be again. He was truly one of a kind. May he finally find the peace that he longed for on earth and may God bless his soul. I found it fitting to close this chapter with Michael Jackson because regardless of what his shortcomings may or may not have been, he epitomizes a person with an expanded consciousness and has demonstrated in his life the things that come to those who have learned how to widen their consciousness to acquire whatever it is that they set out to achieve.

CHAPTER 6 KEY POINTS:

- ❖ Accessing a higher level of consciousness is awakening to a new reality, an expanded reality that allows one to see the truth of who they really are, which imposes no boundaries on what one can be or do.

- ❖ True confidence comes from knowing that you are worthy and deserving of the things you seek and through self-reliance, you pursue those things.

- ❖ Your aspirations are not to be broadcasted to the world before they come into fruition. They are to be revealed to your closest loved ones and your Mastermind Alliance only.

- ❖ There is a need for discernment when it comes to people that you allow into your inner circle of friends. Genuine friends are very rare and you must use discernment to know who is truly sincere with no motives. Acquaintances and associates come a dime a dozen, but true friends will be there when you are up and also down.

- ❖ You will reap the fruit of your efforts if you persist. You will become a person of great power. You will stand out among the rest because of the time, effort, and sacrifice that you put into the achievement of your goals.

7
REMIND YOURSELF OF YOUR WORTH AND POWER

> *Our sense of self-worth is key to being able to appreciate the other factors of fulfillment. Interestingly, feeling compassion for others is the most reliable way to increase our*
> *own self-worth.*
> *Dalai Lama*

In the preceding chapters, I reminded you of your uniqueness from everyone else in this world and the fact that there will never be anyone else identical to you. Your uniqueness has a place in this world and once you find your particular place, you will be gratified and satisfied with your life. Understanding your worth requires you to know exactly where your power comes from. Power can be compared to authority or influence. There is spiritual power and there is worldly power and the two are vastly different. In this world, leadership and power usually go hand in hand and it usually follows that the one with the power is also the one with the control. The perception of worldly power is typically superficial and is based upon conditional elements. In other words, a person is considered powerful if they are in the following positions:

- Have massive wealth and/or an abundance of worldly possessions

- Holds a very high-profile position with influence and clout

- Has authority to hire and fire

- Holds a political office
- Has authority to make major decisions
- Has close connections with influential people
- Has influence over thousands of people at a time
- Is the son, daughter, niece, nephew, grand, or some other relation to an influential person

The list above delineates how the world perceives power. Spiritual power however, is a different kind of power and does not come from any of the above conditions. Spiritual power comes from God and can not be replicated. We need spiritual power more than we need any other power. The majority of the world lives almost entirely in materialism and thinks that things come *to* them from external sources, not understanding that things come *through* them. They do not comprehend the world of spirit. Their faith is in money, positions, people, houses, cars, jewelry, etc. and because they believe so strongly in those things, they actually become worshipers of them. The only powerful life they envision is a life of physical power. However, those who have a sneaking suspension that there is a different kind of power, which is far superior to physical power are beginning to see the kingdom of God. Their spiritual eyes are opening and their minds are becoming illuminated.

THE POWER TO BE FELT

Any man, woman or child may exercise power. Powerful individuals are not "chosen" people who have been given a special gift that others do not have. Everyone has access to the same power that others have in them. Power is right where you are. You are always with it and by use of it, you can call forth forces into your life that will operate in everything you do. The utilization of your power can actualize what you want if the power is strategically directed. The difference between those who use their power and those who do not is that the former have found their inner power, taken hold of it, and used it to greatly enhance their lives. The latter has not discovered that there is power within them, and therefore do not use it. No one's power is denied to them. An example of one who has unified themselves with their inner power verses one who has not can be found in the lives of two speakers. One woman speaks about something and conveys it well. She speaks with knowledge, eloquence and fluency, but after hearing her, the world goes on not thinking twice about what she has expressed, although her presentation was good. Another woman says the exact same thing, but in a different manner. She communicates with less style and less eloquence and does not have as much formal knowledge as the first lady; but the world pauses to hear with great interest and concentration. The listeners take what she has said and resonates on the influence of her words. The second woman has spoken with power. One man writes a book of truth, faultless in technique, content, and inscription. The writing style is also flawless. The world reads the book, lays it calmly down and says, "That was a good book." Another man writes a book containing the same message. The idea is identical, but perhaps with less style and scholarship. However, the book is the topic of conversation on everybody's tongue because every reader *feels* the touch of power from reading that book. The thing that I am trying to make plain is that the power was not in the "words" of the second woman or the second man. The power was "in them" expressing *through* them when they spoke, wrote, or did whatever they did. Both the first woman and the first man had the knowledge, but not the power. The second woman and second man had both the knowledge and the power. When power is in a person, it comes out in everything they do and say. You will see it in their eye. It will be in the tone of their voice, the grasp of the handshake. It will emanate from the whole personality of the person. Power can be felt and it is felt in whatever the person does. If there is no operating power, it can not be imitated. It is either active or it is latent. All power is one power and all power comes from God. It is available to any man or woman who will find it within themselves and use it. It is imperative to convey that when the power within you is discovered and used, it must be used for good and not evil. If used for destructive reasons, it will be sure to destroy in the end. Your power should be used to bring peace, joy, happiness, and harmony into your life and the lives of others, but if it is misused, it will surely deliver terrible consequences in the end.

      The mental attitude of a person who writes a book can also be felt in the pages of the book. In my first book, *Destined for Great Things*, I confessed that writing that book was a form of therapeutic healing for me. When I talked about the death of my daughter, I mentally relived the events surrounding that situation and had to stop writing at different times because of experiencing again the sorrowful emotions regarding that incident. After reading *Destined for Great Things,* people shared with me that they cried when they read that story. Some confessed that they could actually feel my pain as they were reading. While writing the chapter on my marriage, feelings of anger, resentment, and bitterness rose up in me while writing about some of the things I endured. Similarly, people also shared with me their feelings of anger and rage that emanated in them as a result of reading that chapter. My emotions were transferred to the pages of the book as I wrote, and there they remain. My point is that what is inside you will come out and does affect others. Similarly, your mental attitude affects others for better or for worse more than you know. Your mental attitude will cause others to accept or reject you. Take your attitude and place it into the hands of power, love, and wisdom with confidence and faith, knowing that as you absorb yourself in them, you will begin to be felt with power.

      The one God, the one Spirit cares, knows, understands, and responds to you, but only as much as you will allow Him to through your own nature. He operates for you through you, but our mental attitudes often hinder God from operating through us. He is a God of peace, love, harmony, and power. Surely, He will not operate harmoniously in a consciousness that is full of discord, inharmony, and confusion. Power and prosperity are inevitable if a person's consciousness is widened enough to receive them and their mental attitude is right. You should feel as though the entire power of God is for you and never against you. You do not need to go searching after God. He is not lost and the most important thing to know is that He lives within you. Know that the Spirit within you is the Spirit of God. Therefore, you must penetrate more deeply into your own nature and there He is. This is where you meet God, inside yourself. When you begin to let that sink in, you can then talk to Him just as consciously as you talk to people, and if you expect it, believe it, and feel it, you will also get His response.

ALL IS ONE

You must learn that all is one. Every creation is an individual manifestation from the one God. Our God, who rules the universe, is conscious and intelligent. He is Spirit and everything He has created is also Spirit. Since everything that is made comes from God, then everything made has God in it. When He created you, the only material He had to make you out of was the essence of His own being. The only Spirit He had to give you life with, was of His own Spirit. The only mind He had to implant in you was of His own mind. Since the essence of God is Spirit, and He only has the substance of His being to pour into the thing He makes, then there is Spirit in everything. There is nothing but Spirit all around you. You are made in the image of God, thus you are made of spiritual substance. You are spirit clothed in flesh. When your flesh or outer shell disintegrates and your heart stops beating, your soul and spirit will leave your outer shell and return back to God. Your soul belongs to God. The God of Christians, Muslims, Roman Catholics, and the practice of Hinduism, Buddhism, and Judaism all serve the same God. There is only one God permeating the universe. There are not many different Gods with many different powers ruling the world. Man has created things by hand and referred to those creations as God, but those so-called "gods" have no power, no wisdom, or supremacy. A creation can not be greater than its creator who made it. The one Spirit, the God who rules, overrules and superrules the universe is omnipotent (having all power), omniscient (all knowing), and omnipresent (everywhere at the same time). There is only one God and one Spirit. Different religions approach Him differently according to their beliefs, but they are approaching the same God that you and I approach. We, as humans are individual personifications of the same Spirit. Men and women are not separate spirits, but one Spirit expressing consciously and intelligently through different forms.

The one Spirit permeating the entire universe knows all that is known. He expresses Himself through the forms in which He has made although He Himself has no form. We, as the personifications of the formless God do have a form. That which has a form is limited. The one Spirit, being God who has no form, is limitless. If there is no form, there are no boundaries. God has no boundaries and no limits. The intelligence of the unformed Spirit is unlimited, but the intelligence of man, being a form of God is limited. Man can increase his perceptive powers by thought. Knowing this truth leads to spiritual power. The powerful life is that life where the one Spirit, being God, flows through the channels of a person's thought. Before this can happen, the channels of one's thought must be opened and their consciousness must be widened. This comes by way of one's own effort. Spiritual power is an internal awareness. When men and women truly desire to find truth and truly are dedicated to living right and taking the right action in every situation, they advance towards unity with the one Spirit, being God. Power comes when mind, body, soul and spirit are all in harmony with the willingness to be right in every aspect of one's life. When a person earnestly desires to do the right thing, that person begins to think their way towards truth and begins to walk in pathways of power and peace. To have the will to do right, to know the right thing to do, and to do the right thing gives a person the power to discern what God's perfect will is for his or her life and live according to that will.

YOUR INNER SPIRIT

Within everyone is another self, an eternal person. You have two selves, your outer self and your inner self. When you meet your inner self, you find that it contains peace, wisdom, and calmness. This self resides at the very center of your being. It has all answers concerning who and what you are. When you sit to meet that other person within, you will gain an insight and wisdom that will rise up from the inner transcending to the outer self. Let your inner self speak to your outer self and become renewed. Your mind permeates your entire body and it is also responsible for all your circumstances. Call upon your greater mind to mentally carry your outer self to where you meet your inner self who resides within you. There is nothing too small or too great for your mind if you will just open it up to receive. Your inner self is constantly communicating with your outer self. Oftentimes you just don't listen. When your outer self is receptive enough to listen to wisdom, intuition, and creative genius of the inner self, it will flow up and out of you into your circumstances and everyday experiences. You have within you the power to consciously cooperate with your inner self, which is inherent in the spiritual side of your existence. You will not be afraid when you know the truth. God speaks to you every day and is always revealing to you the realities about yourself and life in general. As you cooperate in love, peace, joy and openness with the truths that He reveals, you become renewed. You are given fresh blessings everyday, but you shall not be able to receive them until you can mentally and spiritually digest them. There is no limitation except for the limitations you place on yourself through ignorance. However, since everyone can imagine a greater good that they have not yet experienced, then everyone has the ability to rise triumphantly over their current conditions. God has given you every tool you need to rise above your current situations. You do not have to be sick, broke, miserable, unhappy, frustrated or confused. Just make a decision to "be" what you want to be. Despite what your current situation may be, choose to be happy. Radiate happiness. Think happy thoughts. Speak positive words and just "be". Though you may find yourself in hell, the minute you begin to dwell upon all that is heavenly, you will find yourself in heaven. You may be in heaven, but the minute you begin to dwell upon evil thoughts, you will find yourself immediately in hell. Act the part you want to play in this life. Act prosperous and you will be prosperous. Act positively and you shall be positive. Act healthy and you shall have health. Act the part with conviction and your subconscious mind will make you into the person you have convinced yourself that you already are. Just by your thoughts, you can bring whatever you desire into your experiences if you are thinking right. You will become a living personification of your thoughts. Average people act according to how they feel. If they feel sick, they act sick. If they feel miserable, they act miserable (and make others around them miserable). Feeling and action go hand in hand; but a person who has come into knowledge of the secrets of the ages understands that if you regulate the action regardless of the feeling, you in turn change the feeling. Everyone is seeking happiness. Happiness is not found in outer conditions. It is found in inner conditions. You are an eternal spirit with all power, all wisdom, and all knowledge. Just go deep within yourself and unify yourself with it.

UNDERSTANDING PEOPLE

We have all met intelligent people who were difficult to get along with. Typically, these personality types believe that they do not have to make the point of exchanging pleasantries because it wastes valuable time, which could be used for working. Additionally, they feel that their expertise is so valuable that interpersonal skills are not needed in order to effectively get the job done. Thinking this way is a mistake indeed and is a character flaw. Some people are just difficult because they have become accustomed to being that way. A well-balanced person is one who has both feet firmly planted on the ground. They are down to earth. They know that it takes people to get ahead, and therefore they have someone that they rely on for guidance and wisdom. That person pulls them upward. This person also has people who they mentor and guide. They pull these people up on the ladder behind them. A well balanced person always has someone over them that they look up to and someone behind them who looks up to them. They are fully aware that everyone has something meaningful to offer to the lives of another and they treat every person they meet with kindness and respect. As a result, they are well-liked, admired, and supported. This is the person who understands what it means to treat others as you would have them treat you. This person recognizes any flaws in his or her character and works on correcting them.

Prosperity engenders both accountability and responsibility. As you begin to walk in the unfolding of prosperity, you will not always be liked, but that is fine. It is not your job to be liked. It is your job however, to understand that people are essential to helping you pursue your goals. Despite how others treat you, you are to respond with calmness and dignity. You must learn the art of listening, studying, and understanding people while making allowances for his or her ignorance relating to people. When you treat every person you meet as though they are important, regardless of their position or lot in life, you have mastered a very good skill. As long as you treat people with value, interact with them in a positive way, and make sure that your conversation is sincere, you will be known as a unique individual. Nonetheless, people are going to always find something negative to say regardless of what you do, but you are to continue being the person you know pleases God.

As a result of working for supervisors whose insecurity issues caused them to mistreat, demean, and degrade others, I vowed to never do that. I saw the negative effect that lack of empathy had on employees and I heard the nasty comments made continuously. Nevertheless, I also observed how the same people who complained relentlessly about the boss would feed the ego, laugh and joke with, and be very phony with them. Inwardly they despised their boss. Outwardly, they esteemed them. I learned from this and was determined not to be either type of person. I try and always keep in mind the following quote from George Washington Carver: *"How far you go in life depends on your being tender with the young, compassionate with the aged, sympathetic with the striving and tolerant of the weak and strong. Because someday in life you will have been all of these."*

When I became an Assistant Principal, I brought all my learned lessons and observations of people with me, understanding that as an administrator, I was predisposed to being talked about also. However, I vowed to always conduct myself as a professional. I am very proud to say that I have never demeaned, talked down to, yelled at, or disrespected any person working under me. My expectations have and always will remain high. Yes, there were times that I had to verbally reprimand employees, but I did it in the most dignified manner possible, focusing on the infraction and not the person. There is always a way to get a point across without criticizing. I learned at a very young age by being on both the giving and receiving end that sharp criticisms and rebukes almost invariably end in futility, because as much as we thirst for approval, we dread condemnation. As an administrator in the school system, the nature of conversations that I have with employees is not always pleasant, but if individuals take my admonishments in the spirit they are given, they would understand that I mean no ill will towards them with my words. Unfortunately, difficult conversations must be held at times and regardless of how politically correct they are conveyed, sometimes they are hard to hear and even harder to have to say. If my conversations are taken negatively, then perception comes in to play and all I can do is watch my mental attitude and exercise respect towards the individual. I am able to sleep well each night because I take pride in knowing that I do not mistreat, belittle, or talk down to anyone. I can not emphasize the importance of valuing people. We have to realize that all of us belong to God, and if we treat each other as God's children, we would never have to worry about being offensive to anyone. Everything that is put out comes back full circle, good or bad. If we mistreat others, we will be mistreated by others at some point. Treating others with respect, love, consideration and dignity is using wisdom, and one who has wisdom has the key to being a master of human relations.

<u>CHAPTER 7   KEY POINTS:</u>

❖ The difference between those who use their power and those who do not is that the former have found their inner power, taken hold of it, and used it to greatly enhance their lives. The latter has not discovered that there is power within them, and therefore do not use it.

❖ The one God, the one Spirit cares, knows, understands, and responds to you, but only as much as you will allow Him to through your own nature. He
operates for you through you, but our mental attitudes often hinder God from operating through us.

❖ The one Spirit permeating the entire universe knows all that is known. He expresses Himself through the forms in which He has made, although He Himself has no form.

❖ Act the part you wish to play in this life. Act like a prosperous person and you shall be prosperous. Act positively and you shall be positive. Act like a healthy person and you shall have health.

❖ We have to realize that all of us belong to God, and if we treat each other as God's children, we would never have to worry about being offensive to anyone.

8

INTEGRITY SHOULD GUIDE YOUR ACTIONS

> *It's not what we eat but what we digest that makes us strong; not what we gain but what we save that makes us rich; not what we read but what we remember that makes us learned; and not what we profess but what we practice that gives us integrity.*
>
> *Francis Bacon*

Integrity is a noble and priceless quality. The person who has managed to hold on to their integrity without deviating from it is a rare person. When we hear the word integrity, we naturally think of honesty, holding on firmly to values, having a good moral standing and being ethical. And yes, integrity is all of those things, but once a person's integrity has been compromised and made known, it is extremely difficult, if not impossible to repair that reputation. The bible even says that, *"A good name is rather to be chosen than great riches, and a loving favor rather than silver and gold."* (Proverbs 22:1). A person is somewhat spared from public humiliation if their fall from grace is between them and God only or the few who are privy to have knowledge of the misdeed. It is easier to temporarily deal with a bad conscience than it is to deal with a bad reputation. I think it is fair to say that we all have compromised our integrity at some point in our lives. I for one know that I have compromised mine many times, specifically during my "more youthful" years. I even spoke of my obsession with stealing in my first book, *'Destined for Great Things'*. It is not easy to gain credibility after one has committed so many unscrupulous acts, but with time, a person's integrity builds back up again, *if* they consistently strive towards doing right and becoming right. It is a liberating feeling to be able to stand before the world and say, *"Yes, I used to steal, lie, use drugs, speak profanity, fornicate, etc., but that is who I [used] to be. I am no longer that person."*

CONFESSION IS GOOD FOR THE SOUL

It takes a strong person to confess their disgraceful deeds or talk about shameful things that may have gripped them in the past. The enemy of God and man wants us to forever hold on to those shameful experiences from the past because if we can stay bound up by the chains of guilt and shame, we will never truly be free. Without being truly free, the Spirit of the Lord can not permeate in our lives. *Where the spirit of the Lord is, there is liberty (2nd Corinthians, 3:17).* Keeping hidden secrets deep within is not liberating if those memories continue to taunt you. It is suppressing and draining. One may not realize that shameful memories may actually be holding them back from true freedom, joy, and inner peace because those events have been so nicely tucked away in the back of the mind and seemingly forgotten about; but guilt and shame are not dead things and they are not forgotten. If a person has not been delivered from the effects of guilt and shame, then every time a flashback comes to mind, those feelings rise up and make their effects known. Consequently, those negative, shameful, guilty feelings release the associated poisons throughout the body, which manifests in the form of disease. In order for anyone to move forward from unpleasant past events, he or she must face them, talk them out, then ask the Lord to deliver them from the residual effects of those experiences. One who truly wants to be delivered, can and will be. It is God's desire that we be free! If you know you are no longer the person you use to be, why not help another get freed through confession when the time presents itself? I am certainly not saying that you should divulge all your skeletons to the world. What I am saying is that if the opportunity presents itself for you to help someone through your testimony, then help them. Confession is very good medicine for the soul. Oftentimes, people will look at you and say, *"Wow, look how far that person came from where he or she used to be. If they can overcome, then so can I."*

A person who has integrity has it in every aspect of their life – in their home, on their job, in their business affairs, etc. Everything they do is done with honesty and truth. This person is recognized for being upright and candid. A person with true integrity is honest, balanced, wise, and understands people. This person becomes prosperous through hard work, mental labor, honest dealings, and being straightforward with others. He or she will taste the refreshing drink of pure prosperity in due season. No one will ever taste of that drink until they have put in their share of honest sacrifice and labor. Gratification and fulfillment springs up in a person who has put in honest days of hard work, commitment and perseverance. There is a difference between honest wealth and dishonest wealth. There is no gratification at all in attaining dishonest wealth. There is no fulfillment that comes with it because true fulfillment is a fruit of honesty, hard work and self-sacrifice. If a person has acquired their wealth dishonestly, then how can they experience true fulfillment? The one who has toiled and labored, pursued their goals, consistently prayed, meditated, and persevered, has sweet sleep each night. The one who acquired the world's wealth by dishonesty, lying, cheating, or stepping on others to get ahead does not taste the refreshing drink of pure prosperity, nor do they sleep with the sweetness that comes from an honest day's labor. Their consciousness does not allow them to get pure rest because the conscious mind itself is not at rest. Although this person may walk in the world with the mask of happiness appearing prosperous, there is an inward conflict between their inner self and their outer self. The outer self is the appearance of what they portray. Eventually, the inner self will merge with the outer self and the natural effects will be of a humiliating outcome. Truth always prevails. Regardless of how long a lie is permitted to remain, the truth will always be revealed. Remember, true wealth entails peace, good health, affluence, love, joy, happiness and abundance, not just money. How then can a person possess these qualities if they have only given out the opposites of them? A person can not draw honesty into their world through dishonesty. He or she cannot draw in love through hate, or peace through confusion. God has as much good for you that you can take, but you can only take as much as you give. You can not take love if you only give hate. You can not take peace if you only give discord. You certainly can not take in good if you only give out evil. You get back only the effects that correspond with the causes that you give out. Integrity guides a person to give out good will towards men.

HEREDITARY TENDENCIES

Some hereditary characteristics are visibly obvious in a person's features such as freckles, dimples, a widow's peak, tongue rolling, an

Prosperity is Your Birthright!

attached earlobe, blue, green or hazel eyes, etc. These are physical traits that are inherent in the DNA imbedded in the family bloodline. However, some genetic predispositions that are not so readily noticeable, but are carried from generation to generation are made evident through character and personality. Some of these predispositions are so strong that a person finds themselves being pulled in certain directions and do not understand why. Oftentimes it is because the ancestral tendencies passed down in the bloodline awakens and seeks expression. This can be wonderful if those tendencies are noble and constructive, but when they are not, a person may find themselves in unfavorable situations. I personally came from unfavorable maternal and paternal backgrounds. My maternal grandmother was an alcoholic and died from Sclerosis of the Liver, which is often caused by drinking too much alcohol. From the stories I've been told, she frequently drank, would become inebriated and would then walk the neighborhood using profanity and embarrassing her children (who were my mom and two aunts). Both of my aunts ended up strung out on drugs and alcohol. Both lived in poverty and none of their combined nine children graduated from high school. Many other relatives on this side of the family currently live in poverty, debauchery and limitation. Drug abuse, alcoholism, incarceration, welfare, dropping out of school, uncontrolled anger and belligerence are very prevalent on this side. It has been very seldom that I attended a family function where there was not some form of conflict that arose. It seems obvious that the propensity to cause chaos and confusion is also imbedded in the family traits on this side. There are however, some maternal relatives who are decent, honest, law-abiding citizens. Unfortunately it seems that the "dysfunctional" relatives outweigh the "functional" ones on this side of the family. My biological father spent the majority of his life in and out of prison for various crimes ranging from larceny, writing bad checks, theft, and committing other offenses until he was stabbed and killed by a woman he had been dating while they were at a bar together. Coincidentally, my paternal relatives have comparable characteristics to my maternal relatives as evidenced by the incarcerations, drug abuse, excess in alcohol, dropping out of school and the constant proclivity for publically displaying belligerence. The women on this side are also cantankerous and defiant and debauchery is also prevalent. Many of my relatives on both sides have spent the majority of their lives in prison and some are in there for life. This, my friends, is from whence I came.

GENERATIONAL CURSES

Was I destined for destruction? I had failure in my blood from both maternal and paternal sides and I certainly began following in the footsteps of my father, who by the way was a highly intelligent man in the cognitive sense of the word. Unfortunately, he used his intelligence to mastermind schemes for getting over on people dishonestly. I began stealing at a very young age, then graduated to bigger, more expensive things. I went to jail for my petty crimes just like my family members and I was headed for the same life as them. Some of the troubles that followed certain members of my family also followed me in my earlier years and I often found myself in unpleasant situations. Some people call these inherited tendencies generational curses, which are perpetually passed down from generation to generation. But we rejoice to know that there is not a single family curse that can not be broken through prayer. I did not like the path that I was traveling on, so I chose to walk another path. Through many honest prayers and confessions, much spiritual warfare, many tears, lots of fasting and reading the Bible, I was delivered from those strongholds that gripped me. The forces of destruction tried to keep me bound through my family line. The spiritual fight that I had to overcome was not easy, but with the help of God, I broke loose and I am free! I am not ashamed to tell the world where I came from. It is my duty to share with the world what the Lord can do for them since I am a living testimony. The sins of our forefathers can have a devastating effect on our lives. Family members fight, they hate, and they feud. Such behaviors that are continuously ongoing in a family are often results of curses being placed on a family unit or the whole family line. There are many people today who are bound with spiritual chains because of the iniquities of their forefathers. Whole nations are being destroyed because of the sins of ancestors. My freedom came when I confessed the sins of my ancestors and forefathers as well as everyone in my bloodline. After I did this, the curses were lifted off both my life and my son's life and blessings took their place.

Hereditary tendencies are real and should thoroughly be researched in order for a person to understand why certain desires and cravings rise up in them. When patterns of particular actions are perpetuated in different family members in a family line, those behaviors should be analyzed a little deeper. Scientists, psychologists, and law enforcement criminologists understand the significance of genetics. For instance, when a person desires to apply for a job with the Federal Bureau of Investigation (FBI), regardless of the position being applied for, a thorough background check is conducted. When the FBI performs a background check, they don't just scratch the surface, they go back to a person's high school, middle school, and yes, even elementary school. They ask questions of old classmates, former teachers, ex-girlfriends and ex-boyfriends, old neighbors, and if possible, even the old cashier at the corner store. They get information about the person's mother, father, and grandparents. If they can, they will go as far back as acquiring information on a person's great grandparents. I personally know someone who was denied an interview with the FBI because "his father" smoked a little too much marijuana. Not him, but his father! The FBI understood that the father's blood was in the son and that he was disposed to walking in the footsteps of his father since he came from that seed. Did his father abuse marijuana? Who knows? But his father's use of it caused his son to be denied a job. We have to begin to understand that our actions do not just affect us but our actions may adversely affect relatives that we may never even meet. When we let integrity guide our actions, it is difficult to walk contrary to God's will. When and if we choose to ignore our conscience, we must suffer the consequences that will result thereafter, but God is faithful and is quick to forgive. He is a loving, forgiving, gracious God, but every sin has a price to be paid and although Jesus has ultimately paid the price for every sin, we as individuals must reap the effects of the causes we initiate. We must let integrity guide in every area of our lives. If not, we could be inflicting life-changing difficulties upon ourselves and those who come after us.

MOTIVES

In the world we live in today, one can live their entire life giving service and doing good to people, but then make one public mistake and then they are finished. Immediately they become infamous and everyone seems to forget all the good he or she did and speaks only of the misdeed. It is sad, but it is true that we live in that kind of a world. What really matters to God and also to your conscience is the motive behind your actions. Some people do the wrong thing, but with the right motives. They will eventually be rewarded for their noble intentions. Others do the right thing, but with the wrong motives. They have their reward already. Nothing is ever done without a motive and when the motives are pure, good follows. The motives that cause people to do things are usually because of the incentive that follows. This incentive can be intrinsic or extrinsic. However, there will come a time when the motive has been forgotten but the deeds continue to be performed out of habit. It is your responsibility to ensure that your motives are right at all times.

Everyone has impure thoughts that come to his or her mind. Not everyone talks about it, but impure thoughts come to everyone regardless of what his or her title or position in life may be. The measure of your strength comes when you learn how to identify the thoughts as impure and then dismiss them. Once you release the thoughts by countering them with constructive thoughts, they pass out of the mind. There are several ways in which a person can train themselves to dismiss negative or impure thoughts. You may pray over the impure thought asking the Lord to purify your mind or you may recite scripture as the thought enters the mind. A scripture that I use whenever I find myself thinking negatively or impurely is, *"Casting down imaginations, and every high thing that exalts itself against the knowledge of God, and bringing into captivity every thought to the obedience of Christ." (2nd Corinthians, 10:5).* The moment you identify negative, impure, ungodly or unfruitful thinking and take control of your thoughts, you become a master of yourself. The key is to recognize and destroy those impure thoughts. When you hear stories of preachers, politicians or other prominent leadership figures who have fallen from grace, it is not because of one thought acted upon. In those cases, the fall was only the finished product, the outworking, the end. The person allowed an impure thought to enter their mind. As it entered a second and third time, they welcomed it, fondled it, and entertained it. Each time the impure thought returned, it grew and became stronger until at last it attracted to itself the opportunity for it to manifest into action. That thought, which was nurtured and cultivated gradually undermined the person's character. No-one is so strong that this can not happen them. Remember – YOU BECOME WHAT YOU THINK ABOUT! Everything acted upon always originates in the mind first. If you analyze every thought, you won't have to worry about the actions because if the thought is good, the actions will be good as well. This goes hand in hand with having integrity. When you get down to your true motives, you discover so much about what and who you truly are. In order to learn yourself, begin to ask what your motives are for wanting certain things in your life. For instance, review each goal that you have set and ask yourself, *What is my motive for wanting this particular goal? What is my motive for wanting a promotion? What is my motive for wanting my business to flourish? What is my motive for wanting a new car?* If the answer to each question is "money or status", then go deeper and ask yourself, Why do I want more money? Why do I want status? If the answer is, "*so people will respect me.*" Then you must dig deeper and ask yourself, "*Why do I want or need people to respect me?*" The student of life, who is coming into knowledge of the truth regarding true prosperity, realizes that it is not money they should seek, but wealth, not status, but service, not fame, but humility. If you had all the money you needed to pay off every debt, and you were able to afford anything your heart desired, then what else would you want? You should really explore these questions because they take you very deep. Exploring motives helps you to purify your heart, analyze your desires, and see yourself for who you truly are. It is only then can you become a new person.

THE VALUE OF WISDOM

A person who has true spiritual wisdom also has integrity because wisdom guides a person by integrity. Many people *think* they have wisdom, but in all actuality, very few people do. There is a difference between common sense and wisdom. Having common sense means understanding things from a reasonable point of view. It is knowing what is politically correct to do and say. It is being able to ascertain things based upon the facts that are given. Wisdom on the other hand is much more than that. Yes, wisdom entails all of those qualities but wisdom includes spiritual awareness. This spiritual awareness sets a person apart from those who simply have common sense. We often expect wisdom to come with age, but the sad reality is that age sometimes comes alone. Some people try to do in the second half of their lives what they should have done in the first half and unfortunately some never acquire wisdom. Wisdom is the greatest desire that one should aspire to posses. If a person has wisdom, all other good things follow. With wisdom come poise, calmness, and the power to dwell upon all that is pure, unselfish

Integrity Should Guide Your Actions

and right. Those with wisdom know how to think the right thoughts and avoids the pitfalls and troubles that accompany wrong thinking. The Bible repeatedly speaks of the benefits of having wisdom and explains the value of it. The book of proverbs lists many benefits wisdom. Below are just a few blessings that wisdom gives:

- For the Lord gives **wisdom**: out of His mouth comes knowledge and understanding. He lays up sound **wisdom** for the righteous. (Proverbs 2:7).

- Happy is the one that finds **wisdom**, and the one that getteth understanding. (Proverbs 3:13).

- Keep sound **wisdom** and discretion. So shall they be life unto thy soul and grace to thy neck. (Proverbs 3:21).

- The fear of the Lord is the beginning of **wisdom**; and the knowledge of the holy is understanding. (Proverbs 9:10).

- How much better it is to get **wisdom** than gold and to get understanding to be chosen rather than silver (Proverbs 16:16).

- He that getteth **wisdom** loveth his own soul; He that keepeth understanding shall find good. (Proverbs 19:8).

- **Wisdom** is the principle thing. Therefore get wisdom and in all thy getting, get understanding. (Proverbs 4:7).

- The **wise** shall inherit glory, but shame shall be the promotion of fools. (Proverbs 3:35).

- Get **wisdom**, get understanding, forsake them not. Forsake her not, and she shall preserve thee. Love her and she shall keep thee. (Proverbs 4:6).

- Exalt her (**wisdom**) and she shall promote thee. She shall bring thee to honor when thou does embrace her. (Proverbs 4:8).

- Length of days is in her (**wisdom**) left hand, and in her right hand, riches and honor. (Proverbs 3:16).

- She (**wisdom**) is a tree of life to them that lay hold upon her; and happy is everyone that retaineth her. (Proverbs 3:18).

The bible speaks vividly about possessing wisdom. God has conveyed to us that with wisdom as our guide, we are sure to make the right decisions and walk the path that He has marked for each of us individually. If you don't have wisdom, simply ask for it. God is always ready to give you what you ask for if the desire is noble. *"If any of you lack wisdom, let him ask of God, that giveth to all men liberally, and upbraideth not; and it shall be given him." (James 1:5).* Integrity is an offspring of wisdom.

We can learn integrity from many biblical figures. When I think of individuals who epitomized integrity and wisdom, a couple of biblical characters come to mind, but the one who stands out the most in my mind is Joseph. Joseph was next to the youngest born to Jacob who had 12 sons from which the 12 tribes of Israel are named. Joseph's brothers hated him because their father loved him more than his other sons. As the baby, he told his father of his brother's evil deeds, which is typical of the youngest child. Because his father loved him so much, he gave Joseph a coat with many colors, which he loved to wear and his brothers hated to see him with it on. God gave this child a gift of "seeing" and interpreting dreams. He once shared with his brothers one particular dream he had. In this dream, his brothers were his servants. After listening to their baby brother share his dream with them, they became very angry and conspired against him. One day the brothers were far away from their father when they saw Joseph coming to look for them. When they saw him from a distance, they discussed killing him and telling their father that a wild beast came and ate the boy, but his brother Reuben said, *"Let us not kill him."* He suggested instead that they cast him into a pit in the wilderness, so they did just that. They took off his coat that his father had given to him and they threw him in a pit. As they sat down to eat after they had done this, they saw some Ishmeelites coming from Gilead with camels and decided that it would be profitable for them to sell their brother to the Ishmeelites for 20 pieces of sliver, but when they went back to the pit to get Joseph, he was gone. They did not know where he was or what had happened to him, so they took his coat, dipped it in goat's blood and took it to their father so he would think a wild animal had killed his son. The father mourned for his son many days and refused to be comforted.

Meanwhile, Joseph was found by the Midianites and they sold him to Potiphar, an officer and captain of the guards for King Pharaoh in Egypt. Although Joseph was a slave, the Bible states *...the Lord was with Joseph and he was a prosperous man: and he was in the house of his master the Egyptian.* Moreover, the Bible states that, *...his master saw that the Lord was with him, and that the Lord made all that he did to prosper in his hand. ...Joseph found grace in his sight, and he served him. (Genesis 39:2-4).* Potiphar made Joseph overseer for his house. All that Potiphar had, he put into Joseph's hand. Since the favor of God was upon Joseph's life, *the Lord blessed the Egyptian's house for Joseph's sake (Genesis 39:5). Joseph was a goodly person and well-favored. (Genesis 39:6).*

Even though Joseph was a servant, God still blessed him in this position. However, just because you have God's favor does not mean that you are not subject to being tempted, tested, or mistreated. You are more subjected to temptation because the forces of evil know that you are in God's will and they want you out of the will of God. Joseph was tempted. Potiphar's wife seduced him and tried to get him to sleep with her, but because he had integrity and was loyal to his master, he refused to do such a thing. His response to her was, *...how can I do this great wickedness, and sin against God?* She continued trying to get Joseph to have sex with her day after day, but he continued to resist her. She became angry because of this rejection and snatched off a piece of his clothing. She then ran and told the servants of her house that Joseph had come in and tried to rape her but that she started screaming. She had a piece of his clothing in her hand and told them that he had left it there when he tried to lie with her. When Potiphar came home, she told him this story and he put Joseph in prison. The Word says however, that in spite of this, *...the Lord was with Joseph and shewed him mercy, and gave him favor in the sight of the keeper in the prison.* The keeper of the prison put Joseph in charge of all the other prisoners.

In the meantime, King Pharaoh's butler and baker made him angry and he placed them both in prison where Joseph was. While there, they both had dreams, but were very discouraged because they could not understand the meaning of them. Joseph interpreted both of their dreams and each of his interpretations came to pass. Two years later, King Pharaoh had a dream, but there was no one in his kingdom that could interpret it. The butler who Pharaoh had put in prison and later restored to his original position told

Pharaoh about Joseph who had interpreted his dream two years earlier. Pharaoh called for Joseph and told him his dream. Joseph interpreted the king's dream for him step by step with great accuracy and clarity. As a result, the king was so grateful to him that he made Joseph governor over all the land of Egypt. Joseph was next in command only after the king. The king even took the ring that was on his own finger and placed it on Joseph's finger. He gave Joseph a wife and Joseph went on to perform his job as governor of Egypt.

    Because Joseph held on firmly to his integrity, God rewarded him. In the natural, it may not have seemed fair that Joseph spent years in prison for something he did not do, and to add to that, he was thrown away like yesterday's trash by his own brothers. To the natural eye, it looked like this man was destined for bad luck, but God had a divine plan for his life and he had to go through the fire in order to be purified. The years that he spent in Potiphar's house as a servant and the years in prison was his "essential time for preparation". The reward that he received for his patience and faithfulness while in prison was multiplied many times over. But the story does not stop there.

    There was a famine in Canaan where Joseph's father Jacob and brothers lived. Jacob told his sons to go and see if they could buy some food in Egypt because he had heard that there was food there. Coincidentally, it was Joseph who sold all the food in Egypt. Joseph's brothers came to Egypt to buy food. Not knowing that they were standing before their own brother who they had thrown in a pit and left for dead, they bowed themselves down before him with their faces to the earth. He knew who they were, but they did not know who he was. He asked them a lot of questions about where they came from, their father, and if they had anymore brothers (He realized that his brother Benjamin was not with them). They explained that their baby brother (Benjamin) had stayed back with the father and that they had one other brother who was dead (speaking of him). He allowed them to buy corn, but told them to go and get their other brother who they had left at home and bring him back in order to prove that they were not spies. He only did this because he wanted to see his brother Benjamin with whom he shared the same mother. When they returned back home, they told their father about what the "Lord of the Country" had told them to do. The father told them that he would not allow them to take their brother to this man because he had already lost his youngest son (Joseph) and would not lose another. However, after a year, they ran out of food again and needed to return to Egypt to buy more food, but they knew they could not return unless they had their brother Benjamin with them, who Joseph the governor had requested. Jacob allowed them to take Benjamin this time, but told them that if something happened to him as had happened to Joseph, he would surely die. They returned to Egypt with a gift to offer to the governor as their father had told them to do to show respect. When Joseph saw that they had returned back, he told one of his servants to prepare a setting because "those men" were going to dine with him that evening. When they brought the brothers inside the mansion, they were very afraid, thinking that they had done something wrong. The servants gave them water and washed their feet. When Joseph came in, he cordially spoke with them and asked them how their father was doing. Still not knowing that this governor who was speaking to them was their own baby brother, they respectfully answered and said, *"Yes our father is well and in good health."* He then saw his brother Benjamin close up and asked them, *"Is this your younger brother Benjamin of whom you spoke to me?"* and they replied *"Yes"*. When he saw his brother Benjamin, his emotions got the best of him and he went into his chamber and cried. He came back out and enjoyed a nice meal with them. They all received large portions, but Benjamin's portion was five times more than the other brothers. They enjoyed this time with the governor where they ate, drank, and were merry, but they still did not understand why they were being treated with so much favor. As they were preparing to leave, Joseph had a silver cup put in Benjamin's bag as a setup to accuse him of stealing. As they were on the way out, he had a servant go and accuse the brothers of the missing cup. The servant said that the one who is found with the cup must stay behind and be Joseph's servant. The cup was found on Benjamin. However, Judah, the oldest son begged Joseph to let him be the servant in Benjamin's place. He then explained how his father would die if they did not return back with Benjamin. After hearing this, Joseph could not refrain himself anymore, but revealed to his brothers who he was. He wept very loudly and told them not to be angry with themselves for what they had done to him, but that it was a part of God's plan. He wept on his brother Benjamin's neck and Benjamin wept on his neck. He explained to them that the famine was going to be a total of five years and that they were to go and tell their father of his position in Egypt and to pack up and come live prosperously in Egypt with him. He kissed each of his brothers, filled their sacks with food and money, and sent them on their way to their father. They went back and told their father all that had happened. When they told their father all of this, *"the spirit of their father revived."* God spoke to Jacob in a dream and told him to go. When King Pharaoh found out that Joseph's brothers were coming to live in Egypt, he was very pleased. He and all his family went and lived in Egypt. Had Joseph not had integrity, he would have handled that situation much differently. Had he not forgiven his brothers, he would have tried to get revenge on them, but forgiveness comes with integrity and Joseph loved and forgave. This beautiful story entails so many spiritual nuggets. There are several lessons that can be learned from this story.

Lesson #1: When God shows you something in a dream, vision, or prophecy, keep it to yourself until the manifestation occurs. Revealing it too soon could cause warfare for you.

Lesson #2: Love each of your children the same. If you do adore one more than the other(s), do not let it be known to the other child(ren). It could cause resentment towards you and the favored child.

Lesson #3: You will always be rewarded for holding on firmly to your integrity.

Lesson #4: God can give you favor in the least expected places. When the favor of God is upon your life, it does not matter where you go or what you do, you will still be blessed in the situation.

Lesson #5: The bigger the test that you overcome, the greater the blessing. The level of attack is the best indicator as to the level of blessing that waits for you beyond the attack.

Lesson #6: What appears to be evil can actually be a blessing turned inside out.

Lesson #7: Always forgive. No matter what has been done to you, forgive.

CHAPTER 8 KEY POINTS:

- ❖ A person with true integrity is honest, balanced, wise, and understands people. This person becomes prosperous through hard work, mental labor, honest dealings, and being straightforward with others.

- ❖ You can not take love if you only give hate. You can not take peace if you only give discord. You certainly can not take good if you only give evil.

- ❖ Hereditary tendencies are real and should thoroughly be researched in order for a person to understand why certain desires and cravings rise up in them.

- ❖ Exploring motives helps you to purify your heart, analyze your desires, and see yourself for who you truly are. It is only then can we become a new person.

- ❖ Keeping hidden secrets deep within is not liberating if those memories continue to taunt you. It is suppressing and draining. One may not realize that shameful memories may actually be holding them back from true freedom, joy, and inner peace.

9

TRAIN YOUR MIND TO THINK POSITIVELY

> *You can close the windows and darken your room, or you can open the windows and let light in. It is a matter of choice. Your mind is your room. Do you darken it or do you fill it with light?*
>
> *Remez Sasson*

Throughout this book, I have talked a lot about the power of the mind and the life-changing effects of positive thinking. The ultimate mastery of the human mind is when one entertains only thoughts that are positive, constructive, creative, and peaceful. When a negative thought enters your mind (and it will), the thought should immediately be dismissed. You can not have a positive life and a negative mind. If you have a negative mind, you will have a negative life. The enemy controls your life when he controls your mind. You are changing everyday and as your mind changes for the better, your life changes for the better. Thoughts bear fruit and when your thoughts are good, the fruit of your life is good. You can look at a person's attitude and immediately know the kind of thoughts they most often think. Thousands of thoughts enter into your mind everyday; therefore, your mind filter must be constantly filtering thoughts 24 hours a day. No thought should be able to reside in your mind for long if it is not of a positive nature. You must get to a point where when a negative thought enters your mind, it immediately leaves because of the overwhelming light in there, just as darkness leaves when light comes. Light and darkness can not dwell in the same place. One has to be the dominating force. It is your responsibility to make sure that light dominates your mind.

Light reveals things. Darkness keeps things hidden. We must walk in the light as Jesus is in the light.

There are many ways in which you can fill your mind and spirit with light. Of course, entertaining thoughts that are positive, productive, and peaceful is the main way to stay in the light, but the question is, *"How does one get to the point where the majority of their thinking is positive?"* It is not easy for a person to immediately begin thinking positively if their entire thought life has consisted of negativity; but if there is a strong will, there is always a way. I have therefore, identified three very effective ways that a person's thoughts will change for the better if they implement these things on a regular basis. Take a look at them below:

Prayer. When you pray, you are submitting yourself to God in a very humble manner. When your words to Him are honest and sincere, He hears you because He listens to your heart. When your prayers come deeply out of your heart, they go directly into His ears. *In my distress I called upon the LORD, and cried unto my God: He heard my voice out of His temple, and my cry came before him, even into his ears. (Psalm 18:6).* Keeping the lines of communication open to God strengthens you and gives you faith, hope, and uplifted spirits. The more you pray, the more you open your mind to the hope and expectation of answered prayers. Hope and expectation are positive feelings and as your mind resonates on those feelings, you attract the essence of what you feel back to you.

Study. The Word of God declares in Timothy 2:15 that we are to, *"Study to show thyself approved unto God, a workman that needeth not to be ashamed, rightly dividing the word of truth."* The more you study the Word of God, the wiser you become because the Word is a guide for dealing with every aspect of your life. *"Thy Word is a lamp unto my feet and a light unto my path." (Psalm 119:105).* If the Word of God is a "lamp", then *Train Your Mind to Think Positively* this means that the Word is light. As you read and study the Word with an open heart and mind, you are actually allowing light into your spirit. If there is any darkness in you, then the more you read the Word, the less darkness there will be because light drives out darkness. Jesus is the light and if Jesus is the light, and the Word is light, then Jesus is the Word. *In the beginning was the Word and the Word was with God, and the Word was God. (John 1:1).* Mind renewal takes place when you begin to Let the Word of God *Dwell in You Richly. (Colossians 3:16).*

Fellowship. Webster's Dictionary defines fellowship as, "*An association of people who share common beliefs or activities.*" In Acts 2:42 we read that one of the main things the early church devoted itself to was fellowship. Fellowship was a very important part of their coming together and interacting with each other on one accord. When we fellowship with one another in brotherly and sisterly love, we strengthen our Christian bond between each other. Good, clean fellowship should be a very important part of a person's life because fellowshipping allows you to give love and to receive it from people with like minds and spirits. The need for connection is usually motivated by the desire for love and acceptance. Everyone has a desire to connect with other people. Spiritual fellowship is relatively easy because you typically share your spirituality with those you have religious commonalities. However, when you associate yourself with those outside of your spiritual affiliation, you really begin to see the kind of people you are drawn to and the kind of people who are drawn to you. This gives real insight into what you are sending out because we attract what we are. If you show me the caliber of friends you have, I can tell you a lot about the kind of person you truly are. You must be watchful of the people you choose to maintain close relationships with. They can either help or hinder you as a person. They can enhance or take away from your personal quality. Would you put 22 inch tires and a spoiler on a Mercedes Benz or Jaguar? No you wouldn't (I hope), because it would take away from the quality of the car. Why then would you walk with people with foul mouths, contentious behaviors or a negative attitude? This takes away from the quality of person you are. Having the right friends is a blessing. It gives meaning to your life. It allows you to let your hair down, laugh with, joke with, cry with, and just be yourself with; and we all need that. However, it is critical that you have discernment when it comes to those with whom you let your hair down with. Always analyze yourself first and then your associates. Listen to the language that comes out of the mouths of your associates, and observe how they respond to difficult situations. Just know the people with whom you fellowship. If these individuals have you thinking positively when you leave their presence, then these individuals enhance you as a person. This is effective fellowship for you. These three things, prayer, study, and fellowship all help your mind to think on things that are positive and productive. Of course there are other ways in which you can develop the power of positive thinking, but I know for sure that these three things work.

We all are where we are because of where our thoughts have brought us, and we will be in the future where our thoughts take us. Our character today is the culmination of our thoughts of the past. Your life is what you have made it by your thoughts. Once you get full control of your mind, you will have full control of your entire life. You have no personality and no life apart from your thoughts. Your thoughts are always right where you are. They are never separated from you. You are thinking right now. As your thoughts change, you change. You and only you can change your character and you do this by changing your thoughts. There is so much information on the power of the mind, and yet scores of individuals still do not fully understand the significant power that "thoughts" have on their lives, their circumstances, and their destinies. Life is about cause and effect, sowing and reaping, going around and coming back around. If your thoughts lead you to lie, you will be lied to; if you cheat, you will be cheated; if you give hate, you will be hated; if you give love, you will be loved; if you give criticism, you will be criticized. If you dislike something about a person, it is because that which you hate in them is a part of yourself. What isn't a part of you does not bother you.

STAY POSITIVE

Over the years, I've learned that a positive attitude gets me much farther than a negative one. It is not always easy to be calm and positive in stressful or frustrating situations, but if you will exercise self-discipline, you will see how it will work out much better for you in the end. Calmness is a beautiful nugget of wisdom and its presence is an indication of rich experience. A positive attitude is a rare commodity and it looks very attractive on the person who exhibits it. Needless-to-say, it results from positive thinking. A prosperous person with a positive attitude is a great person indeed; unfortunately, there are some people who are prominent or well-known, have massive wealth, great fame or influence, but display a negative disposition in their interactions with people. That type of personality takes away from one's credibility.

I know it is not easy to be positive all the time. Sometimes you just want to be left alone, but remember, a person who has mastered self-control understands that if you regulate the action regardless of the feeling, you change the feeling. Someone is always watching you. Be sure that what they see coming from you is light and not darkness. You could just be having a bad day, but that one bad day could leave a lasting impact on someone's life in a negative way. Train your mind to think positively, and as you think on positive things, you act in positive ways, even on bad days.

NEVER GIVE UP

Whatever you may be trying to achieve right now, do not give up. No matter how difficult things may "seem" to be, you must persist, persevere, and overcome every obstacle. Sometimes unexpected circumstances arise that knock you to the ground, but you must get up, dust yourself off and with God's guidance and your inner strength, move forward. If you can look up, you can get up. It is within you to succeed and overcome any and every obstacle that comes your way. Nothing ever lasts forever. Things only "come to pass" and they always leave behind a valuable lesson to be learned from them. Your circumstances do not equal your conclusion, but your outlook determines your outcome. When discouragement and frustration try to overtake you, examine your thought life. Remember, you become what you think about. If you think discouraging thoughts, you will become discouraged. If you think condemning thoughts, you will become condemned. If you think powerful thoughts, you will become powerful. Everybody has endured trials, tribulations, hardships and difficulties, but the reward comes to those who endure until the end. It does not matter what happens *to* you, but what happens *in* you that makes the difference in whether you learn the lesson from the experience or not. No great achievement comes without toil and struggle. Yes parents die, and as hard as it seems, we have to find the strength to go on. Children sometimes pass away before parents, but God has allowed such things to happen to certain "chosen" people for His divine purpose. People lose jobs, homes, become sick, get their hearts broken and get divorced. All of these things are a part of this thing called life. Sometimes when hardship and trials come our way, we think that we are the only one in the world experiencing the hurt and pain at that time, but Jesus said, *"There hath no temptation taken you but such as is common to man: but God is faithful, who will not suffer you to be tempted above that ye are able; but will with the temptation also make a way to escape, that ye may be able* to bear it." (1 Corinthians 10:13).   This scripture says that what we go through in life is *common* to everyone. There is nothing new that happens to anybody good, bad, or indifferent. "*That which hath been is now; and that which is to be hath already been; and God requireth that which is past.*" *(Ecclesiastes 3:15)*. Sometimes we need to be purified, and the only way that God can do this is through our tears. After the Lord has purified us to His satisfaction and our benefit, He takes the tears that He has squeezed out of us and puts them in his bottle. He then writes it down in His book. "*Thou tellest my wanderings: put thou my tears into thy bottle: are they not in thy book?" (Psalm 56:8)*. God loves you so much that He would take you through heartache and pain just to make you a great person. You never know what's inside a person until they are squeezed. If you squeeze a lemon, you will get lemon juice. If you squeeze an orange, you will get orange juice. When life puts the squeeze on you, what do you think will come out of you? If there is cursing in you, then when life puts the squeeze on you, cursing will come out. If evil is in you, then it will come out. If faith is in you, then when the trials, tribulations and hardships of life come, faith will keep you. If praise and worship is in you, then no matter what happens, you will praise and worship Him in and through all things. What is inside you? As you endure the mental, psychological and emotional pain, He is there the whole time keeping an eye on you, and although it hurts Him to see you suffer, it is very necessary in order to purge you. When you come out, you are as pure gold - refined, stronger, wiser, calmer, and at peace. He knows the end from the beginning. It is God's desire that you be prosperous, but there is a process that you must go through in order to get to that prosperity.

CEASE FROM CAUSING YOUR OWN WARFARE

In life we will experience good and bad, happiness and anger, sadness and joy, and ups and downs. It is all a part of living; but sometimes we cause our own problems with our mouth and our actions. Wisdom teaches how to act, what to say, and the right time to say it. Once something negative has been said, it can not be taken back. Once a person behaves in a foolish, outlandish, out-of-control manner, that image can not be taken out of the minds of those who witnessed that behavior, no matter how many times an apology is given. To be ill-mannered is to be unlearned and unwise. Ill-manners are the outward expression of inward defects. A person *is* what he or she does. If you act gentle at all times, then you are a gentle person. If you act wisely, then you are a wise person. If you act rudely, then you are a rude person. If you act selfishly, then you are selfish. No one can "make" you be what you are not. If you are not rude, then no matter what the situation, you will not act in a rude manner. Only what is "in" you will come out and that is an indication of what you are. A person can change their outward behavior for the sake of their image, but that does not change what is in the heart, but if a person truly changes what is in the heart, it will change their outward behavior. Therefore we must be very careful with our words and actions. What we say and how we act can bring "warfare" into our lives.

I am personally very leery of people who talk too much. If a person tells you too much of their business, they will tell you too much of other people's business, and it is certain that they will tell your business to others. Be careful with loose-tongued individuals. You are striving to be better and do better in every aspect of your life. You should use discernment regarding your associates and not have the time for gossip, petty foolishness, or fruitless conversations. You are not a garbage can, so do not allow people to dump their garbage into your spirit. Your focus should always be on your goals and on bringing greater meaning to your life. I've learned (the hard way) that when we get "caught up" in gossip, the outcome is never good. We have all been on both the contributing and receiving side of gossip, but we do not have to be on the contributing side of it anymore. That is the side that we can control. Remember "like attracts like", so the less you talk about others in a negative way, the less you will be talked about in a negative way. When you gossip, you are initiating a cause (sowing a seed) and what do you think the effect (harvest) of gossiping will be? No one likes to be discussed negatively and although everyone is talked about, it is not a good feeling when it comes back to you as either the contributor or the object of the gossip. We are all guilty of speaking negatively about others and oftentimes, it is not to hurt the person. Sometimes we are just guilty of being careless with our tongues. However, if we make a vow to never speak negatively about anyone, regardless of his or her reputation or character, then we should never have to worry about anything coming back to us in a negative way. That is a very noble vow to make and one that will stand you out among the ordinary. This sacrifice will cause you to rise above petty foolishness and mediocrity. You are bigger than to allow yourself to get caught up in petty gossip because

Prosperity is Your Birthright!

when you do, a little bird may go back and tell it. *"...curse not the rich in thy bedchamber: for a bird of the air shall carry the voice, and that which hath wings shall tell the matter." (Ecclesiastes 10:20).* You should rise to a level where people will not even feel comfortable speaking negatively about others around you. Great people associate themselves with great people, and great people do not speak negatively of others regardless of who the other person is or how disliked the other person may be. My mother always said to my sisters and I, *"If you don't have anything nice to say, then don't say anything at all."* Those are wise words to live by indeed. If you are using your time productively, then you do not have one second to waste engaging in negative gossip about people. You should be too busy working on achieving your goals, keeping target dates for yourself, and sowing good seeds in good soil.

We can cause our own warfare in others ways as well. Yes, negative speaking is one way to attract unfavorable situations into our lives, but conducting oneself in a manner that does not represent greatness can be another way. Remember that someone is always watching you and you are making some sort of impression on somebody in either a positive or negative way. You never get a second chance to make a first impression, so practice self-discipline, poise, grace, and self-control. Meditation helps with acquiring these things. Your actions are influencing people for or against your interests and desires. People are watching not only your actions, but also your mannerisms, interactions, responses, behaviors, and are also listening to the nature of your conversations. If you will keep in mind that you are always being watched, then you will be less inclined to give in to out-of-control behavior. Practice self-control and good manners. Good manners are the sugar to which people attract themselves to you. A smile enhances your beauty and attractiveness. A wholesome conversation gets people thinking in a good way. Tasteful behavior helps others to see that you are a person of class and worth. Be a light that shines brightly everywhere you go and in everything you do!

UNDERSTANDING YOURSELF

Although it is a great skill to be able to understand people, it is more important to understand yourself. When you truly know who you are, I mean really "know" yourself inside out, you become enlightened on a very deep level. Human nature causes us to scrutinize and "size up" others when we really need to be scrutinizing and sizing up ourselves. A major mistake that most people make as it relates to themselves is thinking that others see them the way they see themselves. Ninety percent of the time, our perception of how we view ourselves is extremely different from how others view us. Very few view people hit the target. Dave Weber, author of the book 'Sticks and Stones' defined seven concepts of self. He states that each of these concepts lives inside of us and help define the person we are. According to him, our composite as human beings is made up from the integration of the seven concepts. Those concepts are: The Me I think I am, the Me I really am, the Me I use to be, the Me that others see, the Me I try to project, the Me others try to make me, and the Me I want to be. If we really look at these different "Me's", we must admit that he is absolutely right because we do act a different way in different environments. When people interact with you, they have their own perception of the "Me's" in you. They look at you a certain way based on their experiences with you. Although you really don't know how people truly see you, you can know that if you strive to always be positive, always treat others the way you desire to be treated – with dignity, respect, and kindness, then you are not contributing in a negative way to how others may be perceiving you. They could very well have a distorted view of life in general, who knows. You must also know that people may also see you in a way that is exalted and honorable and you may not know it or understand why. This could be because everyone else around you sees greatness in you. If you keep hearing the same things over and over from different people with no connection to each other, then you may want to analyze what is being said. When everyone tells you they see a gift in you, or they see greatness in you, or you should take your skills to another level, then God could be trying to send you a message. Do not ignore it. Keep in mind that God uses people to deliver His blessings, convey his messages, and answer prayers for Him.

LIVE LIFE TO THE FULLEST

I've been repeating that life is meant to be lived and that you should live it to the fullest. This means that every aspect of your life should be gratifying to you. When you use your God-given gifts, they make room for you, and this room could be used to bring a flow of wealth and success into your life. *"A man's gift maketh room for him, and bringeth him before great men." (Proverbs 8:16).* Your subconscious mind must get to a place where it accepts only the best of everything and brings the best to you in a constant flow *if* this is your desire. Some people are content with what little they have and nothing is wrong with that, but if you desire to possess quality things, then you must begin to invest in the things that make for quality. You must let it sink in that prosperous people exude prosperity. People with real prosperity on the inside can sense the presence or absence of prosperity in others when they stand in their presence. It does not matter what you portray on the outside. There are people who are very perceptive and will know immediately the real from the fake. Remember that prosperity is an outward manifestation of what is evident on the inside. Act the part you wish to play in this life. If you want to make room in your consciousness for prosperity, then begin doing things with class. There is no lack of anything. Don't worry about anything running out.

INVEST IN QUALITY

I have always been a very cautious spender. My bills are always paid on time, and I have never been a shop-a-holic. I very seldom go to the mall and I have always tried to save money whenever I could. I know how to make a nickel scream. There were times that I would see something beautiful, fall in love with it, and refuse to buy it because of the cost. I would always justify not buying it by saying that I could do three or four other things with the money that I would spend on that. There is nothing wrong with this thinking, but everyone deserves to treat themselves every now and then. I have friends who treat themselves all the time. They have this level of thinking down to a tee. But there needs to be a balance. After depriving myself of the thing I wanted, I would regret not getting it weeks later when I would think about how much I liked it. If your bills are paid, your household and family members are taken of, and there is sufficient money in your savings account, then why not treat yourself every now and then? Why not travel first class? Why not stay at luxury hotels and be treated like the King or Queen that you are? In the past when I traveled out of town and had to stay at hotels, I always said to myself, *"Why should I pay an extra $100.00 a night when I could pay significantly less at a cheaper hotel?"* and so I would stay at the cheaper hotel. However, I would tell a lie when I would run into people who were staying at the Ritz Carlton, Hilton, Radisson, or Sheridan, etc. I was too shame to say that I was staying at the Ramada Inn or Holiday Inn, so I would lie. I've since learned that if I want to be surrounded by beauty and elegance, then I need to pay for beauty and elegance. Money will always come to me. Nothing will ever run out for good and so I am telling you to stay at the finest hotels. Eat at the best restaurants. Dress in quality clothing. Get massages. Visit the spa every now and then. Get a facial. Travel the world and enjoy the finer things of life. Stop penny pinching. Act the part you want to play in this life. If you want money to flow in and out of your life, then you must not penny pinch. If you begin to put out large quantities of money within reason, then large quantities of money will return back to you. Attend professional conferences. The way will be made if the desire is there. I am not saying to be materialistic by no means. If something happens and you have no choice but to stay at a less quality hotel, then you should be down-to-earth enough to stay there without complaining, but if you desire finer things, then go after finer things. Just make sure all other things are in order.

As vain as it may seem, people do judge you based on your appearance and they treat you based on how you "appear" to be. How can you convince people that you are a high-quality individual who can represent them or their business with style and class and yet you look like you are in need of charity? How can you convince people that you can make their business flourish and become profitable when you are driving a fifteen thousand dollar car? How can you represent someone in a persuasive role if your appearance is only persuading them that you are the one in need? I am not trying to sound vain by no means, but what I am saying is that appearance matters and if your desire is for the finer things in life, then you must represent. God wants you to have abundance and live the way your heart desires. He said in 1st Corinthians 2:9 that, *Eye hath not seen, nor ear heard, neither have entered into the heart of man, the things which God hath prepared for them that love him. But God has revealed them to us by his Spirit:* If you love the Lord, He will make a way for you to have what you desire "if" you seek Him, if you are living right, and if your intentions are right. You can have what your heart desires. It is possible if you only believe!

CHAPTER 9 KEY POINTS:

- ❖ You can not have a positive life and a negative mind. If you have a negative mind, you will have a negative life. The enemy controls your life when he controls your mind.

- ❖ When you pray, you are submitting yourself to God in a very humble manner. When your words to Him are honest and sincere, He hears you because He listens to your heart.

- ❖ If you dislike something about a person, it is because that which you hate in them is a part of yourself. What isn't a part of you does not bother you.

- ❖ Someone is always watching you. Be sure that what they see coming from you is light and not darkness.

- ❖ If you desire to possess quality things, then you must begin to invest in the things that make for quality. You must know that prosperous people exude prosperity.

10

YOUR PRAYERS MAKE A DIFFERENCE

> *God shapes the world by prayer. The more prayer there is in the world the better the world will be, the mightier the forces against evil.*
>
> *E.M. Bounds*

Demons flee when even the weakest Christian falls on their knees to pray. Prayer changes things! We all have heard that, but how many people really resonate on the truth of that statement? No major decision in your life should be made without consulting God about it through prayer. Prayer should be the foundation upon which your whole life is lived. Prayer is nothing more than just talking to the living God. The more you pray, the closer your relationship with Him gets and the more receptive you will be to His guidance and leading. The power of answered prayer is not in you or the person who prays. Rather, the praying power is in God, who is being prayed to, but you must have the confidence and faith that He hears you. First John 5:14-15 tells us, *"This is the confidence that we have in God: that if we ask anything according to His will, He hears us."* If we know that He hears us, then whatever we ask of Him, [according to His will] will be answered. You must know that God's "yes" answer to you is always according to His will. It could be His "permissive" will or His "perfect" will, but it's always in His will. Living in God's permissive will is not always for your ultimate good, but because you have free will and self-choice, He allows you to live in that will for a while.

HIS PERFECT WILL

When you ask for His *perfect* will to be done in your life, He guides you and detours you from things that are not in line with His divine plan for you. His perfect will keeps you on the path leading to the unfolding of your destiny. He removes people and situations in your life that are unfruitful, He uproots you from places and circumstances that are contrary to your divine purpose, He leads you to where your destiny can be fulfilled, and He begins to reveal your purpose to you. When you ask God to allow His perfect will to be carried out in your life, you begin to desire only those things that He desires for you. With your desires matching God's desires, how then can you go astray? When God answers prayers, those answers could be yes, no, or wait. A "wait" answer is not necessarily a "no" answer. It could just be the wrong timing. God answers affirmative "yes" prayers that are in agreement with His will for your life at the right time. Remember, He gives you free will, and if you choose to follow your own humanistic logic and reasoning, He steps out of the way and allows your free will to guide you, but only for so far. When He sees that you have veered too far out in the middle of no-where and you don't know what else to do or where to go (because you trusted in your own reasoning), He draws you back to Him, and it is up to you to stay there by releasing your self-will to God's will. He will not force you to do anything; otherwise, you would be a robot. He nudges you by speaking to your consciousness. He gives warnings through various avenues. He sends messages through people, and He guides you. All of these are warnings to prevent you from going in the wrong direction. It is up to you to listen and take heed. When you pray passionately and purposefully, according to God's will, God responds powerfully to you and keeps you on the right track!

A BALANCED CONNECTION

Many Christians have an imbalanced spiritual life, which often leads to frustration and confusion. This is because they are connected to the body of Christ only, the Head of Christ only, or neither. There is a disconnect. Going to church, singing in the choir, teaching Sunday School, sitting on church committees, and fellowshipping with the saints are all examples of being connected to the body of Christ. However, we must also be equally connected to the Head. When we are connected to the Head, we have a strong prayer life, a consistent praise and worship life, constant time for study, and a designated time for fasting with the Lord. However, when we are *only* connected to the Head, we become too spiritually-minded that we are no earthly good. If we are not careful, we can get to a point where we don't love anybody but Jesus. This is not God's will for your life either because He has commanded us to love our neighbors. Being only connected to the Head, makes you too "religious" which spills over into self-righteousness. On the other hand, when you are only connected to the body, you become too "earthly-minded" that you can be no spiritually good. *But the natural man receiveth not the things of the Spirit of God: for they are foolishness unto him: neither can he know them, because they are spiritually discerned." (1st Corinthians 2:14).* To be connected to one without the other is to be disconnected and imbalanced. There must be a balance between being connected to the body of Christ and being connected to the Head of Christ.

There are many spiritual leaders who are strongly connected to the body of Christ and operating in the gifts and callings of God, but have little-to-no connection to the Head, which is Christ Jesus, the Lord. Unfortunately, many of these leaders feel that because the gifts and callings of God are operating through them, their relationship with the Lord is strong and stable. This thinking is error because the Bible states that, *the gifts and callings of God are without repentance." (Romans 11:29).* This means that one does not have to be in a repentant state or be living a Godly life in order for their gifts to operate. God will continue to allow a person's gifts to flow, operate mightily, and bless others, even if they themselves are not living right. Through their gifts, they may be bringing many souls to Christ, and because of the mighty works operating through them, those souls may find themselves rejoicing eternally in heaven after they depart this earth. This does not mean that the one who was used to bring them to Christ will enter in, even though they've led so many others there. The bottom line is that if you are not connected to the head, then the Lord does not know you, even though you have worked many miracles. *"Many will say unto me in that day, Lord Lord, have we not prophesied in thy name and in thy name cast out many devils and in thy name done many wonderful works? And then will I profess unto them, I never knew you: depart from me, ye that work iniquity." (Mathew 7:20-23).* It is my prayer that none of us find ourselves in that position when we face the Lord on that judgment day. The only way to have a strong and stable relationship with the Lord is to stay consistent in prayer and study. There is no other way around it. It is vital to your spiritual well-being that you have a strong relationship with God through prayer. Sincere, open-hearted prayer keeps you from falling, helps you to remain humble, covers and protects you and those you pray for, gives you power, and ushers in the anointing of God. Having others pray for you will not give you credit with the Lord. It will give credit to the one praying. No one can maintain your relationship with the Lord for you, but you. It is a sacrifice that you must make. We must all come to Him for ourselves. *"...work out your own salvation with fear and trembling." (Philippians 2:12).*

OH, YES HE HEARS!

God hears every prayer! I am a witness who will stand on the rooftops and shout that He hears every prayer. The enemy of your faith wants you to believe that God does not hear you, and that your prayers are only hitting the ceiling. That is a lie from the pit of hell. The day that God revealed to me that He is real and that He hears my prayers is a day I will never forget. I was on my knees praying. Part of my prayer consisted of asking Him to cover me with humility from the crown of my head to the soles of my feet. I was led to command the spirit of humility to come down and cover me. Throughout my prayer, the Holy Spirit led me to bind and loose every hindering spirit in my life. I called them each down by name and bound them as the spirit led me. During the course of my prayer, I said, *"Lord, you said that I was precious in your sight."* When I finished praying, I left the house and went to bible study. After the Word was delivered and the service was almost over, the Pastor's wife called me to come up. As I was walking toward the altar, she said, *"This woman has the spirit of humility all over her!"* When I reached her, she said, "God *says to tell you that you "are" precious in His sight."* She then said to me, *"You have been binding and loosing and you must continue to do that because you have much power. You are small in stature, but you are a giant in the spirit."* It was that day, that I knew beyond a shadow of a doubt, that God is real, that He hears prayers, and that He speaks through people to people. He does have modern day prophets and I am grateful to the Pastor's wife for being in a position allowing God to use her. God delivered a message to me that day through His servant. May that powerful woman of God, Sister Vera Jackson continue to rest in peace with the Lord. Every time I pray now, I pray with the confidence and assurance that God is hearing me. We are living in the last days and the Word says, *"And it shall come to pass in the last days, saith God, I will pour out of my Spirit upon all flesh: and your sons and your daughters shall prophesy, and your young men shall see visions, and your old men shall dream dreams." (Acts 2:1).* He has risen up His prophets, His seers, and His dreamers in this day. He gives us messages each and every day and we must be receptive to His spirit and His voice to receive those messages.

THE ARMOR OF GOD

Although prayer is very powerful, you must also keep yourself spiritually covered. The precious shed blood of Jesus does cover you, but you must also put on the *"Armor of God."* While you do not physically see the armor, it is a real thing in the spirit world. It also affects the physical realm. When you clothe yourself with the Armor of God, you step out into the world fully equipped to handle all the fiery darts shot by "the wicked." A soldier would not go out into war without wearing his armor. We are in a spiritual war, and we must certainly not go out into this cruel and dangerous world without the proper gear either. It is crucial to our spiritual body that we put on the Armor of God as often as we can. *Be strong in the Lord and in the power of His might. Put on the whole Armor of God, that you may be able to stand against the wiles of the devil. For we wrestle not against flesh and blood, but against principalities, against powers, against the rulers of the darkness of this world, against spiritual wickedness in high places. Wherefore take unto you the whole armor of God, that you may be able to withstand in the evil day, and having done all to stand.* (Ephesians 6:10-18). Keep yourself spiritually covered with the Armor of God. Be wise as a serpent, but harmless as a dove.

SACRIFICE

Being in the presence of God is a beautiful and glorious experience, but everything has a price. Spiritual necessities must be purchased. Money cannot buy them, but something must be given up before one can receive them. I had to give up my selfish desires and my fleshly cravings in order for me to experience the peace, joy, and love that comes with true worship. One may love their money and their worldly possessions, but must be willing to give them up or the *desire* for them before they can receive the true peace and comfort of spirituality. Essentially, it is the *desire* that must be sacrificed. When you remove the desire for worldly things and replace those desires with desires for spiritual things, you enter into true wisdom. When those worldly possessions return to you, they mean nothing. You see them for what they truly are. When you get to a place where you can live either with them or without them, they come to you in great avalanches.

PRAISE AND WORSHIP

When you enter the throne room to be with the Lord, His Glory is reflected upon your face, and you feel the presence of God permeating all around you. It is an indescribable feeling, one that leaves you happy, confident, strong, and free from fear. It is an awesome feeling to be able to walk in His justification and glory with your head held high! He desires your praise and worship, and *"He inhabits the praises of His people." (Psalm 22:3).* He loves praises and He loves when you sacrifice the time to come be with Him. He will stop what He is doing to come and sit in the midst of your praise. He wants you to acknowledge Him. He wants you to tell Him how much you love Him, how much you admire and adore Him, how thankful you are to Him for who He is. Your lips and heart must praise Him. He is worthy to be praised and although He is no respecter of persons, He does give favor to those who praise and worship Him in Spirit and in truth regardless of who they are. God is both the Giver and the Gift. We should always thank God the Giver, for God the Gift. There is nothing like having an intimate relationship with Him. Your spirit must be open in order to hear what He is saying. He speaks to your needs and gives you guidance so that His will can be carried out in your life. This is only acquired by spending time with Him. Mere knowledge about Him is not the same as a personal relationship with Him. Walk in Wisdom. Keep your prayer life with God constant and strong!

KNOWING HIS CHARACTERISTICS

Getting to know God, learning His attributes, and being familiar with the manner in which He does things puts you in a better position to understand His character. When spiritual mysteries, secrets of the ages, and deep insight are revealed to you, you become spiritually wiser. However, you are also held accountable for that which you come into the knowledge of. When you know better, you are expected to do better. *"And that servant, which knew his lord's will, and prepared not himself, neither did according to his will, shall be beaten with many stripes. But he that knew not, and did commit things worthy of stripes, shall be beaten with few stripes. (Luke 12:48-49).* You see in that scripture how both were given a beating? The one who knew the right thing to do and did not do it was beaten, and the one who did the wrong thing because he or she did not know the right thing to do was also beaten. Ignorance is no excuse because God has made His Word available to all. As you study the Word of God, you see that He is a God who gives warnings many times before destruction comes. If we heed to God's warnings, there will be no destruction. He is also full of mercy if we do error. Let's look at some of the attributes of God so that we can be confident in who He is when we approach His throne:

- He is clothed with honor and majesty and strength.

- He covers Himself with light as with a garment.

- He is a sun and a shield.

- Heaven is His throne.

- Earth is His footstool.

- Righteousness and judgment are the habitation of His throne.

- Honor and majesty are before Him.

- Strength and beauty are in His sanctuary.

- The clouds are the dust of His feet.

- He sits between the cherubims.

- The heavens declare his righteousness.

- He is plenteous in mercy to all that call upon Him.

- He is gracious and full of compassion, slow to anger, and plenteous in mercy.

- He gives strength and power to His people.

- From everlasting to everlasting, He is God.

- He is the same. His years have no end.

- He is good and ready to forgive.

- He is the "I am".

These are but a few of a long list of God's attributes. This list alone should assure you of His goodness and mercy for us. If we had no problems for God to solve, no difficulties to overcome, no challenges to face, and no barriers to cross, then how would we know that God can bring us out, over, or through them? When we ask God for things, He does not just drop them into our lap. We must earn them. For instance, when we ask God for strength, He sends us the difficulties which make us strong. When we ask for courage, He gives us dangers to overcome. When we pray for wisdom, He gives us problems that require wisdom to solve them. A very large portion of our spiritual growth and prosperity will come from eating the bread of adversity and drinking the waters of affliction.

GRATITUDE

When you give thanks for everything, you open a floodgate of blessings that come pouring toward you. You place yourself on a current that draws good things your way. There is always something to be grateful for. I once read the following quote, which really sums up the fact that there is always something to be grateful for: *"Let us rise up and be thankful, for if we didn't learn a lot today, at least we learned a little, and If we didn't learn a little, at least we didn't get sick, and if we got sick, at least we didn't die, so let us still be thankful." Buddha.* Your hands shall begin to touch, feel, and experience the manifestation of things desired through constant gratitude. Begin to *feel* the spirit of gratitude now. Your strong thankful emotion will draw your desires to you speedily. When my daughter died after having lived for only 93 days, I gave thanks to God for giving her to me for that period of time. She could have died at birth and I never would have gotten a chance to know her, love her, feed her, change her, or care for her; but He allowed me to borrow her for 93 days, which I will forever be thankful to Him for. I still have the gift of her memories to cherish in my heart. I am grateful for that.

PRAYING IN THE PRESENT TENSE

I find that when we pray as though what we ask for has already been received, the manifestations of what is desired come faster. Whatever you want God to bless you with, pray as though you already have it. If it is right for you to have, it is right for you to pray for it. There is a power in speaking in the present tense. What happens is that the subconscious mind begins to pick up the vibration of the feeling of the "now" and creates the environment that embodies what you are envisioning. It is really a matter of speaking those things that are not as though they were. However, if you were to go a little deeper, you would understand that the thing you desire already does exist. If you can see it when you pray or when you visualize, then it is already an existent thing in the mental world. Therefore, praying in the "now" makes the transition from the mental world into the natural world a little faster. God honors those types of prayers because He honors faith. Faith honors God and yes, God honors faith. You must take your faith in God to a higher level and everything else will follow. Understand and let it resonate in your spirit, mind, and soul that YOU are a powerful being with the authority to call anything you want into your life. Realize the power that is within you. Get your mind, body and soul in harmony with each other and walk in this world with the grace, wisdom and power that God has placed in you. Use the principles outlined in this book. Rise above mediocrity and stand out among the best in this world - the renown, the movers and shakers. You are everything you desire to be. You already know it and in time the world will know it too! May the knowledge and wisdom of God be unto your soul, when you have found it, there shall be a sure reward, and your expectations shall not be cut off. Look back and thank God. Look forward and trust God. Look around and serve God. Look within and find God!

Remember that,

"PROSPERITY IS YOUR BIRTHRIGHT!"

DISCUSSION TOPICS FOR BOOK CLUBS & MASTERMIND GROUPS

A. Discuss some things that can be done to impress the subconsciousness in order to manifest your vision, desires, and aspirations.

B. How to begin changing the nature of your words and conversations in order to attract all that is desired through what is released from your mouth.

C. How to live in harmony with the natural laws of the universe, specifically the law of cause and effect.

D. Does lack of confidence limit your ability to rise to greatness?

E. Do you feel that hereditary plays a role in one's successes or failures in life? Why or why not?

F. What is the difference between a person with power and a person without power? What are some distinguishing characteristics? How can you begin walking with power?

G. How can we become acquainted with our inner spirit (inner self) and walk in harmony with it?

H. Why is it important to understand people, their behaviors, their actions, their responses, and their attitudes? How can understanding people help you?

I. Why is having integrity important? Can one continue being prosperous and successful and also lack integrity? Why or why not?

J. How to begin changing the nature of your words and conversations in order to attract all that is desired through what is released from your mouth.

K. How to live in harmony with the natural laws of the universe, specifically the law of cause and effect.

L. Does lack of confidence limit your ability to rise to greatness?

M. Do you feel that hereditary plays a role in one's successes or failures in life? Why or why not?

N. What is the difference between a person with power and a person without power? What are some distinguishing characteristics? How can you begin walking with power?

O. How can we become acquainted with our inner spirit (inner self) and walk in harmony with it?

P. Why is it important to understand people, their behaviors, their actions, their responses, and their attitudes? How can understanding people help you?

Q. Why is having integrity important? Can one continue being prosperous and successful and also lack integrity? Why or why not?

Book 2

Destined for GREAT Things!

Life's Trials That Bring out Seeds of Greatness in You!

~~~~~~~~~~~~~~~~~~~

Dr. Mia Y. Merritt

Copyright © 2009 by Mia Y. Merritt, Ed.D
All rights reserved. No part of this book may be reproduced in any form,
except for the inclusion of brief in a review, without
permission in writing from the
author or publisher.

Destined for Great Things!

First Printing August 2007
In the USA

Library of Congress
Cataloging-in-Publication Data
Merritt, Mia

Dedication

This book is dedicated to my eight-year old son
Stephan Raynard Sanders

I pray that you will walk in the Spirit of wisdom, integrity, and humility. As you continue to mature, your understanding will expand and the wisdom of the ages will be opened up to you. You will be limited in your understanding only by your unwillingness to abide by spiritual principles and grow. Always remember that the trials and tribulations that you will encounter in your lifetime are designed to make you stronger and bring out the greatness that is already within you. I pray that God will grant you favor in His sight. Remember to acknowledge Him in all of your ways so that He will guide you through your life's journey. He desires your praise & worship, so give to Him what is due unto His holy name, and He will never leave you nor forsake you. God will be with you always.

I love you sweetheart.

Mommy

In memory of my daughter,
Stephanie Leanne Sanders
Your Spirit will always remain alive
in my heart. I will forever cherish
the 93 days we spent
together.
God Bless You!

Foreword

The number "7" denotes completion. ***Destined for Great Things!*** was originally written in August 2002, but was not revealed for fear of what others might think and say. Since then, I have realized that liberty often comes through confession, and that through my story, others may be blessed, encouraged, and delivered. The time has come to reveal my life story to the world.

This book was inspired by two books that literally changed my life. Those books are, *The Greatest Salesman in the World Part I* and *The Greatest Salesman in the World Part II,* by Og Mandino. The chapter introductions in this book are derived from those two books with variations to some degree. I have simply augmented and modified concepts that parallel the challenges of my life. I thank God for the courage, faith, and wisdom to be able to write this book. Through the Holy Spirit, I have been able to bring forth a gift that has been inside of me. I thank God that although the revelation of this book was delayed, it has still been birthed.

Not everyone will tell their story, but everyone has a story to tell. I've decided to tell mine. By the grace of God, I have come through some difficult experiences. It is through my adversity that He has strengthened my character. It is through my challenges that He has helped me to stay on the path that leads to the unfolding of my destiny. To God be the Glory!

Mia Y. Merritt

CONTENTS

CHAPTER 1 1
Develop Good Habits & Practice Them Daily
Deliverance in the Midst of Praise

CHAPTER 2 13
A Spirit of Excellence
The Gift of Teaching

CHAPTER 3 25
Find the Good in Every Situation
Loving the Unlovable

CHAPTER 4 43
Laugh Often
Know I know How Love Feels

CHAPTER 5 53
Control Your Emotions in Every Situation
Playing With Fire Will Get You Burned

CHAPTER 6 85
Live Today as Your Last day on Earth
Memories Last Forever

CHAPTER 7 95
Believe That You are Miracle
His Love Covers & Protects

CHAPTER 8 111
Plan for Prosperity & Abundance
Live a Life of Vision, Purpose, and Fulfillment

CHAPTER 9 134
Reflect on Your Deeds of Each Day
One Bad Choice Can Change Your Life

CHAPTER 10 147
Pray With an Attitude of Gratitude
He Hears Your Prayers

x

Chapter 1

Develop Good Habits and Practice Them Daily
Deliverance in the Midst of Praise

As a child I was slave to my impulses; now I am slave to my habits. My actions are ruled by emotions, love, hate, appetite, environment, fear, anxiety and habit. The worse of these elements is habit. Therefore, if I must practice habits, let me practice good habits. My bad habits must be destroyed and new fertilizer laid for good seed.

Both success and failure are the result of habit. Successful people practice habits that failure minded people do not like to practice. Good habits will never produce bad results. Bad habits will never produce good results. Only a habit can overcome another habit. In the beginning, I make my habits, but in the end, my habits make me.

I will get into the habit of rising early, praying daily, talking less, listening more, smiling often, and speaking positive in all manner of conversation.

As I develop good habits and practice them daily, they become a pleasure to perform. If they are a pleasure to perform, it is my nature to perform them often. When I perform them often, they become a habit, and I become their slave, and since they are good habits, then this is good.

THOU SHALL NOT STEAL

Bad habits are easy to make but very hard to break. This fact became a personal reality when I began stealing. At the tender age of eight, I was introduced to shoplifting by my babysitter who kept me after school until my parents came home from work. I would go to the stores with her and watch her sneak things into her purse and pockets. I was also given the task of informing her if anyone was coming or looking. I had often seen her sneak money out of her mother's purse. On a few occasions, her mother would fuss about money missing from her purse, and my babysitter would accuse one of her three brothers. Their mother would blame one of the boys as well since they were mischievous. At nine, I began walking to the convenience store after school and stealing candy. When I was in the sixth grade, I began stealing quarters out of my mother's purse and soon thereafter, I graduated to dollars. When I grew into my teenage years, I was introduced to department store stealing. My friends and I would shoplift and take things such as clothing, makeup, costume jewelry, cassette tapes, but mainly clothing. During my adolescent years, I began stealing on my own without the company of my friends. The habit became such an obsession that I could not go into any store, gas station or office without stealing something – lipstick, perfume, lotion, gum, pens, notepads, candy, aspirin, you name it. This went on until the day my friends and I were finally arrested for shoplifting. Since I was then 18 years of age, I developed a criminal record. Unfortunately, it did not stop there. I continued to shoplift until I was arrested a second time. However, for some reason, I never stole anyone's wallet or took money out of anyone's purse other than my mother's. Deep within I knew that was totally wrong, although there is no better sin.

I stole out of stores primarily. I knew that stealing out of stores was taking from someone indirectly, but I felt that whoever owned the store were rich, and I was not hurting them. Surely, I no longer think that way. It was not until I decided to seriously learn about God through reading His Word daily that I was delivered from stealing. The funny, but mysterious thing about the situation is that I was not trying to be delivered from stealing. Learning about God and shoplifting were two separate aspects of my life. I was just curious about God and wanted to know what was written in that Bible. However, one day as I was reflecting over my life, I realized that I did not steal anymore. I had immersed myself into reading the Word, praying, fasting, and learning about Him, that I could not see nor feel the change that was taking place in my life. That is how unfathomable, yet powerful the Lord is. He is a gentleman. He does not force Himself on anyone, but He is faithful and willing to deliver us from all of our sins, troubles, burdens, and strongholds. Stealing was a stronghold in my life, but as I began to learn about my Father's business, He purged me from the things in me that were not like Him. The Word of God is light. Light and darkness cannot dwell in the same place. One has to be dominant. Therefore, as the light of God was entering me through reading, and as my spirit was being washed through fasting, and as my heart was being cleansed through prayer, the darkness had to leave. There is no happy medium with light and darkness nor good and evil. Anything that is not like God is darkness. Stealing is darkness because it goes against what God has commanded us to do. When I lifted my head up to look at my life, I realized that the stealing was gone, the urge to steal was gone, and the profanity that use to come out of my mouth was gone. God is just awesome. He has delivered me from all those bad habits. He is so faithful. In Him, there is no darkness!

TEMPTATIONS

Not stealing anymore was not without its temptations. I knew that I had been freed from taking things that didn't belong to me, but the temptations still came from time to time. There were instances when I would be in the store and had the perfect opportunity to steal something when no one was looking, but I did not do it. I knew that God was watching. Paying for everything that I brought home and refusing to give in to temptation was an exhilarating feeling. When the forces of evil realized that I could not be tempted in the usual way any longer, another approach was presented to me disguised as a so-called blessing. While paying for a few items in the grocery store one day, I handed the cashier a ten-dollar bill. She gave me change for a fifty-dollar bill. As she was counting the change back to me, I realized immediately that it was wrong. She handed me the money and began trying to scan the next customer's items. I discreetly told her that she gave me too much money back. I proceeded to tell her that I had only given her a ten-dollar bill, but that she had given me over forty dollars back. She was very appreciative and gave me the correct amount of change. However, I can not say that the thought of keeping the money did not enter my mind because I was low on cash and could really have used that money. Additionally, I could have rationalized keeping the money in my mind by saying to myself that it was a blessing from God, but God does not cause problems for one person in order to bless another. That young lady could have lost her job for being short in her register. I was very proud of myself when I left that store. The Lord did not give us the "Thou shall not steal" commandment just for our own spiritual discipline. He gave it to us because there is a power in resistance to temptation that crushes the enemy's head. It tears evil out by the root!

THE EXPENSIVE BRACELET

Yes, little temptations came here and there, but I passed every test. Once we resist the temptations presented by the forces of evil, they depart. Every now and then, new schemes are tried to regain entrance, but with enlightenment, comes wisdom and the ability to recognize those evil plots. The ultimate test that really confirmed that I was truly free from stealing happened during the Christmas holiday season. After being driven to my car by mall security after hours of shopping, I noticed a small JC Penney's bag sitting on the passenger seat of my car. I was very perplexed because I had not gone into JCPenneys and I did not purchase anything in a small bag. When I looked inside, it was a beautiful diamond tennis bracelet. The bracelet was in a gift box and the receipt was still in the bag. The cost of the bracelet was $289.00. Immediately, I became very afraid.

I thought that someone was trying to set me up. Fear took over me. I looked around and drove home, terrified the whole time. When I arrived home, I called mall security because they had driven me to my car as I was leaving the mall. I thought that I had inadvertently picked up that little bag in the security vehicle that I rode in. But when the driver called me back, he said that there were no bags in the truck, and that he had just gotten the vehicle when he took me to my car. This was really a mystery to me. How in the world did this beautiful, expensive bracelet get into my car? After the security guard told me that it did not belong to him, I envisioned myself keeping it. I tried it on and it fit me perfectly. I have a very tiny wrist, and for the bracelet to fit me so perfectly, it had to become mine. I was soon led to call JCPenneys. I explained to the person on the phone that I had found a tennis bracelet that was purchased from their store and would like to know if someone had reported a missing bracelet. Yes, someone had. The young lady told me that a gentleman had called and wanted to know if he had left it at the counter after he purchased it. He left his phone number in case anyone turned it in. She took my number and told me that she would have the gentleman call me. She was surprised that I would be calling to turn in an expensive bracelet and told me that I was very honest. Ten minutes later, a gentleman with a heavy accent called me about the bracelet. He indicated that he had lost it, but did not know where he had lost it. We arranged for him to come over to my house and retrieve the bracelet. I told him that he would have to show me his driver's license and credit card number that matched the last four digits of the number on the receipt. I asked a friend of mine to come over as a precaution.

The gentleman came over and immediately I knew who he was and how he had left the bracelet in my car. He did not remember me, but I refreshed his memory. I had been driving around the mall parking lot for about 20 minutes trying to find a parking spot. I was so desperate and frustrated that I was about to drive back home. But then I saw an Arabian-looking fellow walking to his car. I rolled my window down and asked him if he was leaving. He told me yes, so I begged him to let me drive him to his car so that I could get his parking spot. He seemed a bit afraid at first (go figure), but he got in and let me take him to his car.

When he got out, that's when he left the bracelet. His credit card matched the receipt. His wife and baby were in the car and he motioned for them to come inside. He explained to me that they were celebrating their three-year anniversary, and the bracelet was a gift for his wife. The baby was a three-month-old little princess who was absolutely gorgeous. The wife brought me a token of appreciation, two long thin wine glasses. I played with the baby for a moment and then they left. Wow, talk about a 360! Who would have gone through all of that just to return something of so much value? only an honest person who had been truly and completely delivered from stealing. In Jesus, the greatest things that were once a weakness can become a great strength. He is the rock, the fortress, the deliverer; our God, our strength, in whom we will trust. Bless His holy name!

THE COUNTERFEITER

The forces of evil are counterfeiters. They have a counterfeit for every genuine reality that God has. He diligently works against everything that God wants to purpose in our lives. One example of this in my life is the fact that God's Word commands: *"Thou shall not steal."* However, the enemy of my faith tempted me into doing the very opposite of what God had called me NOT to do, steal. How does this happen? Because demonic forces are sent on assignment to tempt us. Whether or not we give in, is totally our decision and a decision that we must live with. The ultimate goal is to destroy us. The spirits are very subtle, tempting in small areas at first. The spiritual reality is that evil forces are sent to sift us as wheat. When something is sifted, it seeps out gradually until all of its contents are completely gone. The enemy of my faith wanted to sift me so that I would not realize what was happening to me until it was too late. By then, I would have been completely consumed. But God, in His mercy did not allow that to happen to me. He intervened just in time. I took the first step and He took the rest. Praise God for grace, mercy, and deliverance.

THE SPIRITUAL WAR

There is a constant, ongoing war occurring in the spirit realm and the more we deny it, the more likely we are to be used by the forces of darkness without realizing it. The first time I stole, a feeling of guilt and conviction overtook me. When I stole the second time, I felt less convicted, but I continued to steal, until I had very little feeling about it at all. What I did not realize is that each time I gave in to temptation, the spirit that was sent to tempt and destroy me grew stronger, making it much more difficult for me to resist. I became obsessed with stealing and eventually could not control myself. Nobody is exempt. The enemy continues to tempt in other areas as well, and if we submit to temptation, doors open for other demonic spirits to enter our lives until a transformation has happened for the worse. This is what happens to drug addicts, prostitutes, adulterers, and even murderers. If you were to ask them, they would tell you that they all felt guilty after their first offense, but each time they repeated the sin, those convictions diminished to where they were completely eradicated. Resist the enemy, and he will flee from you. Develop good habits, and practice them daily.

DELIVERANCE, PRAISE, & WORSHIP

As I grew in maturity and wisdom, I consumed myself in reading God's Word and the Word became life inside me. It became alive in my heart and soul. When I began reading and praying diligently, God took care of the areas in my life that needed repairing or obliterating. It was a liberating day when I woke up and realized, *"I don't steal no more! I don't curse no more!"* I am a witness and God is my judge that when you give Him your whole heart and focus on pleasing and learning about Him, He will purge and deliver you from everything that is not like Him. His visitation will become habitation. Whatever or whoever is exposed to the manifested presence of God, begins to absorb the very material matter of God. Once God delivers from demonic strongholds, resisting the flesh and walking in the spirit is a must, otherwise, the deliverance will not be maintained. Although the temptations will leave for a season, they do come back, and we must be prepared to resist. Yes, I was delivered from stealing, and I know that God did it, but what exactly is deliverance?

Deliverance means to be freed of the demonic forces that are assigned to kill our spirits, steal our joy, and ultimately destroy our lives. Deliverance can be as mild as reading the Word daily while God purges you of evil spirits to as serious as a deliverance team commanding demonic spirits to leave a person. Demons are enemies of the gifts and fruits of the Spirit. They try to keep the fruit from coming forth in the life of a person. They are spirit beings. They are enemies of God and man. Their objective in human beings is to tempt, deceive, accuse, condemn, defile, resist, oppose, control, steal, afflict, kill, and destroy. They enter through open doors, but they have to be given an opportunity to enter, an invitation, if you will. Otherwise, they cannot just come and go in and out of a person's life as they please. Whenever you commit a sin, you open a door. That is the invitation.

There is much controversy on the subject of demons, demonic forces, ungodly spirits, etc., but they are real and do exist whether we believe they do or not. And the sad reality is that many demons work directly with Christians. Many of these Christians are well dressed, respectable, and have the "appearance" of being refined and educated. While many profess Christian truths in order to appease their consciences, they live their lives in agreement with demonic forces, and the assigned demons grow and direct their actions very easily. It is critical, that we realize that the majority of demons influence Christians from the outside. They operate *around* them and not *in* them as with some non-Christians. Believers need only to stop agreeing with evil influences in order to get freed of them. The power of demons is rooted entirely in deception. Satan's power depends on the agreement of Christians with the ways of evil. Man is able to change his outward behavior for various self-centered and deceptive reasons, but only the spirit of God can change a man's heart. But although Satan may be able to counterfeit form, he can never counterfeit the fruit of the spirit. *You shall know them by their fruit* (Mathew 7:16) Deliverance must be maintained through prayer and fasting.

After overcoming temptations, I then realized that temptation is not a lasting condition. It is a passing phase, and once it is conquered, it ceases to be a temptation. As a student, ready to learn and understand knowledge and wisdom, I discovered that temptations come from inside a person, not circumstances surrounding a person. Temptations show us where we are sinful and ignorant. The source and cause of all temptation is the inward desire. Outside objects are really powerless to move a soul to be tempted. The outward object is just the element of the temptation, but the *desire* comes from *inside* of the one tempted. If the source and desire was in the object, then everyone would be tempted by the same things, but that is not the case. However, without temptations, a soul could not grow and become strong.

THE ARMOR

As I continued to fall in love with God, I realized that He is worthy of daily praise and worship, so I made a decision to develop a *good* habit of sacrificing my sleep and rising early to praise and worship Him. With this spiritual self-discipline, I began rising at 4:30 in the morning. It was very hard, but I forced myself to get up at the moment the alarm clock would sound. It eventually became second nature to me. There were days that I would forget to set the alarm, but would still be awakened by the Holy Spirit at exactly 4:30a.m. When it first happened, I thought it was merely a coincidence, but it happened too many times after that, so I knew it was God waking me up. God is not a respecter of persons, but He does give favor to those who praise and worship Him. As we draw closer and closer to Him, we no longer want just His gifts, but we want the Giver of the gifts. We no longer desire the blessings only, we want the Blessor. Although prayer is very powerful, we must also keep ourselves spiritually covered. The precious shed blood of Jesus does cover us, but we must also put on the *"Armor of God."* While we do not see the armor, it is real in the spirit world, and it also affects the physical realm. When we clothe ourselves with the armor, we step out of the house fully equipped to quench all the fiery darts shot by spiritual enemies. A soldier would not go to war without his armor. We are in a spiritual war, and we must certainly not go out into this cruel and dangerous world without the proper gear. It is vital to our spiritual body that we put on the Armor of God. *Be strong in the Lord and in the power of His might. Put on the whole Armor of God, that you may be able to stand against the wiles of the devil. For we wrestle not against flesh and blood, but against principalities, against powers, against the rulers of the darkness of this world, against spiritual wickedness in high places. Wherefore take unto you the whole armor of God, that you may be able to withstand in the evil day, and having done all to stand. Stand therefore, having your loins girded about with truth, and having on the breastplate of righteousness, and your feet shod with the preparation of the gospel of peace; above all, taking the shield of faith wherewith you will be able to quench all the fiery darts of the wicked. And take the helmet of salvation, and the sword of the Spirit, which is the Word of God; praying always with all prayer and supplication in the Spirit, being watchful with all perseverance and supplication for all the saints...* (Ephesians 6:10-18). Keep yourself covered. Be wise as a serpent, but harmless as a dove.

IN THE THRONE ROOM

Being in the presence of God is a beautiful and glorious experience, but everything has a price. Spiritual necessities must be purchased. Money cannot buy them, but something must be given up before one can receive them. I had to give up myself, my selfish desires, and my fleshly cravings for material things that were not mine nor rightfully mine to have. One may love their money and their fleshly possessions, but must give some of those things up or their desire and love for those things before they can receive the true peace and comfort of spirituality. Essentially, it is the desire for things that must be sacrificed. When you enter the throne room to be with the Lord, His Glory is reflected upon your countenance, and you feel the presence of God permeating all around you. It is an indescribable feeling, but one that leaves you confident, strong, and free from fear. It is a wonderful feeling to be able to walk in His justification and glory all day with your head held high! He desires your praise and He inhabits the praises of His people (Psalm 22:3). He loves praises and He loves when we sacrifice the time to come be with Him. There is a song from Donald Lawrence and the Tri-City Singers that I love to listen to. It is called *In the Presence of a King*. Some of the lyrics are the following: *Do you know what it is? Can I tell you how it is?...oh, to know how it feels, to be in the presence of a King... It's an honor and a privilege to be in the presence of a King... such an honor and a privilege to be in the presence of the King.* Oh yes, I know what it's like to be in the presence of the King. Do you? He will stop what He is doing to come and sit in the midst of your praise. He wants you to acknowledge Him. He wants you to tell Him how much you love Him, how much you admire and adore Him, how much you appreciate Him for who He is. Bless Him for this very moment. Thank Him right now for your health, your strength, your family, your friends, your job, your stable mind, and the ability to be able to read this book. Honor Him for what He is getting ready to do in your life. Most importantly, thank Him for His son Jesus, your Lord, Savior, and Redeemer. Our lips and hearts must praise Him. He is worthy and although He is no respecter of persons, He does give favor to those who praise and worship Him in Spirit and in truth, regardless of who they are. God is both the giver and the gift. We should thank God the giver, for God the gift. There is nothing like having an intimate relationship with Him. Our spirit must learn to listen to what He is saying. He speaks to your needs and gives you guidance so that His will can be manifested in your life. This is only learned by spending time with Him. Mere knowledge about Him is not the same as a personal relationship with Him. For without Jesus, you would have no access to

~~ LESSONS LEARNED ~~

1. When you truly desire to serve the Lord, He will deliver you from every stronghold that would keep you bound.

2. The "Armor of God" protects from the spiritual bullets that are shot at men and women of God. No longer will I go into battle without putting on the whole *Armor of God* daily.

3. Character is not permanent. It is one of the most changeable things in nature. By a conscience act of the will, it is being constantly modified and reformed for the better by the pressure of circumstances.

~~REFLECTION QUESTIONS~~

1. What is the stronghold in your life that you need God to deliver you from? How do you plan on obtaining your freedom from it?

2. How do you handle temptations when they come your way? Do you resist, or do you give in? Are you passing the tests of temptation?

3. Do you put on the Armor of God during your prayer time before you leave the house? Are you walking into battle with your gear on?

Chapter 2

A Spirit of Excellence
The Gift of Teaching

The person who is constantly hesitating between which of two things he or she will do, will do neither. If you waver from plan to plan, goal to goal, and constantly bend back and forth in the wind like a lily, you will never accomplish anything great or useful. It is those who concentrate on but one thing at a time who advance in this world.

Not many things scattered, but one thing focused on is the demand of our world. If you scatter your efforts, you will not succeed. Decide on your goals and keep them forever in your thoughts until they have been effectively achieved.

The great difference between those who succeed and those who fail does not consist in the "amount" of work done by each, but the amount of "quality" work. Never again should you lay only your hands on your work when you can give your entire being.

Whatever you begin to do, you must do, as if nothing else in the world is of greater importance. Concentration and perseverance built the great pyramids.

*One of the great joys of this life comes from doing everything you attempt to do to the best of your ability. There is a special sense of satisfaction; a pride in reviewing such a
work, a work which is accurate, full, exact, and complete in all its parts, which a mediocre person who leaves his or her work
in a half-finished condition, can never know.*

The smallest task well done becomes a miracle of achievement. Accomplishment of whatever kind is the crown of effort, the diadem of thought. You cannot pursue a worthy goal steadily and persistently, with all the powers of your mind, and yet fail. Work with excellence each task performed.

A SPIRIT OF EXCELLENCE

An excellent spirit clearly means working with pride, pleasure, and significance in all one does. When I think of the spirit of excellence, I think of the Prophet Daniel, who had a flawless character. There is nothing written in the scriptures about Daniel that would cause one to taint his image. Daniel always stood for God and always endured every test with wisdom and integrity. Daniel's spirit was impeccable in terms of being holy and committed to his God. It is written that Daniel was preferred above all the presidents and princesses, because an "excellent spirit" was found in him (Daniel 6:3).

In the book of Daniel, the Jews were taken into captivity because they were continuously rebellious and refused to turn from their wicked ways, even after they had been given multiple warnings. They had practiced idolatry, which was an abomination, and because of this, God allowed various nations to take over their government and rule over them. Daniel was about 13 years old when he was forced to go into the Babylonian captivity. While there, he was made to learn a new language and respond to a new name given to him. They also wanted to change his diet and his religion. He was Hebrew, and it was against Hebrew religion to eat certain food and meat. But King Nebuchadnezzar wanted Daniel to abandon his dietary laws and conform to the

Babylonian lifestyle, their culture, their religion, etc. The psychology behind changing a name is to change a person's identity so that they would forget everything about their past. Therefore, the king gave Daniel the new name of Belteshaz'zar. He offered Daniel the best of his meat and the best of his wine, and basically told him to, "*Eat my meat, drink my wine, and be a part of my kingdom.*" What the king was really saying was, *"Forget about your past and what you are use to and embrace your new life, a good life."* This not only interfered with Daniel's religion but also his relationship with his God. However, this 13-year-old young man possessed something inside of him that would not allow him to accept what the king offered, nor would he eat the king's food. *Daniel purposed in his heart that he would not defile himself with the portion of the king's meat, nor with the wine which he drank* (Daniel 1:18). He said *"no"* to the king because of the spirit of God that was inside of him. At such a young age, this child was filled with the Word of God and clung to it with his heart. Daniel had an excellent spirit!

A GOOD NAME

Daniel had developed a reputation for being a good and credible young man. He had a gift of interpreting dreams and all of his interpretations came to pass (*... and Daniel had understanding in all visions and dreams.* 1:17). But it was not only his spiritual gifts that made him favored. It was the way he carried himself. There was something characteristic about Daniel that caught the eyes of the leadership. When he spoke, he answered with counsel and wisdom (*Daniel 2:14*). He was a diligent young man, who was given to precision. He was described *as ...having no blemish, but well favored and skillful in all wisdom, and cunning in knowledge, and understanding science and such as had ability in them to stand in the king's palace...* (*Daniel 1:4*). Daniel was dependable to the point that he was elevated in various heathen kingdoms to be a leader over many. Can you imagine a slave becoming a leader? It was because of his excellent spirit.

There is something about the spirit of a person that tells you where that person stands spiritually, emotionally and intellectually. There is something about a person's attitude that tells you whether or not you can trust him or her and whether he or she is a person of worth or not. Today we value people by their personality, charisma, and social skills, and are disappointed later on because we failed to realize that it is "character" that makes that person worthy more than charisma and social skills. Personality and charisma may open doors but character and integrity will keep them open.

THE "*A*" WORD

Accountability seems to be a nasty word today. People do not want to be held accountable when they know their work is sloppy. If both you and I are mediocre in our performance, then that's fine because no one stands out, but when I perform with mediocrity and you perform with excellence, that makes both of us stand out, one for good and one for bad. It also puts pressure on me to work harder. The "excellent" pays attention to all his duties and does everything wisely, thoughtfully, and efficiently. Unfortunately, mediocrity seems to be the standard for today's time, yet everyone wants a great employee evaluation. God wants and deserves the best in everything we do, whether it is washing the dishes, cleaning the house, making the bed, taking out the trash, sweeping the floor, or entertaining a guest. Whatever you do, do it as unto the Lord. When you give of yourself to your local church family or community, but neglect to ensure that your own household has been taken care of, you are not walking in a spirit of excellence. When you feed the hungry, but have not fed your own children, you are not walking in a spirit of excellence. When you teach Sunday School, but have not taught your own children the Word of God, you are not walking in a spirit of excellence. When your appearance is flawless, but your own children are unkempt, you are not walking in a spirit of excellence. One who has a spirit of excellence does *everything* to the best of their ability whether others are watching or not, and there is One above who is *always* watching. Those who are elevated naturally and spiritually are those with a track record of accomplishment.

Daniel had to be accountable to heathen kings, but God still gave him favor because of his excellent spirit. It is written in the scriptures that the king was so impressed with Daniel's spirit that he ... *made him a great man and gave him many great gifts, and made him ruler over the whole providence of Babylon* (Daniel 2:48). However, people were jealous and envious of Daniel because of it, and they plotted against him. And so it is today. People will plot against, talk bad about, and scrutinize everything you do when you have an excellent spirit. There is a price to be paid for being outstanding. Not everyone is going to like you when you walk in a spirit of excellence. Whenever you want things done accurately and efficiently, people begin to complain about you. Whenever you strive to do your best, people become suspicious and begin to watch you closely. However, God will keep you covered and protect you on every side. People may plot and plan against you, but it is very dangerous to plot against a praying saint! One cannot wickedly plot against a child of God without consequences. A praying saint has angels with them everywhere they go. They have angels on the right side and angels on the left side, and angels in the front and back of them. They have goodness and mercy that follow them all the days of their life. They are well protected. They may not seem like much or look like much in the natural, but a praying child of God is a dangerous person to plot against! Continue walking in the spirit of excellence. Let what happened to the men who plotted against Daniel be a lesson to those who would think to plot against you: *And the king commanded, and they brought those men which had accused Daniel, and they cast them into the den of lions, them, their children, and their wives: and the lions had the mastery of them, and brake all their bones in pieces or ever they came at the bottom of the den* (Daniel 6:24). We always reap what we sow.

THE COST OF DISCIPLINE

Discipline goes hand in hand with having a spirit of excellence. Daniel prayed in the morning, in the afternoon, and in the evening. As busy as he was, he found the time to meet God. In order to have an excellent spirit, you must have a lifestyle of prayer. Only God can give you an excellent spirit and it comes by spending time with Him. Daniel had a busy schedule, yet he was disciplined. We are too busy working, going to school, doing so many things that we do not have designated time for God. We sometimes hang out so late that we can't even get up in the morning to pray. Daniel found time to pray not just once, not just twice, but three times a day. He met God in the morning, at noon, and at night. Meeting God should be a daily event. You may not be able to keep the same time every day, but you must be consistent. The secret in Daniel's excellent spirit was consistency. Do you desire to walk in the spirit of excellence? Then walk with God consistently and you will walk in an excellent spirit.

THE HIGH SCHOOL CHALLENGE

I can recall many instances where I performed mediocre to below what I had the potential to do. High school is what stands out the most. Without much effort, I was always at the top of my class in elementary school. The potential to excel above normal has always been in me, but I did not demonstrate it during middle nor high school. I goofed off and made bad grades from junior high on through high school. I just did not care. Socializing and modeling my clothes were my primary reasons for going to school. My grades were so low that I almost did not graduate. In fact, most people had already counted me as a lost case. No-one expected that I would graduate from high school or amount to anything worthy. Had it not been for my mother, I probably never would have finished. She stepped in and insisted that I take night classes and do whatever else I needed to do in order to graduate high school on time.

When it was time for graduation, I still needed one half of a credit. My mother went out to the school and talked to the principal about the situation. She managed to convince him to allow me to participate in the ceremony and she assured him that I would take the last class needed. God touched his heart, and he said that if I came in for one day to help out in the main office the following Monday after graduation, he would give me my diploma, and I would not have to take that half-credit course. He warned me that I'd better show up and be on time. My mother thought that was a miracle. That was all I needed to do to receive my high school diploma.

I walked across that stage, shook my principal's hand with pride, and enjoyed the sense of accomplishment and bliss that my friends and I were experiencing. Monday came and the alarm clock sounded. I turned it off and rolled back over in my bed. My mother came in my room and snatched the covers off me. She told me that I'd better get dressed and get out to that school to work in that office so that I could get my high school diploma. Needless-to-say, I worked in the school's office and received my high school diploma.

Things never should have happened that way. I should have graduated with honors at the top of my class. I did not take my education seriously at the time, and I almost paid dearly for it. After graduation, I had no plans of going to college. The thought did not even cross my mind. After high school, I managed to get a job making seven dollars an hour, which was an excellent salary at the time. I thought I had it made earning that kind of money when the minimum wage was $3.35 an hour. I was still living with my mother, going to work and hanging out with my friends (the wrong crowd). My acquaintances, at the time were uneducated, had many children, lived in low-income housing, and frequented the clubs every week. These were the same people with whom I shoplifted.

THE DORM ROOM

The situation at home was not good between my mom and me. We constantly argued and all I wanted to do was move out of her house. I just could not stand her. Every woman needs her own house when she gets to be a certain age. I was then 19 years old, a woman, and needed my own place and my own space since I did not want to mind nor obey my mother's rules. I will never forget the day I had just arrived home from work when the phone rang. The man on the other end said, *"Hello this is Mr. Butler calling to let Michelle know that her dorm room at the college is ready."* I said, *"There is no Michelle at this number, but can you tell me a little bit more about the dorm room?"* The man began explaining how I could move into the college dorm. I continued to ask questions about this dorm room and he, perceiving that my only interest was in the dorm room, proceeded to say, *"You can't just live in the dorm. You have to enroll in classes as a college student."* I had not thought about that. I just wanted to get out of my mother's house and living in the dorm seemed just the right thing for me. I scheduled an appointment to meet him, registered for classes, and moved in the dorm the next day.

REALITY SINKS IN

My classes were all in the evening since I worked during the day. I continued my daily routine of going to work and attending school in the evening until one day... I had an awakening. Out of nowhere, it hit me that I was actually a real college student. I was a college junior, making straight As and Bs and was on the path to becoming a teacher! Initially, when I registered for classes, I never chose any major. I simply went to an advisor who I was directed to see, and he chose my classes for me every semester. He was in the school of education, so naturally, all my classes were education courses.

I walked in a spirit of excellence while in college. I was a good student. I attended all my classes on time, was never absent, studied hard and made good grades. Yet, I never really gave any thought to what I was doing. God was navigating the circumstances of my life. My destiny was unfolding right in front of me, and I was oblivious to what was happening until that day when I was awakened. From that moment on, I consciously took control of my life. I began to reflect on how I had gotten to that point. The more I reflected, the more astounded I was at how everything in my life was falling into place. I was humbled and grateful for what God had done for me. I had been reading the bible during my leisure time and also going to church on Sundays. I did not steal anymore, did not use profanity anymore, and did not hang with the same people anymore. Praise God! I graduated Cum Laude from Florida Memorial University in the spring of 1994. I had earned a college degree!

Becoming a teacher was very exciting for me and I eagerly anticipated the undertaking. However, getting hired did not come without obstacles. Since I had managed to get myself arrested in my adolescent years, I had to give an account of what happened for each arrest, explain why I did it, and convince a panel of people at the Office of Professional Standards why they should hire me. God, in His grace and mercy saw to it that I was hired.

THE ALTERNATIVE STUDENTS

I couldn't wait to bring my creative teaching styles into the classroom. I felt that there were too many children in this world who were below grade level and way too many who could not read or write. I had purposed in my heart to be the best teacher that I could be. I was determined that my students would learn and would leave my tutelage with a wealth of knowledge. I had a successful first year teaching third graders, and I could really see that teaching was one of my God-given gifts. My second year however, was a bit more challenging. Upon completion of my first year, the principal approached me about teaching the 4th grade Alternative Education (AE) class for the next school year. This class consisted of students who displayed severe behavioral and emotional problems although they had not been professionally diagnosed as having such problems. I had seen those students around the school and it was obvious that they were in a "special" class. I had seen their antics and display of disciplinary problems, so I knew that it would take a strong teacher to educate those types of students. They were very intimidating. I was very hesitant to accept the position at first, so she asked me to think about it. She stated that she felt I would do an excellent job with those students, and that she saw the ability in me. There was also a $1,200 stipend that came with teaching in the program. I knew that the position had to be challenging if the school district was willing to give extra money for teaching the class. Nevertheless, I accepted the position.

My first week with the students was a huge test. They walked in my classroom with attitudes out of this world, throwing temper tantrums, knocking over desks and chairs, using profanity, yelling and screaming, refusing to sit down, refusing to do any class work, etc. I knew that I could not show any sign of intimidation, but I had to do something. So I did some of the same things they did. When they knocked over a desk, I knocked over one. When they threw a chair, I threw one, and so on. I told them that there could not be more than one crazy person in the class at a time, and that the crazy one was me. They began to realize that I was just as crazy as they wanted me to think they were. I stood my ground, did not waver, laid down the rules, was consistent in what I said, set the tone in the classroom, and it was smooth sailing after that.

I put my entire being into getting to know each and every one of my students personally, and I succeeded. I learned that many of them had been psychologically wounded and emotionally scared. However, I taught them with excellence. There were students in my class who had been abused, neglected, some raped. Many of them were living with grandparents because their parents were incarcerated or on drugs. Some lived with foster parents and some were in shelters. Others were just plain defiant and needed firm discipline. That's when I learned that we must get to the root cause of the misbehavior in children. They are not as adults, in that they can express themselves effectively and tell us what is wrong with them. They don't know how to say, *"I'm hurting because my mother is on drugs, and she lives in the street. I miss my mother, and I think about her at night when I'm in my bed. I just want my mom to come home."* When children are hurting, most often they misbehave as an escape mechanism. They need to understand that no matter what outer behavior they find themselves presenting, there is still goodness inside of them. When we cannot see beyond the behavior, we begin to dislike and sometimes mistreat the children. All too often, we neglect to separate the behavior from the person. It is imperative that we begin to articulate to children that although we reject their behavior at times, we still accept them and love them.

Working with those young children helped me to realize that there is a great need to reach out to underprivileged youth. Unfortunately, many in disenfranchised communities are often compromised in the school system academically, financially, and also psychologically. Unfortunately, the unmet needs of our children impact their ability to be effective in their learning. Children need to be able to talk about their fears, hurts, and pains. They need an outlet. They need the same things adults need, to feel loved, to be able to give love, to feel safe and secure, accepted, appreciated, and respected.

I became so close to my students that I prayed for each one of them individually. They made tremendous progress in their attitudes, their outlook on life, their respect for others and themselves, and their academic performance. When their attitudes changed for the better and they allowed light to shine in their hearts, their academics improved. Every morning after the Pledge of Allegiance, I would have a student recite a thought for the day in front of the class to start off the day positively. They would stand up and say something like: *"The thought for the day is: Don't look for miracles because you are a miracle."* There were positive affirmations all around my classroom. We would then have a discussion regarding what the statement meant to them, and how they were going to apply it into their lives.

My students were overprotective of me and there was a strong bond between all of us. They trusted me, and I was able to trust them. When it was time for the school year to end, I cried because I did not want to see them go. They had blossomed. They had flourished. They had developed a sense of pride. They had just completed the fourth grade. I was adamant in making a positive change in those students, and I did. I worked with excellence towards the task at hand. I taught alternative education students every year thereafter, and I still kept the same attitude about making a difference in the lives of those challenging students who are only crying out for love and attention. I make sure I give it to them too.

~~ LESSONS LEARNED ~~

1. Displaying love towards God's children will bring out the best inside of them and cause their gifts to manifest into the earth realm.

2. When we focus on walking in righteousness, reading the Word and praying, God will navigate our lives so that our feet will walk on the path that He has pre-destined for us.

3. If you look at children the way they are in the natural, they only become worse, but when you see the good that God has placed inside of them, they become what they should be.

~~ REFLECTION QUESTIONS ~~

1. Do you strive for excellence in what you do, or are you a mediocre person who does only enough to get by?

2. Is there potential inside of you that you are not allowing to manifest into your life?

3. Are you disciplined enough to designate a specific prayer time each day to spend with God?

Chapter 3

Find the Good in Every Situation
Loving the Unlovable

Look at all things with love and become renewed. Speak with love. Behave with love. React to the actions of others with love. Face each day and every person you meet with love, and love yourself.

Love the sun because it warms you; Love the rain because it cleanses your spirit. Love the light because it shows you the way; Love the darkness because it shows you the stars.
Welcome happiness because it enlarges your heart; Endure sadness because it opens your soul.
Acknowledge rewards because they are your due;
Welcome obstacles because they are your challenge.

Find the good in every situation!

How should you speak? Extol your enemies and they will become friends; Encourage your friends and they will become brothers and sisters. Always dig for reasons to applaud; never look for excuses to gossip. When you are tempted to criticize, bite your tongue; when you are moved to praise, shout on the roof!
Find the good in every situation!

HOW WE THINK IS HOW WE ACT

Has anyone ever said to you, *"I see you woke up on the wrong side of the bed this morning?"* What exactly do they mean when they say that? They mean that your disposition and attitude seems to be negative that day. The energy that you are releasing is negative and you may be walking with a bad vibration. Some people refer to this as bad karma. We probably are exhibiting moody or contentious behaviors. Because of our negative mood, folks tend to stay away from us, not wanting to be around the negativity that we are giving off. As true men and women of God, we must walk in stability, not allowing our thoughts and feelings to control our behaviors. Our attitudes must be positive regardless of what we may be thinking, feeling, or what circumstances we may be facing. Attitudes parallel with what is in the mind, and attitudes do reflect thinking. We must begin to think about what we are thinking about and force our attitude and behavior to be positive. Our thoughts are revealed in how we act and how we act, determines how others act towards us. People do read attitudes through body language, voice tones, and inflections. We must realize the impact that a positive attitude has on every interpersonal relationship in our lives. I once heard the Reverend Jackie McCullough, one of my favorite Christian Ministers recite a quote that her mother use to say: *"Even if you don't have money, if you have a positive attitude and good manners, that can take you all over the world."* That quote resonated in my mind, because I thought that it was so simple and yet so true. When our attitude is right, our abilities reach a maximum of effectiveness and good results will follow. Winston Churchill said, *"Attitude is a little thing that makes a big difference."* The ability to maintain a positive attitude, especially in the midst of challenges, is an asset that can never be measured. This asset is used for making meaning out of our environment, circumstances, relationships, conversations, and problems that are experienced in life. Maintaining a positive attitude is about choices in emotional responses. People with this ability choose their focus instead of allowing circumstances to dictate their focus. They tend to remain in a rational state of mind, and make the most of whatever life offers them. These individuals know how to seize the day and create good memories by projecting a positive future.

They solve problems as quickly as possible. They often do more, go further, and experience more enjoyable, fulfilling and satisfying lives.

Yes, it is true that we do not always wake up bright-eyed and bushy tailed, but we can *force* ourselves into having good days regardless of how we may feel when we wake up in the morning or how terrible the day has started off to be. We cannot directly choose what our days will entail, but we can choose our thoughts and indirectly, yet surely, shape our circumstances. Walking in a negative vibration will open doors to all sorts of stressful situations to be drawn to us, which work against us. When others see constant patterns of negative dispositions and different personalities in us, derogatory opinions are formed and this creates adverse situations in our lives. When there is constant conflict, discord, and confusion in a person's life, that is an indication that there is conflict, discord and confusion inside of that person. Whatever is experienced on the outside is only a tangible manifestation of what already exists on the inside. As the within, so the without. We must let the light that God has placed in us shine daily. We cannot hide it on bad days, and let it shine on good days. Doing this is indicative of instability and double-mindedness, and according to the bible in James 1:8, *"a double-minded man is unstable in all his ways"*.

One who dwells day by day in thoughts of peace towards every person, will bring a wealth of peace to themselves. What you say of another will be said of you, and what you are wishing for another, you are wishing for yourself. Life is a mirror, and as we look with admiration, those God-given characteristics in others, we are actually looking at what God has placed inside of us. We find ourselves reflected in others.

THE POWER OF LOVE

Genuine love is selfless and free from fear. Its joy is in the joy of giving. Love is the strongest force in the universe. It is God in manifestation. It is our greatest weapon, piercing the hard hearts of many. Love is also our shield to cast off arrows of hatred and spears of anger. When adversity and discouragement beat against our shield, they will eventually become the softest of rains. If you do everything out of love you will always triumph. Love is the source of courage and it will prevail in the end. There is perfect peace, courage, and power in love. If we are really committed to walking in love, speaking in love, and encountering others with love, then when facing difficult people, the spirit of love will break down their hard exteriors and penetrate to the goodness inside them, causing them to love in return. It may not happen immediately, but a persistent drop in the same spot, will cause the strongest cement to soften. If you find yourself in a situation wherein you must interact with a difficult person and it really bothers you, try this: In your quiet time alone, address the spirit of that person in prayer and say to their spirit, "*I love you.*" Though spoken in silent prayer, these three words will open the heart of the individual, and you will eventually win him or her over with your newfound love and perception of him or her. You can never receive what you have never given. Give a perfect love, and you will receive a perfect love.

Many of us try to change other people. To live in peace with others, we do not need to change them. We need to change ourselves. Others will change as we change our thoughts and feelings about them. Regardless of what they have done, you absolutely must find the strength to forgive and release them, not for them but for you and for the sake of your sanity and your health. Contrary to what the enemy speaks to your mind, it does not take much to forgive and release. In fact, it takes more strength, effort, and energy to hold grudges, harbor bitterness, hatred, and unforgiveness. Do not think that courage lies only in physical boldness. The greatest courage is the courage to be higher than your anger and to forgive a person who has offended or hurt you.

THE RESULT OF KINDNESS

It does not take much effort to smile and be kind. You never know just how much your kind words or deeds will impact someone's life who has been feeling down, depressed, hopeless, or distressed. Your smile alone may brighten their day and give them hope for a better tomorrow. On the contrary, your mean attitude or ugly look may push a person over the edge. You do not want that on your conscience. Every chance we have to be kind and show mercy and grace, is a great opportunity for us to receive more mercy and more grace from the Lord. We must begin knowing one another after the spirit and seeing each other as God sees us. When we start to see the good in that which seems worthless, and begin speaking to it and drawing it out in one another, we will become the men and women who God has created us to be. Let us stop crucifying Christ again when He comes in even the least of His children, but let us start recognizing Him, honoring Him, and calling Him forth in one other. Find the good in everyone and every situation!

The words in this book or any book may be easy to read but hard to apply. It is also easy for me to write these words, but can be very challenging to apply to my own life. I am however, speaking from experience. I am still struggling with finding the good in everyone and every situation, especially when I cross paths with those who have hurt me, lied on me, used me, betrayed me, or hated me. But the more deliberate I am in trying to look at them with love, the less harder it becomes, until it is not so hard at all.

THE PRINCIPAL

In all my years of living, I have worked with many types of people with varying personalities, but there is one person who really stands out. She was the principal at the first school where I began to teach. I had completed my internship at her school and during the internship, she approached me and told me that she had been watching me and was very impressed with what she saw. She stated that my teaching skills were impeccable and she thought the way that I interacted with the students was very positive. She hired me fresh out of college.

I enjoyed working with the teachers, but it did not take me long to see that the principal was needless-to-say, a very disturbed woman. She seemed to gain a distorted sense of power by embarrassing, mistreating, and demeaning people. She was a liar and her unethical leadership practices, lack of decorum, and overall sadistic behaviors had caused a very large portion of the teachers and staff members to have very little respect for her. Ironically, she professed to be a devout Christian Minister. There were others however who walked in peace and true Godliness on the job, but strangely, she did not gravitate to those individuals. In fact, it seemed as though she tried to avoid them. Just as Cain could not tolerate Abel, those who seek to stand by their own righteousness find the presence of those who stand by faith in Jesus, intolerable. The self-righteousness of those seeking to be justified by their own works is very shaky and deep inside they know it; because of this, they are easily threatened by anyone who would challenge their delusion. I had a wonderful first year of teaching and received many compliments from veteran teachers at the close of the school year. I loved teaching children, and I knew that teaching was my gift.

As time passed, I continued to see the unscrupulous behaviors displayed by the principal. She was very unprofessional and had a proclivity for publicly humiliating teachers. In one particular staff meeting, she told a teacher that she dressed like a hobo. The teacher was mortified. Her face turned red and her entire countenance changed. When I spoke with her the next day, she told me that she had cried all the way home. This principal would harass teachers for no apparent reason and try to force them to socialize only with certain individuals. She had several harassment complaints filed against her, but was never held accountable because her uncle was a very high executive within the school system and protected her. Many were afraid to file complaints because of who her uncle was, so she got away with many improprieties as the principal of that school.

IT'S MY TURN

She was very kind to me when I first started working there, but I began to dislike the way she treated others. It bothered me to see her mistreat and demean adults in the presence of other adults. She also disrespected teachers in the presence of their students. She began to perceive how I felt about her and the mistreatment towards me began. I was one of two union stewards, and when I would speak in faculty meetings, the teachers would be very attentive to the information given and would clap when I was finished because they appreciated the valuable information being given to them. I have learned that people appreciate valuable information that is beneficial to them. The principal told them that there was no need to clap for me, as they were not being entertained, but only receiving information. She approached the other union steward and told him that she did not want me giving the union updates anymore. Why did she not want me to speak? Was it because the teachers listened too attentively to the information that I was conveying? When he told me what she said, I told him that I had no problem with him disseminating the information to the teachers, but if he did not attend the union meetings as I had been, then how was he going to convey information that he had no knowledge of? When he told me that I needed to tell him the information and he would give it, I immediately realized what was happening. I told him that made no sense and to tell the principal that no one was going to stop me from talking. It was my job as a union steward to ensure that teachers receive information to which they were entitled. Furthermore, I told him that when he went to the Union Meetings and received the information himself, he then could disseminate it to the teachers. Until then, I would not neglect to give teachers first-hand information, simply because the principal had insecurity issues.

This woman, a minister of the gospel caused those who were not saved to remain unsaved, substantiating their views of Christian hypocrites. The reason why people who knew her were not interested in her god is because she did not have enough of the presence of God in her life. The main reason why people do not turn their lives over to God based on what we say, is because they may be seeing too little of God in our lives, and too much of flesh. We absolutely have to practice walking upright and loving one other because souls are at stake. Our behavior does not only affect us. It affects many others - having a domino affect on people we don't even know. Those who truly know their God, are the most confident, peaceful, and humble people on earth. What does it profit a person to be able to profoundly discourse the Word of God, if he or she is void of humility and thereby displeasing to the Lord? The fruit of corruption that manifested in this woman's everyday walk was evident in her life and everyone could see it. *A corrupt tree cannot bring forth good fruit; neither can a good tree bring forth corrupt fruit* (Mathew 7:8). Fear, intimidation, strong controlling forces operated through her and made it difficult for anyone to speak out for what was right. Therefore, everyone continued to endure mistreatment and overlooked this woman's unethical practices and ineffective leadership skills. Sadly, teachers eventually became immune to the behaviors and accepted her antics as the norm. Although many teachers left, many also stayed, and I began to see and hear justifications made for her by those who had been teaching many, many years. It was amazing, yet sad to hear those who once stood up against what was wrong now justifying and compromising for what was wrong. I knew it was time for me to leave before my perceptions for what was right became distorted as well.

WHISPERING GRUMBLES

People constantly complained amongst each other about her, but did so secretly. They smiled, laughed, and continued to feed her insatiable ego while in her presence. Her lust for power was fueled by her insecurity. Her drive for control seemed to be a defense mechanism to protect her from rejection, but those who have truly surrendered to Christ will not be intimidated by others with knowledge or dismayed by rejection. On the other hand, those who exercise authority with selfish motives are corrupt, regardless of their pretentious piety. It is important and very critical to realize that when we are truly surrendered to Christ, we should handle authority with the greatest care, knowing that we are His servants. No one is established authoritatively unless God allows it. God does share His authority with His people, and used in humility and submission, authority is a powerful tool. But when that power is used for self-exaltation, our leadership, effectiveness, and credibility is significantly diminished; and we do those under our leadership a great disservice. This principal was so self-exalted that she demanded children to stand up and greet her whenever she walked into a classroom, as though she were a Greek Goddess. To the unwise, authority is an opportunity for self-exaltation and self-promotion, but in Christ, the call to authority is a call for self-sacrifice. I could not conform to what I knew was wrong, and as a result, I was ostracized and mistreated.

The children were not allowed to speak to her while sitting down. They had to stand up, push in their chairs, and then greet her in unison. I absolutely detested that, but it was a school-wide rule, and I could not tell the children not to obey the principal. I prayed about it. We may not understand God's purpose in many things, but every authority that He permits to come into power is to bring about His purposes. I knew that. With that in mind, I tried to be respectful and humble when interacting with her, but it was very difficult to look past the natural exterior in order to understand the forces at work through her.

Everyone at the school saw the mistreatment towards me and others who she had targeted. People would hear negative comments that she would make about teachers and that put a bad taste in the mouths of many. Nonetheless, they still would not interact with or even look at us if she was in the vicinity to see it. When she was not around however, people would shower us with kindness to alleviate their guilt. Others would tell me that they appreciated me for who I was and what I stood for. Some expressed that they felt that the mistreatment towards people was wrong, unnecessary, and downright wicked. Many offered words of encouragement. However, those same individuals would not openly speak with those who had been targeted by her for fear of reprisal. It was an unspoken rule that if anyone interacted with those whom she did not like, those individuals were automatically against her and would be subjected to the same mistreatment.

DIVISIONS IN THE WORKPLACE

This was a major test for me, but I continued to teach my students to the best of my ability and I gave them all I had on a daily basis. Regardless of how I was being treated by the principal, I never let it affect my performance in the classroom. I loved my students and I served them with commitment and diligence. I could not understand however, how one person could lead such a large group of individuals into conforming to what they knew was wrong. I had watched over the years how people who once spoke out for what was right had compromised what they stood for to appease this woman. They had been silenced and did not realize what had happened to them over the years. The spirits that controlled that woman were strong, and the desire of others to be on her good side was also strong. I observed how people would backstab their own friends by divulging their friend's personal business, all in the name of favor from this woman. We should never strive for man's approval. We need to be concerned about whether the King approves of us, not man. That school had become so divided that visitors could feel the polarity when they walked into the building. The tension in that school was so thick that it permeated the very atmosphere and the principal was the root cause for all of the dissension.

    Although I loved teaching my Alternative Education students, I also loved the $1,200 stipend that came with it at the end of each school year. I looked forward to receiving that money because I usually did not work summer school and the money came in handy for the upcoming summer months. I will never forget the last 4th grade AE class that I taught. I loved them, but they were really a challenge. I had to run a really tight ship with that class. I was basically a drill sergeant for the entire first semester. This class had a total of three girls only and the rest were boys and they were rough. I really earned my salary with that class. When it came time for me to receive my stipend at the end of the school year, the money was not in my last paycheck, so I asked the principal about it. I was absolutely shocked at her response to me. She told me that I had not taught the AE class that year and that I had taught a regular 4th grade class. A regular 4th grade class? Everyone knew that I taught the AE class because they knew my students. At the beginning of each school year, letters were sent home informing parents of what the Alternative Education Program entailed and how the class was slightly different from a standard class. The principal herself had sent one of the clerical personnel to me at the beginning of the school year to make sure that I had received each letter back signed by the parents. These letters were kept in the main office. I had received a letter back from each student and I filed them into each cumulative folder myself. When I reminded her about this, she told me that I should not have sent those letters home, although she was the one who gave me the letters. They were pre-written and she gave them to me at the beginning of the school year and told me to make sure that I sent them home and received each one back.

When I asked her why I wasn't told that I was not teaching the class anymore (on paper), she told me that she and I had had a conversation about it, at which time she told me that I would no longer be teaching the class and therefore would not be getting a stipend at the end of the year. How in the world could I have not remembered such a conversation? The conversation never took place and she knew it. I asked her what my response was when she told me this, and she said that she did not remember. I was so angry that I blatantly said to her, *"You are a liar!"* and I walked off. I was so infuriated and shocked that an administrator would stand in the face of an employee and lie about something as significant as that. This was my livelihood that she played with just as she had done so many times before with other people. If she didn't have the money in her budget to pay me (and I don't know if that was the case) all she had to do was tell me from the beginning. I would have been disappointed, but would have gladly taught the children, because the gratification in seeing them turned around at the end of each school year was my reward; but she used and deceived me. I knew that it was time for me to go.

TIME FOR ACTION

Realizing that I must practice what I profess, I prayed for a change in me so that I could love this woman with an agape love regardless of her evil doings. It wasn't easy. After all, she was my superior, and I had to exercise respect and submission to her since she did have authority over me. It was really difficult because I wear my emotions on my face, and my facial expressions reveal how I feel about a person or situation
without me having to say a word. Although I would try and smile at her when I spoke, I would deliberately send subliminal messages letting her know that I did not like nor respect her. Other than the time that I called her a liar and walked off, I never again disrespected her. Trying to change for the better and being

sincere about it was hard, but God gives us the strength to tear down those walls of pride in ourselves so that we can love others in spite of their ways. Loving the unlovable is not easy, but as we continue striving to be like God, He will transform us by the renewing of our mind so that we can love unconditionally. We must work out our own salvation with fear and trembling, but the working it out part is a process and a challenge. I made a decision to leave that school. It was difficult because I had been there for a few years. I knew that I eventually wanted to become an Assistant Principal, and in order to apply for the program that enabled aspiring administrators to be trained, their immediate supervisor needed to complete a recommendation form and checklist. I did not trust that her completion of the form would be honest or favorable. Therefore, after prayer and fasting, I humbly went to her and handed her a Transfer Form to sign. Initially, she seemed to be surprised but immediately collected herself and signed the form with a sinister, yet disappointing look on her face. She asked no questions and made no comments, at least not to me. Having already secured a position, I left the very next day. After I was gone, I decided to pursue getting the AE money that was rightfully owed to me. I called the Alternative Education Department and explained my situation. I was told that their records indicated that the principal had placed me in a regular 4th grade slot for that school year and unless I had proof that I taught the class, they could not pay me the stipend. I told the gentleman that I had sent letters home, which parents had signed at the beginning of the school year. He told me that if I could show him those signed letters, that would be proof enough. I needed to bring those letters to his office and I would be able to get paid. But there was only one problem. I no longer worked at the school, and therefore did not have access to the student records anymore. I called a friend who still worked there and asked her to copy the set for me. She called me back and told me that the letters had been taken out of the students' cumulative folders. After hearing that, I called and spoke with the clerk who had asked me for the signed forms at the beginning of the year. I distinctively remember making her a copy of the complete set before filing them in the students' cumulative folder. When I asked her what happened to the forms, she reluctantly told me that the principal made her shred them. The principal had gone to such measures just to ensure that I wouldn't get paid. I knew that I would not be getting the money then, so after that, I left the situation alone. I knew that God would take care of me.

THE LOSS OF A GOOD TEACHER

After I had been gone for a few days, I was called by ex-colleagues who told me that the principal was not happy about my leaving and was very upset by it. That was strange to me considering how indifferent she was when I handed her the transfer and how mean she had been to me. The truth is that I was extremely good at what I did because it was my gift, and when something is a God-given gift, you are good at it. I know that I had a positive impact in the lives of my students and the school. My commitment to excellence would not let me do it any other way and as a result, my dedication and loyalty to the children made the principal as well as the school shine. When standardized test scores were released, my students always ranked in the top three compared to the other classes on the grade level. One year, their writing scores were the second highest in the grade level. Some may ask why falling in the middle such a big deal? Because I taught the 4th grade Alternative Education Class. This class was comprised of at risk "low-achieving" students with severe behavior problems. Needless-to-say, there was an overrepresentation of Black boys in the class compared to any other ethnic group or gender. These children had been given up on and basically counted out. Although they called it what they wanted, the class was really a dumping ground for Black boys with behavior problems. But those are the students I wanted. They called them trash, but when I was finished with them, they became treasures. The expectation was that their test scores would be at the bottom of the barrel, but that would not be the case so long as they were in my class. Children can and will learn once their behavior has changed for the better and when they have a good teacher willing to teach them. Learning will not take place until behavior is changed. The discipline gap mirrors the achievement gap. Discipline is love and in my class, they were loved much. I was later told by the principal's secretary that the principal secretly admired my strengths and intellect, but that her pride would never allow her to tell me. She revealed that the principal constantly bragged about what a great teacher I was and how she wished she had a memory like mine. She said that the principal had a high level of respect for me. Wow, is that how you treat someone you respect? I was confused and did not understand, but I did not spend a lot of time pondering on it. I had my future to look forward to at the new school.

    After leaving that school, I never spoke negatively about her and although I would hear others say derogatory things about her, I never commented. I felt that speaking negatively about another person, particularly a former boss, diminished that person, so I refused to diminish myself. I remembered a quote that I read from Benjamin Franklin when he was asked about his gift for positively interacting with people. He said, "*I will speak ill of no man... and speak all the good I know of everybody.*"

    I left that negative experience behind me, and I looked with optimism to the future that I knew had many blessings waiting for me. I needed that experience to recognize what ineffective leadership looked like and the effect that it had on others. God was preparing me for effective leadership, and I needed to know the difference. Finding the good in everyone and every situation will also strengthen the spirit of discernment within one and open the spiritual ear to hear the voice of God clearly.

    I thank God for the experience that I had at that school. Had I not worked there, I may not have had the opportunity to work with AE children, bring out their potential, and help to raise their self-esteem and respect for themselves and others. I also thank the principal for seeing the ability inside me and helping me to be successful in that position. I thank her for hiring me and teaching me by example that ineffective leadership can have a detrimental effect on staff morale.

No man is your friend. No man is your enemy. Every man is your teacher. She taught me well and yes, I love her for it.

THE HOTDOG MAN

Speaking of love, I also recall a time when I was on my way to an interview for an Executive Secretary's position. It was for a huge pharmaceutical manufacturing company, and the position for which I was applying was way out of my league. I was in my early twenties, in college, and had to find a good paying job because I had accumulated bills that my current job salary of $7.50 per hour was not covering. The position for which I was applying paid $8,000 more per year, and although it was out of my league, I knew that if given the opportunity, I could do it. My clerical and interpersonal skills were pretty good, and I had always had a knack for interviewing well. I had managed to secure myself an interview. On the day of the interview, I was about 30 minutes early, so I walked to the hotdog stand across the street. The vendor was a tall, slender man from the West Indies. Somehow he and I began talking. I discerned that he had a wounded spirit and was disheartened about something. He revealed that his wife had just left him the day before. She said that she was not happy in the marriage anymore. He was devastated and began to weep as he talked to me. His heart was broken, and the compassion that I felt for him caused my heart to hurt. I offered him words of encouragement and assured him that I would pray for him. I meant that I really would pray for him because all too often, we hear the trials and tests that others go through, and we are so quick to say, *"I will pray for you"* and we never do. I guess that statement is a natural response when we know there really is nothing else that we can do or say, but if we say we are going to pray for someone, we need to pray for them. After I told him that, I went to the interview.

The interview went very well, and I was told to come back for a second interview days later. When I arrived home that evening, I not only prayed for that man, but I went to warfare for his marriage. I prayed as though he was my own

Destined for Great Things!

relative. I went into the spirit realm and pulled down every force of darkness that came against his marriage. I prayed for comfort and peace for him. Then I prayed that his wife would return to her husband with a change of heart. I honestly felt a breakthrough in the spirit as I was praying and an overwhelming sense of assurance fell on me. I was extremely excited and full of joy because I knew that God had moved.

WHAT A GREAT DAY!

Days later, I returned back for my second interview with the company. I went to the hotdog stand to see my friend and to buy another hotdog. His face lit up when he saw me. This day, he was not selling hotdogs alone. He was with his wife who had come back home the day after I met him. I knew in my heart that God had heard my prayers because I had prayed for him with love in my heart. I went on to my final interview. God blessed me with that new job, where I became the Administrative Secretary to the President/CEO of that company, and where I remained until I graduated college and began teaching. I received two blessings that day!

~~ LESSONS LEARNED ~~

1. Taking a stand for what you know is right, will strengthen the character within you. Even when the mistreatment is not directed toward you personally, it should not be tolerated when we see others targeted.

2. Although it may not be easy working with certain individuals, look for the good in the situation and evaluate what you think the reason is that you have crossed paths with them in that season.

3. God hears and answers our prayers quickly when we pray with total love and compassion for others.

~~ REFLECTION QUESTIONS~~

1. Is your personality stable, or does your moodiness show in your thoughts, feelings, behavior, and actions?

2. When encountering difficult people, do you look for the goodness in them, or are you quick to treat them according to their faults and behaviors?

3. When you tell people that you are going to pray for them, do you really go home and pray for them?

Chapter 4

Laugh Often
It's Better to Have Loved and Lost

*N*o *living creature can laugh except human beings. Only humans have this gift of laughter, and it is*
ours to use whenever we choose.

When you smile, your digestion improves; When you chuckle, your burdens are lightened; When you laugh, your life is lengthened, for this is the great secret to long life, and now it is yours.

Can you laugh when confronted with person or deed, which offends you so as to bring forth your tears or makes you want to curse? Certainly! Four words you can train yourself to say until they become a habit so strong that immediately they appear in your mind whenever good humor threatens to depart from you. These words will carry you through every adversity and maintain your life in balance.
These four words are:
THIS TOO SHALL PASS.

For all worldly things shall indeed pass. When you are heavy with heartache, you shall console yourself with, "This too shall pass." When you are puffed up with success, you shall warn yourself with, "This too shall pass." When you are burdened with

wealth, you must tell yourself, "This too shall pass." If all worldly things shall indeed pass, why should you be of concern for today?

And with laughter all things will be reduced to their proper sizes. Laugh at your failures and they will vanish into clouds of new dreams. Laugh at your successes and they will shrink to their proper sizes. Laugh at evil, and it will die untasted! Laugh at goodness, and it will thrive and abound!

Never should you allow yourself to become so important, so wise, so dignified, and so powerful, that you forget how to laugh at yourself. In this manner, you will remain as humble as a child, for only as a child are you given the ability to look up to others.

THE MYSTERY MAN

Many of us have heard the saying *"It's better to have loved and lost than never to have loved at all."* That may very well be true, and there is nothing like the "feeling" of being in love. In all my years of living, I have been in love twice. I thought that I was in love at other times, but looking back in retrospect, I was in love with the *idea* of being in love. A friend of mine once told me that unconditional love between a man and a woman does not exist. He said that unconditional love existed between parents and children only. Love between men and women was, in his opinion conditional. As I pondered on his reasoning, I began to realize that he was right. We think that we are in love with people because of how they treat us and how they make us feel, but as soon as they begin to mistreat us or step out of the boundaries that we have created for them, we don't love them anymore. Our love is indeed conditional. Let me introduce you to Robert. I had been seeing him in services, and I noticed how faithful he was in coming to church. He was always quiet and seemed to be very attentive to the Word of God as it would go forth. He always sat alone and would leave immediately following church services. I really liked how he carried himself and for months, I admired him from afar. I didn't even know his name.

One Tuesday evening following Bible Study, I arrived to the parking lot to find a note under the windshield of my Eclipse. The note read: *"Hi, my name is Robert. I think you are gorgeous. I have seen you in church many times and I admire the way you praise the Lord. If it's not too late, please give me a call tomorrow,* and he left his number. I was flattered to get a note, but I did not know who this secret admirer was, so I did not call, at least not right away. I wondered for a couple of days who could have left the note. In the back of my mind, I wished it was the person who I had been secretly admiring for so long, but I knew that was a long shot. I did not want to call the number for fear that it would be someone that I would be completely unattracted to, so I held off on calling. Our church was so big that it could have been anyone. After all, New Birth Baptist Church had over 7,000 members at that time.

MYSTERY MAN REVEALED

About four days later, I called and had a conversation with my secret admirer. He told me that he would reveal himself to me the next Tuesday night at Bible Study. He explained that he had to leave church early the night he left the note on my car because he had to be to work at 4:00a.m., and needed to get some rest. Otherwise, he would have approached me personally, he stated. He was a supervisor at United Parcel Service. We had interesting conversations, and he seemed very intelligent, but I still was hesitant about talking too much without seeing him first. Bible Study finally came and all throughout the service I thought about the revelation that I was to get that night. I could not concentrate on the Word that evening because my mind kept wandering off.

When service was over and the congregation was walking out, I wondered if he had seen me because I was almost out the door, but just before I stepped out completely, a man approached me and said, *"Hi Mia, I'm Robert. I am the one who put the note on your car."* It was him, the guy that I had admired for so long! I was so excited, but of course I did not show it. I was as smooth as silk. I remember thinking, *"Thank You Jesus!"* Maybe I had sent him some sort of subliminal messages that led him to me. That was not the first time that a man I had admired from afar had come to me. We talked in the parking lot for a while, and I gave him my phone number. After dating for a couple of weeks, we decided to become exclusive, and he insisted that we begin going to church together. He possessed many of the characteristics that I was attracted to and desired in a man. He was handsome, had a great job, was educated, a complete gentleman, and was very attentive to my wants and feelings. He was divorced and currently living with his mother because he was having a house built at the time. He was eight years older than me, but I didn't mind because I always liked older men. During the course of our relationship, we did many things together. We constantly went to dinner and outings. We would walk on the beach, go bowling, skating, concerts, comedy shows, have picnics, and take weekend vacations. He would even surprise me with little cards and gifts sporadically. I really enjoyed being with him, and it was obvious that our feelings were mutual. He made me happy. We talked about getting married, raising a family, and moving into the house that he was having built. He was anxious to get married soon and wanted children right away. I loved him, but I was not as anxious to marry as he was. I was only 26 years old and wanted to be triple sure that we were doing the right thing at that time. After all, it hadn't been a year since we were dating, and he was already talking marriage. I felt that we needed to continue getting to know each other for a while.

THE PERFECT COUPLE

Most thought that we were the perfect couple, and he made no secret about how he felt about me in the presence of others. He was very good to me. He valued and respected me and truly cared for my feelings, my aspirations, and my goals. But he had a dark side. He was very possessive and had a habit of pushing, grabbing, or shoving me when he would get angry. He wouldn't punch or slap me, but he would still put his hands on me in that manner. He would get upset over what seemed to me to be very petty things such as other people conversing with me; not only men, but women too. He would become extremely angry if anyone of the opposite sex would hug me, even though he would be standing right there. The hugs were very innocent and even though he would be right there, he still did not like it. Whenever someone approached me, I always introduced that person to Robert to make him feel comfortable. I knew that he was very jealous and although I tried to make him feel secure, I would still get the heat from him when people would hug me after church, so I stopped allowing men to hug me. He then started answering the telephone at my apartment and became very controlling. He became jealous if I would talk to my sister or anyone else too long on the telephone, so everyone eventually stopped calling.

As time passed, I started seeing more and more of his dark and ugly side. Our first really bad argument was during the summer on a day that I had been home all day doing nothing but reading and watching television. The phone had not rung except for when he would call to check on me from work. On this particular day when he got off, he called to say that he was on his way over. The minute he knocked on the door, my telephone rang but I answered the door first. He walked into my apartment and went straight to answer the telephone. It was Bill, an old friend who I had not spoken with in a long time. He was just calling to say hello. Robert questioned him, cursed him, and told him never to call my house again. I tried to explain to Robert that I had not spoken with Bill in months and that he was a plutonic friend who I had never dated. He did not believe me, and accused me of talking to men on the phone all day while he was at work. He grabbed and pushed me against the kitchen wall. He was so angry that he took the porcelain collectibles that were on my coffee table and threw them all over my living room. I was so scared that I went to my bedroom and climbed into the bed as he was destroying my apartment. I had never seen that side of him before.

I had some understanding of a man's ego, and I strategically tried to cater to his. I had no fear of competition from other women because he made me feel secure so I tried to do the same for him to no avail. He had a bad temper that often got out of control. After he would cool off, he would apologize and tell me that he loved me. He would then buy me roses or take me on a vacation to make up for what had happened. That soon became very old. I had gotten tired of trying to make him feel secure when I was doing absolutely nothing to make him feel insecure. Everyone had stopped calling me because of him, and I was no longer happy. Finally, I prayed. My prayer to God was: "...*if this man is not the man that you have ordained for me, then please remove him out of my life.*"

I had gotten tired of the constant arguing, and I knew that it was just a matter of time before we dissolved the relationship. During our last argument, he hit me in my face, and I said, "*You have hit me one last time.*" He asked me what that meant and I said, *"It means exactly what you think it means."* We broke up that day, which was the very next day after I had prayed that specific prayer. He called a few days later apologizing and asking if we could work things out. He reminded me that we had made plans to marry and raise a family. He asked me why I was willing to throw all of that away when we both loved each other. I was adamant in my decision and I told him that I really did not think things were going to work out for us in the future.

PAIN OF A BROKEN HEART

As the days turned into weeks, I began to really miss him. I called him and talked about reconciling. His attitude was very nonchalant, and he was totally not interested in talking to me. Needless-to-say, I was very shocked, considering this was the man who had showered me with love, went over and beyond to please and satisfy me, would buy me cards and roses for no reason and was relentless in trying to marry me. I couldn't believe that he had such a drastic change of heart. I had a hard time dealing with his attitude change so I began to continuously call him. When I realized that he was serious, the pain in my heart surfaced. It was one thing for me to break up with him, but it was quite another for him not to want to be with me. That was rejection and I did not handle rejection well. My heart was broken. The pain was unbearable and indescribable. I cried out to the Lord everyday to heal my broken heart. I began to lose a significant amount of weight. It was so significant that one could see the bones in my face. I couldn't eat, and the little that I did eat was not enough to make me gain weight. I only went to work and back home. I stopped going to church. I wanted to call him, but I didn't. The feeling that I was annoying him when he answered the phone was the thing that stopped me from calling him. There were times that I would sit by the phone, stare at it, and hope that it would ring and be him on the other end. The pain in my heart hurt so badly. I just wanted it to go away. As the days turned into weeks and the weeks into months and the months into years, my heart was still broken. I cried and cried. I couldn't eat or sleep. I had sunk into a depression. I didn't want to be with anyone else but him. I made myself believe that I was in love with him and that I had a broken heart. It was all an illusion.

GETTING THROUGH THE PAIN

As I look back and reflect now, I realize that I was not hurt because I loved him so much. I was hurt because of the rejection. If he and I would have reconciled and I would have broken up with him again, I would have been just fine, but since he was the one who rejected me, that was a devastating blow to my self-esteem, self-confidence, and self-worth. It took me every bit of five years to get him completely out of my system, mind, body, and spirit. The first two and a half years were really hard and very lonely because I would not date anyone else. I stayed home secluded in my apartment. After work and especially during weekends, I did nothing but cry myself to sleep. The pain was still so fresh and so real, and it hurt so bad. It did not seem to be getting better. I needed to focus my thoughts on something positive. I enrolled in school to work on a Masters Degree. Two evenings a week and one full Saturday had me in school. The days I was not in school, I did homework. This was very productive for me because my thoughts were now diverted to something other than the pain from being rejected.

Robert called me one Saturday morning about year and a half after we broke up. He seemed to be nervous but happy to hear my voice. He stated that he needed to discuss something very important with me. He asked if he could see me that day. At the time of his call, I was headed for school, but I did not tell him where I was going. I said that I was on my way out and that he could call me later if he'd like. Although I was surprised to hear from him, and was still struggling to heal from our breakup, I did not stay on the phone to hold a conversation with him. My tone was very indifferent and I deliberately acted as though I didn't care to speak with him. I did not say that, but my tone did. Needless-to-say, he did not call back until a year later. He revealed the reason why he had called a year before. He had gotten someone pregnant and was confused about the circumstances surrounding the situation. He wanted to know if I still loved and wanted to be with him because that would have been the deciding factor to whether or not he would marry the young lady. He indicated that he loved and missed me immensely, but that his pride did not allow him to return back to me since I had rejected him. According to him, my actions on the phone a year before, helped him to make his decision. He had always told me that if he ever got anyone pregnant, he would marry that person. I don't think he wanted to marry the young lady who was pregnant with his child. She already had a son, and she wasn't the type of woman that I know he was attracted to. Nevertheless, he did marry her and had a baby girl.

THE RELEASE

Years later, he came to visit me at the school where I was teaching. Seeing him after all of those years was weird. I was on the telephone talking to a parent when I looked up and saw him walking around the corner. I ended the call with the parent and greeted him in a friendly manner. He put his arms around me and would not let go. I had to push him away. We talked for a few minutes and exchanged pleasantries. I was married at the time and told him that I was *happily* married (which was a lie) and had a son. He bragged about his daughter, and felt the need to remind me that he had gotten married and had a big wedding. I said to him, *"You did the right thing by marrying her when she was pregnant with your child."* I know that my statement wasn't nice, but I felt that it wasn't nice of him to brag about his wedding either, especially when he and I had so many conversations about how *our* wedding was going to be. I did not want to continue the conversation, so I explained that I had to return to my classroom to teach my students. They were in Physical Education at the time but he did not know it. He hugged me again, and asked me if I missed him. My response was, *"That doesn't matter because I am married now."* He left. I had finally gotten my release. After he left, I realized that I was completely over him because there were no feelings that surfaced in me when I saw him that day. I felt nothing when he hugged me and I was even turned off by his looks. He had shaved his mustache, and that was a complete turn off to me. I was finally over him!

I can look back and really laugh now. It's amazing how when we are in relationships, we don't see anything wrong with the person that we profess to love so much, but when we are no longer in love, we can sure see clearly. After the fact, we say things like this: *"Girl, I saw Robert today and he looks bad. He shaved his mustache, walks with a limp, has a huge flat nose, a bald spot, crooked teeth, and bad breath. Girl he is all messed up."* The reality is that he looked just like that when you dated him, but now that you are no longer in love and can see clearly, you can see all his flaws (Robert did not have those flaws, but you get my point). A man's conversation might sound something like this: *Man, I saw Mia today and she sure doesn't look like she looked when I dated her. Everything about her is fake. She had fake hair, fake eyes, and fake nails. She also had crossed eyes and facial hair.* But the truth is that, girlfriend looked like that when you dated her and all your friends knew it. You shared the same razor with her. But now that you are no longer in love, she isn't all that you thought she was.

It's amazing what time does. It not only heals wounds, but it brings about change. Thank God for experiences, for they are our best teacher. I have no regrets for having had a broken heart and falling in love. At least I know what both feel like. It would be nice if the falling in love part could last forever. Who knows, maybe it can with the right person. But I will not cry because it's over, but laugh and be thankful because it happened. Walk in wisdom. Laugh at your experiences, be grateful for them and laugh at the world.

~~ LESSONS LEARNED ~~

1. We cannot shield ourselves from rejection. Rejection is only destructive when you internalize it and allow it to creep into your belief system. The forces of evil love to fuel the fires of low-self esteem with different forms of rejection. But if we accept rejection as a part of human experience, we can take every negative situation and become a stronger person from it.

2. Some people have never had the opportunity to be in love. Some people have never had a broken heart. I was blessed to have experienced both. Now, I can encourage someone else as they go through the same things.

~~REFLECTION QUESTIONS~~

1. Do you appreciate the experience of having had a broken heart or are you still holding on to yesterday and allowing yourself to continue feeling the pain? Have you released the person to whom the broken heart is associated?

2. Are you still holding on to the successes or failures from the past or have you learned to laugh at them so they can finally vanish in order to make room for present possibilities?

Chapter 5

Control Your Emotions in Every Situation

Playing With Fire May Get You Burned

All nature is a circle of moods, and I am a part of nature and so like the tides, my moods will rise, my moods will fall.

I will remember that every adversity carries with it the seed of tomorrow's victory and every sadness carries with it the seed of tomorrow's joy. I will master my emotions so that each day will be positive, for unless my mood is right, my day will be a failure. I will do this by learning the secret of the ages: "Weak is she who allows her thoughts to control her actions; Strong is she who forces her actions to control her thoughts."

Each day when I awaken, I will follow this plan of battle before I let the forces of sadness, self-pity, and failure capture me:

When I feel depressed, I will sing.
When I feel sad, I will laugh.
When I feel sick, I will double my labor.
When I feel inferior, I will wear new clothes.

When I feel uncertain, I will ask questions.
When I feel poverty, I will think of the wealth to come.
When I feel incompetent, I will remember past successes.

If I feel insignificant, I will remember my goals.

Those such as depression and sadness are easy to recognize, but there are others that approach with a smile and the hand of friendship, and they too can deceive me. Against them, I must never relinquish control. Therefore, I will remember the following:

When I feel overconfident, I will recall my failures.
When I overindulge, I will think of past hungers.
When I feel complacency, I will remember my competition.
When I feel moments of greatness, I will remember moments of shame.
When I attain great wealth, I will remember those in poverty
When I feel overly proud, I will remember a moment of weakness.

Remembering these moments will keep my life balanced. With this new knowledge, I will understand and recognize the moods of others whom I encounter and I will make allowances for his or her anger and irritation of the day, for they know not the secret of controlling their thoughts. From this moment, I am prepared to control whatever personality awakes me each day.
I will master my moods through positive action, and when I master my moods, I control my destiny. Today I control my destiny, and my destiny is to fulfill God's perfect will for
my life.

NEVER SAY NEVER

Through experience I have learned to, "never say never". I had heard stories of women and their awful experiences with men. I had heard of instances where men had used women for money, ran up credit cards bills, beat them, verbally abused them, cheated on them, driven other women around town in their cars, etc. As I would listen to these women tell of their horrible experiences, I would distinctively remember thinking how stupid they were and how desperate for a man they must have been to allow those things to happen to them. I was always quick to judge and say that if a man did not have anything intellectually, financially, or spiritually to contribute to what I had acquired, I would never get involved with him. It was not until I experienced first hand what it was like to be used, disrespected, abused, and disgraced that I realized it could happen to anyone.

We are not forced to give in to temptation. We can either succumb or we can resist. We make our own choices, and we must live with the consequences of the choices we make. I will never forget that Wednesday afternoon in 1996 when I was in Burger King on my lunch break. I felt very uncomfortable being stared at, but I tried to ignore it. The man finally approached me and said, *"How are you? My name is Victor. I'm sorry for staring at you, but I think you are gorgeous."* I responded in a very nonchalant way and said, *"Thank you"* continuing to review the menu. Victor proceeded to say, *"If you don't mind, may I have your name and phone number so that I may keep in contact with you?"* Again, very curt, I said, *"No, you may not have my number."* And I continued looking up at the menu. The persistent man then said, *"Well, here's my number. If you get some time, give me a call."* Aggravated at that point, I said, *"Don't waste your time, because I won't be calling you. Have a nice day."* I had just gotten out of a bad relationship and was still trying get over that, therefore I did not want to talk to or get involved with anyone else. I just wanted to be left alone. He then walked out of the restaurant. Walking back to my car with the food, I noticed that Victor was still in the parking lot. He said, *"Oh, I see you like red too."* He had a red Nissan 300zx. I had a red Mitsubishi Eclipse. I did not respond. I got into my car and drove off.

SO WE MEET AGAIN

Approximately 8 months later, while in the grocery store, a man began walking toward me on the same aisle in which I was shopping. As he was walking by, I stared at him because I knew him from somewhere. He turned to me and said, *"Is there a problem?"* I said, *"Yes, I know you from somewhere."* He said, *"Yea, I'm the one that you were very rude to in Burger King."* Instinctively, I began laughing. Naturally, that broke the ice. I was not rude to him this time and I noticed that he was a fairly decent looking guy. He spoke well and seemed very charming and mannerable. He was nicely dressed and had a nice physique. We exchanged phone numbers, and he called me as soon as I arrived home from shopping. I gathered from talking to him that he lived with his brother and was unemployed. He stated that he was a recording artist awaiting a record contract. He told me that he could not get a regular job because it interfered with his singing career since he needed to be in the studio working on his next album. He went on to say that he had a significant amount of money saved up for bills and that he was financially secure. He called almost everyday thereafter and was insistent on coming to my apartment. He eventually stopped calling when I would not allow him to come over. Between the time that he stopped calling until I spoke with him again was about three months.

    One day, while home alone, or should I say lonely, I decided to give him a call on his beeper. Without delay, he started asking if he could come over, so this time I allowed him to do so. He no longer had the Nissan**,** but was driving a very nice Lincoln Town Car. He told me that he had traded in the Nissan because it was too small and he needed extra room for his two daughters who were elementary aged at the time. While at my apartment, we talked for a while, then he left. Although I was single, he was not the caliber of man that I was use to dating or one with whom I would consider having a relationship. Even though he was decent-looking, charming, well spoken, and seemed to be very mannerable, there was something sinister and dark about him that I could not put my finger on. It did not really matter however, because he did not appeal to me. He was someone to talk to and pass the time. He had nothing to offer me spiritually, financially, or intellectually, and I knew I could never get serious with someone of his caliber. I allowed him to entertain me because there was no one else in my life at the time, and I soon learned that when you play with fire, you get burned.

THE TRUTH COMES OUT

As I reflect back, I remember how he used to ask me questions such as, *"If I needed a place to stay, would you help me?"* That is not a typical everyday question that people ask when you meet them. That question alone should have told me half the story of his life. Because of the fact that I had allowed myself to spend too much time with Victor, I had sex with him and became pregnant. It was not soon thereafter, I found out that he did not live with his brother, but he in-fact lived with a woman. The woman somehow found my phone number and began calling me leaving strange messages and hanging up. I also learned that his red Nissan had been repossessed and the woman with whom he was living had financed the Lincoln Town car for him in her name. He began asking to "borrow" money to make the car note, pay the car insurance and buy things for his daughters. I loaned him the money when he asked for it. I honestly thought that there was a record contract forthcoming as he had told me, and that he would be able to help out financially when the baby arrived. I also expected the money that I had been loaning him to be repaid. I had never had a man ask me for money before, and I felt strange about it at first, but I figured it had to take a lot of courage for a man to ask a woman to borrow money. Therefore, I figured he must have really needed it. I was used to dating stable, accomplished men with gainful employment, so this was new to me. I thought that he was just going through some hard times as everyone does at some point in life. I believed in helping people when and if I could. However, I soon began to see that he was taking my kindness for weakness.

WHO IS THIS WOMAN?

In the meantime, I was carrying his child. The woman continued calling and asking me questions, none of which I would answer. She would call and ask to speak with him. I would tell her that he was not home. She would then ask, *"Who are you to Victor?"* I would hang up. On another occasion she asked, *"Are you Rodney's girlfriend?"* I would hang up. Finally, she decided to be straightforward and talk to me like a mature adult. She told me that her name was

Jennifer and said that my so-called man was her man. She proceeded to tell me that Victor and her had been living together, but that he never came home claiming he had to sleep in the studio at nights. She explained that she had financed the Lincoln Town Car for him, but that he was in arrears with the car payments. She went on to complain that he did not contribute financially to her household expenses, ran up her home and cellular telephone bills, ate all of her groceries, and was leeching off of her. She continued to tell me that Victor had disrespected her constantly by having other women call there for him. According to her, he talked to women directly in her face and would tell her that the conversations were business. She warned me that he was an compulsive liar and that she constantly baby-sat his daughters while he would be elsewhere. She said that he would come home at five and six o' clock in the morning and would say that he had been in the studio all night. She also claimed that she would buy food, school clothes, Christmas toys, and birthday gifts for his daughters and spent more time with them than he would. When I told her that I was five months pregnant from him, she told me that she had been pregnant from him twice, but had miscarried one and aborted one. She was not

disrespectful during the conversation, but seemed to be more angry and hurt than anything else. I was calm while speaking with her and we were very cordial. I was almost to the point of being apathetic. I told her that she could have him back because he had been nothing but a financial and psychological burden to me. Surprisingly, she said that she loved him, but that she was not going to be played for a fool by him any longer. She may not have realized it at the time, but she made a very wise decision in leaving him alone. She should thank God that she had no connections to him that a baby would have required.

INVASION

There came a time for me to visit my sister in Tallahassee, where she attended school. The day that I was supposed to leave, I inadvertently locked myself out of the apartment and had to go to the rental office to get a duplicate key. I did not have time to take the key back to the rental office, so I asked Victor if he would take it back for me because the people at the rental office were very adamant about returning their keys. I went to Tallahassee and stayed there for a week. When I returned, I discovered that Victor never returned the key, but had used it to move all of his belongings into my apartment. He no longer had the Lincoln Town Car or any car for that matter. Jennifer had put him out and taken her car back. I guess I did not mind him moving in because I did want to be with or "appear" to be with the father of my child although I did not love him. However, the way he moved in was deceitful, especially since I had been speaking with him from Tallahassee and he never mentioned a word about it. He had deliberately kept my apartment key so that he could have access in and out while I was in Tallahassee. When I returned, he began driving my car and staying out with it for two and three days at a time without calling me. The first time he did that, I was worried and actually called the police to report a missing person. I could not fathom a man leaving a pregnant woman home alone for three days with no transportation and no contact. That was incomprehensible to me. When I approached him about coming in at 4:00 o' clock in the morning and staying out for days at a time, his reply to me was that he was grown and nobody could tell him when and what time he needed to come home.

    Without my permission, he had a sound system installed in my car, filled my trunk with speakers, and had my cassette player removed and replaced with a compact disc player. I was very upset about that, and I expressed it to him because at the time, I did not own one cd, and I listened to cassette tapes when I would drive my car. Needless-to-say, he never put the cassette player back in. He would be gone for days at a time with my car leaving me stranded with no where to go. Oftentimes I would be stranded in the house with no way of going anywhere. He would not return my pages and I had to cancel doctor appointments as a result of not having a way to get there. All I did was make the car payments because I never drove my own car anymore. He almost never slept at the apartment at night and I almost never saw him. His excuse was always that he had to be in the studio for days at a time so he slept there at night, but when I would call the studio, I was always told that he wasn't there.

MEETING HIS DAUGHTERS

The time came for me to meet his little girls. He had one biological daughter and claimed her sister as his own. Their mother had previously been a stripper and had three children from three different men. She was not married and rarely spent time with her children. They were always with other people, and in my opinion, neglected. One evening, he brought the older two girls to the apartment without informing me of their coming. He dropped them off and said that they were spending the night. He then said that he was leaving to go to the studio. So I asked him who was going to baby-sit them. He boldly said, *"You."* After leaving, he did not call nor return back for two days. They would ask me where their father was, and I did not know what to say. The oldest one was nine at the time and the other one was seven. One would think that since his daughters were there, he would have at least called to check on them. He never did. I learned very quickly that Victor was an inconsiderate, trifling, selfish liar who had no regard for anyone other than himself.

THE LEECH

The rare times that Victor came home, he would talk to women on my phone directly in front of me. I would look at him as if he was crazy, but I did not open my mouth. I remember thinking in my mind, *"Does this man really believe that I am just that gullible and dumb that he would actually sit in my face and talk to other women?* I never questioned him or said a word. I was planning my leave from him after the baby. He ran up my telephone bill every month with long distance calls, causing the phone bill to be over $170 a month. Prior to that, I had never paid more than $40 per month. Needless-to-say, he never contributed a dime towards the bill. When I would show the bill to him, he would not mention anything about paying it. But he continued running it up to the point that it was disconnected. Without contributing a dime to groceries, he ate all the food in my kitchen. I would buy food, but when I would go in the kitchen to eat something, everything would literally be gone from gallons of ice cream, entire packs of cookies, loaves of bread, packs of lunchmeat, everything! That was extremely frustrating for me, especially since I was pregnant. One would think that since he knew he had not contributed a dime towards groceries, he would have used a bit of constraint when eating. This man was a parasite with no respect for women and had no home training. He was the perfect example of how boys turn out to be when they have no positive male role models in their lives to look up to. Victor had no wisdom and was oblivious to how women should be treated. He was one of those men who hunted for established women with good paying jobs, credit cards, money in the bank, and good credit, so that he could charm his way into their lives and leech off of them. It is so sad that there are so many single women who want and deserve a good man, but compromise their values and expectations for men like Victor. Unfortunately, they eventually find themselves in relationships that tear down their sense of self-worth. I guess I was one of them. Such non-affirming relationships can be devastating.

IS THIS REALLY HAPPENING?

I was in a state of shock experiencing these things as a result of this man. I really could not believe that a person could be so trifling. I was used to being wined and dined by well-established dignified men who cared for me emotionally, affectionately, and intellectually. I had dated men who cared for my feelings and respected me like a lady should be respected. I had never had a man use me or even ask to borrow money. To go from that to this was a major and drastic change. Everything that Jennifer had told me about him became my living reality. He was a habitual liar. Ninety-eight percent of everything that came out of his mouth was a lie. I honestly believe that since I never questioned him about anything, never raised my voice, never argued or caused a problem while I was pregnant, he assumed that I was naïve and gullible. He thought that I was the sweetest, nicest, lady that a man could have to walk all over. That was not the case. I had mastered my emotions because of my unborn baby. I was only exercising calmness because I was carrying a child. I am a firm believer that one's actions and feelings can have a devastating affect on their unborn child leaving lasting impressions on that child's subconscious mind, which causes unexplained mental tendencies and behaviors later on in that child's life. Therefore, I tried not to bring any stress on myself.

He did nothing to financially prepare for the baby's arrival. He caused me nothing but problems and was a huge financial and psychological burden on me. Once, the FBI came to the apartment complex looking for him for possession of stolen property. There were so many other incidents that made me realize that I had really gotten myself caught up with a con artist and common thug. The mistake of associating with this man was bigger than I had realized, and I asked myself over and over how I could have gotten so deeply entangled with this caliber of a man. Depression had started to creep in, but I recognized it and fought it off by praying and reading the Bible.

THE EARLY ARRIVAL

Time was approaching for me to have the baby and I had secretly arranged to move into a two-bedroom condominium alone. Everything was finalized and Victor had no knowledge of it. I had planned to have some male friends do the moving for me while he was gone on one of his three or four day excursions. Everything was ready. After the move, I was not going to contact him because of the baby, but initially, I knew that I needed to be away from him. I thought that since he was gone 95% of the time, he would not be there when it to contact him for a while. I knew that at some point, I had to co was time for me to give birth. After all, I very seldom paged him, but the few times I did, he never returned the calls. I had my plans ready to leave this man, but it did not happen quite the way I planned.

My baby girl decided to come a month early, and it just so happened that Victor had been home for about 20 minutes (from being gone three days) when my water broke. So yes, he was right there when I gave birth to Stephanie. She was such a precious and delightful sight. She looked so angelic as I stared into her tiny face. Looking at her seemed to eradicate all that I had been going through prior to her arrival. So many emotions emerged when the nurse placed her in my arms. The love seemed to spring forth as I held her and admired her beauty. From that moment on, I was only focused on caring for and protecting that innocent child. Nothing else mattered.

However, Stephanie's early arrival put a monkey wrench in my moving plans. Victor found out about those plans and certainly planned on coming right along. After all, he did not have a place to live, no job, no car of his own, and no money. I guess the woman he had been sleeping with only allowed him there for a couple days at a time. After I brought Stephanie home, he insisted that *"we"* move right away. I knew that he wanted to move because the FBI had been watching the apartment complex and was looking for him.

It was nothing but hell in the condo with him. The same things were happening, but to a greater degree. The situation was exacerbated because I was no longer pregnant, and I began to voice my anger and aggravation towards how I felt about him. Everything I had been holding inside came out in very hostile, cruel, and wicked ways. He still had not paid a bill, but was still running up bills, staying out for days at a time, stealing money from me, eating all the groceries, talking to women on my telephone, running up the electricity bill with the air-conditioner, utilizing the washing machine and dryer with only one and two articles of clothing in the machine, having women call my home, and taking my car for days at a time.

LOSING CONTROL

After three months of living in the condominium, he told me that he wanted his daughters to move in - permanently. I asked, *"Who is going to take care of them?"* His response was, *"us."* I then said *"How are [we] going to take care of them, when [I] am the only one who works?"* I told him that they could not live there, and I was very adamant about that, and made it very clear.

I was totally miserable and I had allowed him to bring my spirits and character down to street-woman mentality. I did not care anymore. I would curse at him so loud that I am sure the entire complex could hear it. I had lost total respect for him and total control of myself. The sight of him disgusted me. I would say things to him that no self-respecting woman should ever say to a man, or anybody else for that matter. The tongue is a powerful tool that can be used for good or evil. Words have power, and I was using my words to speak negativity and death into his life from every fiber in my body. My words were lethal. There was so much hatred inside me for this man, that I would tell him to do me and the baby a favor and go catch a bullet in the head. That is how poisonous my words were. My personality had drastically changed for the worse. Almost every word that came out of my mouth towards him was profanity. My personal life was even reflected in my job. I had become a negative person who saw the negativity in everything. Misery loves company. I had allowed this man to bring out every repulsive, evil, and horrible characteristic in me. Being with him was a disgrace. One of my close friends called me crying when she found out that her sister had had sex with him. As a friend, she felt that she needed to tell me. I appreciated her honesty and sincerity, but at that point, I did not care who he slept with because I wasn't sleeping with him. I just wanted him out of my life. During their lunchtime, some of the teachers I worked with would see him driving around other women in my car. An associate of mine who worked at another school called to ask if I was still with Victor because she knew his new "girlfriend". She told me that Victor came to the beauty salon quite frequently (in my car) to see the girlfriend where she worked. She said that she knew my car and recognized him to be the man who dropped me off to work. She said that when she told the girl, *"That's my friend's husband"*, the woman said, *"Not anymore, he's divorced"*. That was not the case. I was humiliated because I knew that everything I was being told was true, and that I was being talked about. I knew that people must have thought I was desperate for a man to have been with him. These were the same thoughts I had about other women when I would hear of things their boyfriends or husbands had done to them, so I knew that people were thinking and saying the same things about me. What goes around comes around, thoughts, words, and deeds. After the many reports of people seeing him all over town in my car while I would be at work, I stopped him from driving me to work. It was already embarrassing to have him dropping me off in my own car because I had that car long before I met him and everyone knew it, so for him to drop me off to work, people had to know that he did not have a car of his own. After I stopped him from driving my car, he hated the fact that it would be sitting in the parking lot all day while I was at work because he felt he could be driving it. While I was working, he would be soaking up the air-conditioner, running up the electricity bill and talking on the phone. I had to have a lock put on my bedroom door because of his stealing. I also had to lock laundry detergent and certain non-perishable food items in my room so that I could have a snack when I desired one and had items to use when I needed to.

I expressed to him many times that I wanted him to move out. I tried being mature about it when I first asked him to move, not realizing that I was not dealing with a mature adult. My spirits were so low because I wanted this man completely out of my life and it did not seem like he was going anywhere. The baby did not change things at all. In fact, he got worse after she was born. There were no benefits with him in my life, not for me, not for my daughter. For him, there were many benefits. He was living rent free, paid no bills, driving a car without making a car-payment, had a bed to sleep in, food to eat, stealing money, unlimited phone access, and the leisure of coming in and out as he pleased. Why would anyone want to leave that? It was very hard getting rid of him to say the very least.

ROOM 203

One Saturday morning as I was lying down in my bedroom at the condo, Victor was in the living room on the phone talking to one of his female acquaintances. I had heard him asking for room 203 many times, and I was already fed up,
so I got up and asked him to take out the garbage. He told the woman that he would call her back, but that he would be there shortly. When he walked out of the house, I pressed the redial button and wrote down the phone number. She was expecting him to come over, so he eventually left. While he was gone, I called the number, and it happened to be the number to a motel called *The Vagabond Motel* (go figure). I asked for room 203. No one answered in the room the first time I called. When I called back, I asked the attendant if there was

Destined for Great Things!

a room in the name of Victor Thomas. The attendant told me that the room was previously in two names, Victor's name and another name, but that Victor's name had been recently removed. He went on to explain that the room had been in Victor's name for about seven months until the recent switch (it is amazing how people willingly give out information). Later on, I called back and asked for room 203 again. This time a female answered. So I, (being the drama queen that I am), pretended to be calling from the motel's hospitality office with a few questions regarding her motel stay. After asking the preliminary questions such as how satisfied she was with the stay, would she be likely to refer someone to the motel, would she return back, etc., I mentioned how I noticed the recent name change under which the room was in. The woman informed me that the room had been in her boyfriend, Victor's name, but that she had his name removed so that she could add her new roommate's name instead, who had just come in town to stay with her. When I asked if she would be checking out soon, she stated that she did not know. She told me that she lived out of town and anticipated being at the motel for a while. I immediately perceived that she was an exotic dancer who had been living in the motel for quite some time.

    I decided to pay a little visit to room 203 when Victor returned with my car. As I approached the motel door, I could hear loud music playing from the outside of the room. A very rough-looking female with many scars on her face answered the door in a bad wig, a T-shirt and no bottoms. I was a bit startled at first sight of her because she looked like a man trying to imitate a woman. After I told her who I was, she seemed a bit intimidated, but answered my questions regarding Victor. She told me that he was only a friend of hers who frequently came to visit with some of his other friends to "hang out" with her and her (stripper) friends. She added that there was nothing going on between the two of them. She seemed to be fumbling over her words a whole lot, however. While she was talking to me, I was trying to figure out if she was a man or a real woman. I finally concluded that she was a real woman.

    When I returned back home, Victor was sitting on the couch with a nasty attitude and angry look on his face because she had called him and apparently did not tell him what she had told me. She told him that she had confessed to me about the two of them. What he did not know is that she lied for him and I still did

not know the whole truth. He was the one who confirmed their relationship. I did not say a word to him when I walked in the house. I checked on my baby, fed her, and cooked dinner. I fed his daughters who were there, was preparing a plate of food for myself and was just about to sit down and eat, when the phone rang. It was my mother. She told me that Victor had called her and told her that I went to the home of one of his friends, confronted the man's wife, and accused her of sleeping with Victor. I did not appreciate my mother calling me and questioning me about what went on under my roof between the father of my child and myself. Furthermore, when he called her, I felt that she should have told him that he needed to work out his problems with me and that she did not want to get involved. Instead of doing that, she had the audacity to question me about a lie that he told her. I was extremely angered by her phone call, especially since I had never been close to her and did not share things with her. I had always been a private person, and I did not permit many people into my personal business, not even her. So, when she questioned me about that, I proceeded to tell her the truth, although it was none of her business. It was very typical of him to come home after being gone for days, get on the phone, call family members and fabricate outlandish stories about me. In a distorted way, I think he did that to alleviate the guilt from what he had been doing in the streets. Those things were, at the time unforgivable to me. In my mind, a man who speaks lies and negativity about his woman, can never be trusted. In my eyes, a man should be his woman's best friend and greatest protector. He should defend her honor, and not allow anyone to speak derogatory about her. This man was the extreme opposite of what I thought a man should be. In fact, he was a poor excuse for a man. It takes an evil and malicious person to make up lies about another person in an effort to make himself or herself look good. I had been very good to this man, and there was no justification for the lies that he told about me. Assassinating my character, misrepresenting my motives, and trying to taint my image were typical things that Victor had done
to me, and it really did hurt, especially since I had done nothing but try and help him. Lies always hurt.

    When I hung up from speaking with my mother, he said, *"Yo stupid ass out there running the streets questioning females like you straight out the ghetto!"*

Destined for Great Things!

My response: *"You hang out in sleazy motels with low-life strippers as if you are from the ghetto.* His response: *"She's a better woman than you!"* My response: *She probably got AIDS!* His response: *"If she got it, you got it!"* The plate that was in my hand was thrown in his face with a side order of broken plate pieces to go, because he then had to get out of my house. This led into an extremely violent domestic altercation in front of his children and my baby, which ended with the police at my front door. When they came, he was arrested because there was a bench warrant for his arrest for having a suspended license and not paying for speeding tickets. After he was taken to jail, his daughters were still at my house, so I called their mother to come and pick them up. She never did, even after my persistent phone calls. What kind of woman would leave her children someplace after she had been called, told what happened, and asked to come and pick them up?

As I thought about the situation, I began questioning myself. Although I did not love him, and I knew he did not love me, I couldn't help but wonder what it was about me that turned him off to the point that he had to turn to a woman who looked like a man. I felt horrible. If I would have beheld a beautiful or even decent-looking woman on the other side of that motel door, I would have had to step up my game a notch, and maybe even for the sake of pride only, tried to fight for him, but after seeing the kind of woman that he was drawn to, it gave me a deep reality check of the type of man this really was. What real man would want that caliber of woman? What kind of man was this?

After he was released from jail, I did not want him coming back to my house. I had the locks changed and asked him to send someone to get his possessions so that I would have no further dealings with him. He had not done one thing for me or my newborn, and she was then two months old. He had not even purchased one pack of Pampers for her. He called everyone that he could from jail, begging them to talk to me, telling them that he loved me and wanted to be with me and his baby daughter. No one had any knowledge of all the things this man had already taken me through. They did not know that he was a leech, a womanizer, a user, and a con-artist because I was very private and never told anyone what I had been going through with him I was also too embarrassed to tell anybody. I let his oldest sister and my mother convince me that I should take him back because they said my daughter needed both parents. They explained that it was not easy raising a child alone, no relationship was easy and that I should aim towards making it work. But I was already taking care of the baby alone. He was never there and never did one thing to help support her. And as far as the relationship goes… what relationship? I received lectures and speeches from well-meaning people on why I should take him back and like a fool, I did. Of course, he apologized, cried like a baby, and swore that he would never cheat again, lie again, would get a job, start paying bills, and take care of his baby. They were all lies. After two weeks, it was the same cycle all over again. He was just a little bit more discreet, but still sloppy with his disloyalty and infidelity.

SAME STUFF DIFFERENT DAY

He continued to stay out for days at a time, would come home in the daytime and continued his relationship with the stripper. It was commonplace for him to come in the house at five in the morning and go directly to the guest bedroom after having been gone for days. How could a person be gone so long then come in the house and go directly to the guest bedroom? I could have been cut up, beat up, raped, or even murdered in the next room. He would never have known it because he never checked on us. After having had sex with other women and being gone for so long, his guilt would not allow him to even come and check on me or the baby in the next room. After three weeks had passed since he was back from jail, he said to me during an argument, *"She's no longer in a motel, she has her own apartment now, and it's very nice."*

The day that he was arrested, I called her and asked her why she lied to me. She was bold, belligerent, loud, cantankerous, and very slick with her mouth over the telephone, totally different from how she had been in person. I threatened her and I'm sure she took me seriously. I did not do it because she was seeing him. I threatened her because of the disrespectful tone in which she was speaking to me. During the course of the conversation, she told me that Victor picked her up every night from the club where she danced and would stay with her all night. Her exact words to me were, *"He sleeps with me every night."* This,

I knew had to be true because it was very consistent with him never being home at night. In addition, she said that he had been doing it for almost a year. This statement also had to be true, because he had never been home with me while I was pregnant, nor was he home with me after his baby was born. The woman was very confident when telling me these things because she knew they were true. The feeling that I picked up from her was this: *"If he loved or even respected you, he would spend his nights with you, but he is always with me."* She never said it, but it was clearly indicative in her voice.

    This woman was seemingly uneducated and had a vernacular consisting of profanity and very poor grammar. However, she conveyed herself to me quite clearly, and I knew exactly where she was coming from. She also told me that whenever she called him, he knew to come, which was consistent with his pager going off, him immediately calling her back, and then leaving the house. I was not upset with her, because I was at the point to where I had lost total respect for him and really didn't care. But I asked her why she felt that she had to lie to me when I came there. When she said to me, *"I don't have to tell you a Goddamn thang."* that's when I told her that if she cherished her life at all, she would not go back to that motel that night, and if she did, they would find her body floating in a lake with her tongue missing in the morning. She checked out of the motel the very same day and never returned. So yes, I certainly believed that she had a new apartment.

    There were many situations involving other women, some worse than the one I just explained. I didn't care anymore. I just wanted him out of my life and out of my house. I took out a restraining order against him and changed my locks. He would try and come in through the windows four and five o' clock in the morning, yelling for me to unlock the door. People would see him and call the police. He would leave the complex when they arrived and returned when they left. It was a nightmare. He broke my sliding glass doors and windows trying to get in the house and caused me problem after problem. He would steal money from me and also out of his daughter's piggy bank. He would take my house keys out of my purse and hide them so that he could get in the house while I was at work since I had changed the locks and did not give him a key. It was at the point that when I left in the morning, he had to leave. I was living a nightmare.

He was a sorry, poor excuse for a man, and I wished over and over that I had never met him. I would go to bed at night and wish that the whole situation was a bad nightmare. When I would wake up and realize that it was real, I would cry. I had become depressed and could feel that I was on the verge of a nervous breakdown.

ABOUT TO EXPLODE

Absolutely no one knew what I was going through. Since I was a private person, I would hold things inside. I was about to explode because I was enduring so much mistreatment, and it seemed as though there was no way out. As close as my sister Lisa and I are, I never told her because she was (and still is) so sensitive, and I knew how she would react. She would cry, then curse, then scream, and go from one extreme to the other. However, I sensed that she knew things weren't right because she made a statement once when I was pregnant. She said that it wasn't good for me to be by myself so much in my condition. Every time she called, I was alone, so she perceived that I was alone a lot. I finally broke down and told Teresa, whom I thought was a friend, but she turned out to be the worst person to tell. She told others what I had been telling her, including my mother, and she also added many lies to the situation, making it worse. We must be very careful about who we choose to divulge personal matters to.

In spite of all that he had taken me through and knowing that he had made me miserable, he still would not leave! I had told him what I thought of him many, many times. I held nothing back. Most men, for the sake of their pride and manhood would have left once they knew that the woman did not want them beyond a shadow of a doubt. Not this man. He was going to stay there and suck all the life out of me. My negative feelings towards him never changed, never fluctuated, nor deviated. They remained consistent. There were no mixed feelings being sent to him. Even when things appeared to be better, I wanted him gone. I was very consistent in conveying daily that I wanted him out. There was no swaying back and forth with me. He knew by no uncertain terms that I wanted him out of my house and life. He would use the baby as an excuse to stay. I knew that I had made a very big mistake when I allowed others to talk me into doing something that I was totally against by allowing him back after the jail incident. I only did it for my daughter, but ultimately, I am the one who had to live with him, not them. My peace of mind is a priority and I should have considered that before letting him back in. Big mistake. Every time I looked into his face, I would see the darkness in his soul. I simply could not get rid of that man because the demon in him was stubborn and strong. He was a bloodsucking leech that I could not shake off.

ON THE EDGE

I was on the verge of a nervous breakdown. The man would not leave. He had never slept seven consistent nights at home. Not even after his baby was born did he stay home. After Stephanie arrived, I had to find work immediately. As a teacher on maternity leave, the school system would not allow me to return back to work before the six weeks was up, so I had to find work elsewhere until I was cleared to return back. I literally had to make him stay home and keep his baby while I worked a temporary job. Why should I have paid a sitter when he sat home all day and did nothing? That was the least he could have done, but he asked me to pay him for keeping his own child. I would have been a bigger fool than I already was had I done that. After I returned back to work, I worked three jobs at one time to stay afloat. I was teaching elementary school during the day, preparing taxes at night during tax season, and teaching college students at the university one night a week. Other than Stephanie, nothing good had come out of my meeting Victor. I had to do what I could to keep a roof over my head, keep food in the house, and care for my baby girl. He was just another mouth to feed. I was literally taking care of a grown man. Stephanie was the only motivation that kept me going from day to day. I awakened every morning and went to work for her. Unfortunately, that motivation soon vanished. Stephanie died at three months old from Sudden Infant Death Syndrome, commonly called SIDS.

I had no more ties to Victor, and so I felt that I finally had way out. After Stephanie's death, I tried talking to him maturely by asking him how long he thought it would take him to move out. He would suck his teeth, take my car keys, and leave. Being in the house alone everyday was dreadfully depressing because my baby was gone. After she died, the grief overwhelmed me, and I had to take a leave of absence from work. While on leave, I received grief counseling. During one session, the counselor told me that I was a positive person who was surrounded by negative people. What was I to do?

Stephanie died on August 29, 1997. After her death, I was oblivious to anything that was happening in the world. It was two weeks later that I learned about Princess Diana's death. The Princess died on August 31, 1997. Mother Teresa died on September 5, 1997. My baby, a princess, and a saint all died within seven days of each other. Stephanie is in good company.

A NIGHTMARE MARRIAGE

In the second week of September, 1997, after Victor came home from having been gone four days, I tried once again talking to him and asking him how soon he thought he could find a place to live. I was very calm when I spoke with him because Stephanie had died, and I was emotionally depleted and did not have the energy to fuss, argue, or yell. I told him again that I did not love him and never did. I expressed the fact that since there were no more ties between us, there was no need in trying to be together. I told him that he had been a burden on me and that my life was extremely unhappy because he was in it. His question to me was, *"Can I be a roommate?"* I explained that roommates pay rent and besides that, I just wanted to be by myself. He became desperate and started talking about marriage. I told him that he was not the type of man that I wanted to marry, and I needed a husband with gainful employment who knew how to pay bills. I also reminded him that I did not love him, which is the foundation of a marriage. This was the first mature and cordial conversation that we had ever had. I was very composed and respectful at this point. For the first time, I think that he really comprehended that from the core of my soul I wanted him out of my life. He told me that if he left, I would have nobody. I told him that if he stayed I would have nobody.

The next day, I had to report to jury duty. Victor came with me and pressured me hard and relentlessly about getting married while we were at the courthouse. The man was desperate. He thought about the conversation that had occurred the day before, the fact that he had nothing, no place to live, no where to go, no job, no car, no money, absolutely nothing, so he figured that if he married me, he could secure those things for himself. Stupid me. I allowed myself to become persuaded to marry him simply because he pressured me hard and I wanted him to shut up. While exchanging vows at the courthouse, I developed a huge knot in my stomach. I knew in my heart and soul that I was marrying the wrong man, and I was screaming inside. I believed that I had just forfeited the man that the Lord had for me, the real man that God destined for me, my soul mate, gone forever. I wanted to vomit. How could I have let myself get into this horrifying situation? How could I get out of this? There was no getting out.

There is nothing worse than giving the right thing to the wrong person. After I was married, I knew that I had to be a faithful and devoted wife, and in order to have a happy marriage, I had to release all that he had done to me in the past and forgive, otherwise, the marriage would be sure to fail. Therefore, I decided to forget every horrible incident that I had experienced with him and focus on the future. I wanted the marriage to work although I knew I didn't love him. I didn't even like him. I had always said that once I got married, I wanted to stay married to the same man until death do us part. I did not believe in divorce. I meant that in my heart. However, when envisioning my marriage, I always imagined being in love and having a simple, yet elegant wedding. I had dreamed about those things since I was a little girl. All of those visions were out the window in five minutes. There would be no wedding, no wedding ring, no love.

After I was married, I said, *"I would like to have a wedding ring."* After all, I had paid for the marriage license and everything else, so I felt that surely he would try to buy me a wedding ring. However, his response to my request was to go and buy myself one. Four days after we were married, he cheated. The woman called my house at three and four in the morning when he would not answer his beeper. There were no sexual relations between us after we got married and he still stayed out for days at a time. When he would come home at five and six in the morning, he went straight to the guest room where he would talk on the telephone all night while I would be in my bedroom. There would be times when I would wake up in the morning with no way to go to work because my keys and my car would be gone. I caught a cab to work a few times because of it. One day he came home awfully upset and told me that I had ruined his reputation because everyone had found out that he was married.

THE LONG DISTANCE CALL

While opening the phone bill one day, it was so high that I refused to pay it. There were so many unfamiliar long distance telephone numbers on it, but pages and pages of one particular number that was being called every day, several times a day. It was in Ft. Lauderdale, so I called it. Prior to calling, I called Josephine, a church member and friend to be a witness on the telephone because Victor had been telling so many lies about me to his family, my friends, and the church members. Sister Jo, as we called her, was a sister from the church who had been trying to minister to both Victor and me. She had encouraged me greatly and was trying to give both Victor and me words of wisdom, while being impartial. She was a true woman of God who loved the Lord and loved His people. Victor had been playing on her sympathy and telling her how I was mistreating him and how hard he had been working at making the marriage work. He would also tell his family and other people from the church all sorts of twisted stories about me. Moreover, he would tell people that I needed psychological help, told people that I made up stories, and that I had a mental problem. I would say to him: *"You have no job, no car, no place to live, no money, have been evicted your entire life, have never paid a bill, and you say that I have a mental problem?"*

I called the number with Josephine on the phone as a witness. I introduced myself and explained that I was calling to find out whose number this was on my telephone bill. The woman who answered told me that Victor was her boyfriend. She worked at the Division of Motor Vehicles and told me that she had looked up the tag on "his" car. When she questioned him about the name that the tag was under, he told her that he lived with his sister "Mia," and that "his" car

was in his sister's name. The woman told me that Victor said he was single and she believed him because he spent his nights with her. I had heard that before and knew it to be true because of course, he was never at home with me. She then said, *"He's here with me right now."* I asked her to put him on the phone. When he picked up the phone, I asked him where he was. He said, *"I'm at a friend's house, why?"* I said, *"because I'm wondering if you are going to be moving in with your friend. I would be more than willing to pack your things."* I asked the young lady to come and get his belongings. Actually, I begged her to come and get his belongings. She claimed that she did not know he was married and that she was going to leave him alone. That was a lie. I later found out that she did know he was married but did not care as long as she could be with him. While speaking with her, she asked me why I did not seem angry or surprised and mentioned how calm I was. I told her that it was because I had been through this with Victor many, many times before, and that she was not the first, second, third, or fourth, and that she would not be the last. I became angry when she told me that she had been to my home. She stated that there were times when she would come and pick him up because his "sister" needed to borrow his car, so she would come and pick him up to spend the night with her. That infuriated me. It was obvious that the man had no respect for me, but to bring a woman to my house was despicable. I had terminated his use of my car, and on those occasions when I made sure that my purse and keys were safely hid, he would tell her that "his sister" had to borrow "his" car, so the woman would come and get him. There were times that I would be taking a shower, and would come out of the bathroom to find my keys and my car gone. I cannot count the number of times that he brought my car back with no gas. Having to hide my purse, my wallet, and my keys in my own home was more
than I could bear. Why should I have to hide my purse in my own home?

BUSTED

Just as he had called my mother and others with lies about the stripper, like clockwork, he called Sister Josephine from church the very next day. She had listened on the phone and knew the whole story already, but she allowed him to talk. She admitted that if she had not known the truth for herself, she would have believed every word that he told her. He had a knack for being very charismatic and seemingly sincere, which is how he had so many people fooled. After he finished telling her his well thought-out, fabricated story, she told him that she was on the phone, had heard everything from beginning to end, and knew that he had been committing adultery and lying about everything else. She further told him that what he was doing to me was wrong and that he could not expect to get blessed with the kind of fruit that he was bringing forth. She continued to tell him that she did not appreciate him taking her kindness for weakness when she had only been trying to minister to him. She said that he should be ashamed of himself for all of the things he had done to me and was still doing. Lastly, she told him not to call her anymore. Needless-to-say, he turned on her and made up lies about her to the members in the church. She apologized to me and told me that she had believed all of his lies and that she actually felt sorry for him because she thought that he was really the victim and was being mistreated.

MARRIAGE COUNSELING

The church intervened and tried to help salvage the marriage. Victor lied to the Pastor and the Pastor's wife. He had won them over with his charisma and fabrications and had them thinking that everything was my fault. He would call them without my knowledge and make up all sorts of stories about me just as he had been doing with family and others. However, when the Pastor would ask me about the accusations in Victor's presence, it would be revealed that he was lying. It did not take them long to find out the truth about him. The Pastor became annoyed and asked him one day, *"Why do you lie so much?"* It also did not take the men of the church long to find out about him. But Victor avoided the men. He would approach the women in the church and play on their emotions and sympathy. He did not talk to the men much.

Although the Pastor and his wife knew that Victor did not perform the duties that a man should fulfill as the head of household, they still tried to save the marriage. Victor played with the church and used the Bible when it benefited him.

He began quoting scriptures to me such as, *"A wife should submit herself to her husband."* I would come right back with a scripture such as, *"... if any provide not for his own, and especially for those of his own house, he hath denied the faith, and is worse than an infidel"* (1 Tim 5:8). He constantly lied in marriage counseling and as soon as the counseling was over, he would call me all sorts of names and say horrible things to me. He did not care about the marriage at all. He just wanted to stabilize his security. I reciprocated. I was just as bad as him at this point. I was no longer the sweet, kind, mild-mannered person he knew me to be before the baby. I had turned into a monster, who had no respect for him, and would say anything that came to mind, and my words were lethal. He knew my position on marriage, and would often tell people, *"She will never divorce me because she doesn't believe in divorce."* During a counseling session, the Pastor plainly told him to start coming home every night. He said, *"When the sun goes down, you should be at home with your wife."* Victor tried it for six days, but on the seventh day, he had to rest – right in the bed of another woman. He was gone for two days. Had he come home on the seventh day, I would have been able to say that for the first time, my husband spent seven consecutive nights at home, but it never happened.

Both the Pastor and his wife were shocked beyond belief when I told them that Victor had never paid one bill, had never bought me a Christmas gift, birthday present, or Valentines gift. When I told them that we had never been out on a date, never been out to dinner, or seen a movie together, they were flabbergasted. But when I told them that we had never kissed, one could have knocked them over with a feather. The Pastor repeated, *"You have never kissed?"* He had never heard anything like that in his life from a married couple. I tried to convince them that the man did not love me and that he had married me for convenience. They didn't want to believe it, but was finally seeing the truth of the matter after coming into revelation of the things I had been telling them all along. Victor was sitting there the entire time. The Pastor turned to him and said: *"Why did you marry her if you didn't love her"?* His answer was, *"because I do love her"*. I interjected and said, *"Name one thing you ever did to show me that you love me, one thing."* I told them that I knew he didn't love me and I was okay with it. I was at the point that I just wanted a divorce. All that "I don't believe in divorce" stuff was out the window. This man had given me a run for my money, and I was ready to throw in the towel. I thought that after hearing about my horrible marriage, they would have said, *"We think that a divorce would probably be the best thing."* But, they still believed that the marriage could be saved. I guess that I appreciate what they were trying to do, but what they failed to realize was that the marriage was founded upon lies and deceit, not love. It was built upon sinking sand from day one, and there was never any hope for it because there was never a solid foundation on which to build. It was unhealthy from the beginning. A lasting relationship begins a healthy relationship. Many couples who end up in divorce start off being in love. Then, for whatever reasons, the love diminishes, and they grow apart. However, they have memories of the good times they shared and sometimes the good times outweighed the bad. Victor and I never had any good times. We could never say, remember when we were in love, or remember when we used to hold hands and walk on the beach, go out to dinner, watch movies, look at television together, laugh and play together, or talk to each other and share dreams and visions with each other.

We never did any of those things, so we had no memories of any good times. There were none. The marriage was built on lies, deceit, manipulation, and quick sinking sand.

During marriage counseling with the Pastors, I had not slept with Victor in almost a year. In an effort to help the marriage, the Pastor recommended that we start dating. He suggested that we watch a rented movie and begin sleeping in the same bed. I became pregnant. That was the first time in a year and also the last time that we were ever together sexually. His antics became excessively worse. The pregnancy was as horrible as the first one. I was constantly left home alone with no way of getting anywhere, because he would take my car and be gone for days.

One morning when I was seven months pregnant, I heard Victor getting up early to leave with the car. There was absolutely no food in the house, so before he left, I told him that I needed to go to the grocery store because there was nothing in the house to eat. That was around 9:10a.m. He told me that he would be back in 20 minutes. He did not return until 11:30pm the next day. I was so hungry and being pregnant made it that much worse. After he hadn't come by the evening, I called the Pastors, and they brought me something to eat. By then, I think they knew that it was effortless to try and salvage the so-called marriage, but they never said anything. I tried to get a divorce while I was pregnant, but no attorney wanted to represent me in my condition. This pregnancy was different from the first one. With Stephanie, I never argued or fussed, never questioned him about anything. I purposely remained calm for the sake of the baby. With this pregnancy, I had gotten so used to yelling and screaming, that I did not have the inner strength to force myself to be calm. It was just a horrible experience and an awful pregnancy.

When the police were called out, they would say that someone had to leave the home for the night. Victor would say, *"I am not leaving because I live here."* I was the one who always had to leave. Twice, I was pregnant when I was made to leave my home because he refused to go. The first time, I was six months pregnant, and the second time, I was eight months pregnant. The second time I left, I drove my car to a park and slept in it all night. This man, knowing that I was pregnant, would agree to make me leave my own home, where I paid every bill. That was the kind of man that I attracted into my life and I had to painfully ask God what was inside of me that could attract something so repulsive? Even the police officers felt sorry for me. Most times, it was the same two officers who came out. One day, as one of them was walking me to my car, he asked me, *"Don't you have a father or any brothers?"* When I answered, "no" to both, he said, *"I wish you were my sister."* Men like Victor love women who have no father or brothers in their lives to protect them. It is so sad.

TIME FOR FREEDOM

When it was time for the baby to be born, that man called me every name in the book on the way to the hospital and would not even stay the night after his son was born. He came back to the hospital two days later when it was time for me to be released. I tried with every fiber in my being to get along with him because I had this newborn baby boy, and I did not want negative energy around him. There was no contending with this man. The day that the baby and I were coming home from the hospital, I asked Victor if he would stop by the store so that I could buy some purified water. He told me that he did not have time to stop because he had somewhere to be (in my car). I told him that I really needed the water and that he needed to stop so that I could get it.   An argument ensued. I had totally lost respect for him and I was so disgusted at the fact that he knew I had just had a baby and needed purified water, but his desire to go be with another woman was more important than seeing to it that his wife and child had what they needed. If there was any shred of respect for him, it was totally eradicated after that day.

    I finally came to grips with the fact that I had to be the one to move if I was going to get rid of this man because he wasn't going anywhere, and he had made that perfectly clear. It would be a major inconvenience for me because I would be breaking a rental contract. I had also been discussing purchasing the condo with the owner. It was a nice condominium on the lake and had a very nice deck out back, but I had to make the sacrifice of moving for my sanity and peace of mind. I needed to make a move because Victor certainly was not going to. I had a newborn baby, but I could not take anymore of the hell. I thought constantly about how my baby girl had died, and I did not want what happened to her to happen to my son, because I believed deep down inside, that Victor's demonic forces contributed somehow to my daughter's death. I had to protect this little boy at all costs. Therefore, one day, while Victor was on one of his excursions, I called Derrick, a friend of mine, who I had not spoken with in years, but he had always been a good friend to me, and one I knew could be counted on. I told him about Victor and all I had been going through. He rented me a U-Haul, brought some guys with him, and they moved every piece of furniture out of that Condominium. I had already made arrangements to move in with a friend until I could get on my feet, and that is exactly what I did. When I left, I had the electricity and
water turned off. The phone had already been disconnected. I was leaving my past behind me. I had finally done what I should have done long before that. I was off to a new and fresh start.

THE TWO BLESSINGS

  Finally getting away from that man was the best thing I could have done. When he came home to an empty house, it was three days later. He called my cellular continuously, desperately begging me on the voicemail not to leave him. He begged and cried claiming that he had no place to go. I reminded him that he had boldly told me on many occasions that he had plenty of places to go. I also reminded him that a man who had never slept home must already have an alternate home somewhere. His personal problems were not my concern, and I did not care to hear about his sad story. He continued to call for days, weeks, months and even years. I would look at my caller ID and not answer. When I did answer I would quickly end the conversation. I had finally freed myself, and I was not going to allow him to yoke me up again! My life immediately became better, my head became clearer, I began to gain weight again, and I found myself laughing more. I had peace of mind again. I divorced him eight months after I left him. I purchased my first home a year later and God has blessed me abundantly since.

  As I look back in retrospect, I can clearly see how playing with fire got me severely burnt. I had third degree burns on most of my spiritual body. I allowed the spirit of loneliness to lead me to call a man that I was not compatible with nor equally yoked to, all for the sake of having someone to talk to. I can also now see that it was a setup to destroy me by the enemy from the very beginning. This man was sent to me at Burger King, but I resisted. He was sent again at the grocery store, but I did not resist. I gave in to temptation and paid the price for it dearly. Inasmuch as I judged others for allowing themselves to get into destructive relationships, I was judged. I had blamed and talked about other women until I had to walk in those very same shoes. Unfortunately, I had the devastating and agonizing experience of living the nightmare of every woman's story I had heard. The experience was so awful for me that I had completely lost control of myself. Through my lack of self-control, I had inflicted upon myself far-reaching sufferings of indescribable torment, both of mind and soul. But once I was able to clearly reflect on all that I had gone through, I realized that regardless of what I endured, I was still responsible for my every action and had to regard the wrong actions of Victor as a test of my own strength. All of my weaknesses, sins, hurt, pain, disappointments, and rises and falls, originated in my own heart. I, and only I was responsible for that. Yes, there was and will always be tempters and provokers, but temptations and provocations are powerless to those refusing to respond to them. Once I came to grips with that, I knew that I was on a path that led to wisdom and peace.

Always remember that if you are with someone who brings out the absolute worst in you, that person is definitely not the one for you. You need to be with someone who brings out the best in you, who makes you laugh, who will cry when you cry, but not make you cry; hurt when you hurt, but not deliberately hurt you. If you find yourself changing for the worst and doing and saying things that are uncharacteristic of your personality, remove yourself from that situation quickly. The longer you stay, the worse you will become. Don't waste your time on a person who is not bringing out your best qualities.

I have always heard that every adversity carries with it the seed of tomorrow's victory, and every sadness carries with it the seed of tomorrow's joy. The Lord always leads us to victory if we persevere. If we stay close to Him, we will never fail. Every trial is for the purpose of changing us into His image. Never waste a single trial. If your path is more difficult, it is because of your high calling. Discipline yourself for righteousness. I must admit that the things I went through were devastating for me, but I made it through them. There is always a way over, around, or through. I refuse to grieve over my bad choices and denied gratifications. I will not live in the past and have constant regrets of my bad experiences. I give thanks for the seeds of joy that emanated from such challenges. There were two seeds of joy that came out of those trying times. My two children Stephanie and Stephan. Stephanie is in heaven with God and Stephan is peacefully in his bed asleep as I write this sentence. Perhaps that was the only purpose for me meeting Victor – for him to give me those specific children that no one else in this world could have given to me. Who knows?

~~ LESSONS LEARNED ~~

1. Exercising control over your tongue and actions strengthens and refines your character.

2. We must live with the consequences from the decisions we make, but God always make a way of escape when we are truly ready to be freed of the burden.

3. There is always something good that comes out of every adversity and pain. We must not let the pain blind us from recognizing the good.

~~REFLECTION QUESTIONS ~~

1. How have you dealt with relationships that were burdensome and psychologically draining? Did you let them linger, did you free yourself from them, or are you still in them?

2. What type of people are you attracting into your life? Do they bring out your best qualities?

3. Do you allow your thoughts to control your actions or do you force your actions to control your thoughts?

Chapter 6

Live Today as Your Last Day on Earth
Memories Last a Lifetime

Why have you been allowed to live this extra day when others far better have departed this earth? Is it because they have accomplished their purpose in life when yours is still yet to be achieved? Is this another opportunity for you to become the person you know you can be?

Destroy procrastination with action. Bury doubt with faith. Dismember fear with confidence. Today is the tomorrow that you worried about yesterday, and all is well! This moment, this day, is as good as any moment in all eternity. Make this day, each moment of this day, a heaven on earth.

The duties of today you shall fulfill today. Today you shall spend time with your children while they are still here. Tomorrow they will be gone, and so will you. Today you shall embrace your sweetheart with tender kisses; tomorrow they will be gone, and so will you. Today you shall lift up a friend in need; tomorrow they will no longer need your help, nor will you hear their request. Today you shall give yourself in sacrifice and work; tomorrow you will have nothing to give, and there will be nothing to receive.

Each minute of today will be more fruitful than the hours of yesterday. Your last will be your last, then you will fall to your knees, and give thanks.

WHAT'S WRONG WITH THE BABY?

May 26, 1997 was the day that my baby girl was born. Stephanie was very aware of her surroundings from the day she arrived. It seemed as though she understood everything that was happening around her. It was obvious that she was a special little baby. However, she never seemed to be happy here on this earth. She never slept peacefully, so I would often lay her on top of me. She would seem to be a little more peaceful when I was holding her, but she still would jerk and jump in fear as if something was tormenting her. It tore me up to see my newborn baby like this. I would pray for her, anoint her, and ask God what was wrong. She seemed to have a little peace when she was in my arms, but I could not always hold her. Whenever her father, Victor would come home, she seemed to get worse. At night, she slept in her crib in the nursery, but I would hear her whimper from the baby monitor. I just did not know what was wrong with her.

MOMMY HAS TO GO TO WORK

Two weeks after Stephanie was born, I had to find employment to bring income into the home. I was an unwed mother with zero financial support from her father. He did not have a job, did not try to find one when I became pregnant, and still did not have one after she was born, so I had to go to work. I secured a temporary job after just having had a baby two weeks prior. Stephanie was born in May and since school was out in June, the summer should have given me time to recuperate and establish a bond with my newborn, but unfortunately, I had to work to keep a roof over our heads.

SICK ON THE JOB

It was time for school to start again, and as a teacher, I had to report back to work two days prior to the students. Unfortunately, I had caught a bad cold a few days prior to returning back, so on my first day, I felt awful. I woke up late and did not have time to dress the baby, so I asked Victor to do it for me. As we were leaving the house, I remember looking at Stephanie in her cute little white outfit and thinking that she was so adorable. This would be her first day with her new Hispanic caregiver. Being born and raised in Miami-Dade County, I knew that the benefits of being bilingual were great, and I wanted Stephanie to be bilingual. Her new caregiver came highly recommended by my mother's neighbor, and when I interviewed the lady, I was very impressed. She had a sweet and loving spirit and an immaculate home with a designated area for the babies she cared for. She had three others babies, and individual cribs for each of them. I felt very comfortable with leaving Stephanie in her care.

So here I was being dropped off to work, feeling sick with the Flu and running late. As Stephanie's dad drops me off, he says, *"Aren't you going to kiss the baby?"* I said, *"I want to, but I don't want to be in her face with this bad cold. I'll see her later."* Well, the next time I would kiss Stephanie would be hours later, after her death.

While at work, I felt awful. I had no energy, a sinus headache, and my nose was stuffed up. All I wanted to do was go home. I told my boss how I was feeling and she told me that I could leave. I called Stephanie's father who had my car and asked him to pick me up. It was about 12:00 noon at that time. I was ready to collapse by then. I just wanted to sleep, and I expressed that to him, but he insisted that we pick the baby up right then. That way, he could drop us both off and not come home until the next morning when it was time for me to go to work as he usually did. I, on the other hand was thinking that since the baby had to be picked up before 5:00 p.m., I could go home, take some medicine, get some rest and then pick her up when I felt a little better before 5:00 p.m. After a heated argument, I managed to get him to take me home before picking Stephanie up. I do not think there was ever a time that Stephanie's father made any sense, and even though he did not make sense that day, perhaps I should have picked her up, because she was still alive at the very time I left work.

On the way home, I stopped and bought some Flu medicine. When I arrived home, I took the medicine, took the phone off the hook, and climbed into bed. I woke up around 3:00 p.m. and put the phone back on the hook. Stephanie's dad had left me a message saying that he did not think he would be able to pick her up before 5:00 p.m., and could I find someone else to get her. I called my mother and asked her if she could pick the baby up for me. She agreed. In the meantime, I forgot to turn the telephone ringer back on and I missed all calls after that.

THE TELEPHONE MESSAGES

About 45 minutes later, I realized that the ringer was still off, so I turned it back on and there were many new messages. The first one was from Stephanie's dad saying that he in fact was going to pick her up, and was on his way. When I picked up the second message, it was my mother saying, *"Mia, I am here at the baby sitter's house and there are police officers here and yellow tape everywhere. The baby is not here. They say that she had problems breathing, and she is at Parkway Hospital."* I frantically fell down on my knees and prayed that she was okay. At that moment, all I could think about was how tormented she always seemed to be. I just wanted to pick her up and hold her in my arms. I ran outside to find anyone in a car to ask him or her for a ride to the hospital. I did not see anyone. I went back inside and called my cousin, Keith who came immediately, although it seemed like an eternity.

WHERE IS MY BABY?

When I arrived at the hospital, everyone seemed to know who I was. When I asked the security guard where the children's ward was, he said *"Are you Mrs. Sanders?"* and he showed me where to go. As I entered, I asked the nurses at the station, *"Where is my baby?"* they said, *"Are you Mrs. Sanders?"* They contacted someone on the phone and immediately a female doctor came out to talk to me. I kept asking, *"Where is my baby? Where is my baby?"* She said, *"I need to ask you a couple of questions first."* She asked if the baby had been sick, if there were any unusual problems with her lately, had I noticed anything different about her. The answer to each question was, *"No, where is my baby?"* I finally said, *"Is my baby all right?"* The doctor said, *"No, it's serious"*. She took me into a conference room where I saw my mother, Stephanie's father, medical personnel, and police detectives. My mother's eyes were bloodshot red and Stephanie's father was crying. I asked the question one last time, *"Where is my baby?"* The next five words that came out of that doctor's mouth pierced my soul like a sharp sword. She said, *"Your baby was found expired."* All I remember was me screaming to the top of my lungs. The baby had died at the baby sitter's house around 2:30p.m. I was at home sleeping. No one called me until 4:45p.m., rather no one left a message until that time. All of my numbers where in the baby's bag. Stephanie's father and my mother had arrived at the sitter's house at the same time. They both left and headed straight to the hospital. No one came by the house to get me. The baby was dead.

    The medical examiner determined Sudden Infant Death Syndrome (SIDS) to be the cause of death. Stephanie was buried Wednesday of the next week. I felt an overwhelming sense of grief and guilt. I felt as though I should have picked her up from the sitter when I left work that day. I should have spent more time with her. I should have been the one to dress her that morning. I should have kissed her when I got out of the car that morning. Maybe she felt like I didn't want her since I was almost never there for her because I was working all of the time. Finally, I had to come to grips with the reality that she was never happy on this earth and she was going to leave anyway. As I look back on everything in retrospect, it was better that she died while I wasn't around because I would have been a basket case had she done it at home while I was in the house. I thank God that it happened the way it did because it also removes doubt from others that I contributed in any way to her death. I know how some people think when babies die at home with the parents in the house. What if we would have picked her up when I left work and she died while I was in the bed asleep? Imagine how I would have felt awakening to find my child dead in her crib. God knew what he was doing. He makes no mistakes.

THE 93-DAY VISIT

I am thankful that I had the opportunity to have Stephanie for 93 days. I often still thank God for her. I can't help but wonder why she had to die. What was making her so frightened here? Why did she have to come and go so abruptly? I needed to be in the presence of the Lord right away, so the day she died, I came home from the hospital, lifted my hands to God, and began to Praise and Worship Him. Every pain we suffer brings us closer to divine wisdom and brings us closer to God. My heart was shattered into pieces, but I needed to praise him to keep my sanity. Do you have a better understanding of why it is so important to live each day as if it were your last? If I had the chance to repeat that day, all of my actions would have been different. It was a long road ahead for me, and I am still healing. Stephanie would have been ten years old on May 26, 2007. May she be at peace now, and may God bless her little soul.

PRECIOUS MOMENTS

My grandfather died on June 14, 2002. His body was consumed with cancer, but his mind was sharp and still full of wisdom. Although he wasn't my biological grandfather, he always treated me as if I was one of his own. He called me every year on my birthday until he became ill. I did not spend as much time with him as I would have liked to, but I still spent some time in his presence before he died. I had an opportunity to talk to him and ask him questions about his life. He shared some of his life's experiences as well as some of his youthful indiscretions with me and I enjoyed our little talks. They made me feel good. Prior to his death, he asked to see all of his grandchildren and great-grandchildren. He knew that his days were numbered, and he was ready. He was eighty-two years old, and would often tell people that God had blessed him with three-score and two years. He shared with me that he had no regrets, and that he had lived a full life with a faithful and loving wife. He had cancer, but endured absolutely no pain. The doctors were astounded and could not understand how he experienced no pain.

We can still be blessed in the midst of infirmities. On the day he died, I called to check on him, and my grandmother told me that he had died about an hour before my call. Initially I cried, but then I wiped the tears from my eyes and rejoiced because I knew he was spiritually ready to go. He had said at some point before he passed that he had seen a white cloud and that he was ready to step on to it. Had I not been to see him, I would have felt extremely sad and guilty. We must live today as our last day on earth.

IN PERSPECTIVE

As humans, we take so much for granted. We oftentimes don't show appreciation for the small, yet important things that bring meaning to our lives. We love to place emphasis on things with an expensive price tag and yet place little emphasis on things that are free. We value big houses, luxurious cars, designer clothes, expensive jewelry, name-brand purses, boats, yachts, etc. Living the American Dream in the good ole USA has gotten us caught up in materialism. Houses, cars, clothes, jewelry, and boats can all perish in a matter of seconds and yet can all be replaced. However, when a life is gone, that life can never be replaced, yet we seem to place little value on human life. We should highly value the free gifts: our health and strength, family and friends, knowledge and awareness, and our thoughts, because when those *free* gifts are gone, they are gone forever. You cannot put a price tag on those things. They can never be replaced.

Unfortunately, many of us do not have that revelation yet because we are still trying to be like, and keep up with the Jones'. Sometimes it takes a tragic situation to have our perspectives put in proper order. If you talk to a suffering cancer patient who was once strong and vivacious and lived an abundant life, they will tell you how very insignificant materials things seem in comparison to their deteriorating health. They will tell you that none of their material things meant a hill of beans because without health, they can't enjoy them. Priorities immediately change when a terminal diagnosis is given. Talk to a person who has endured a life-threatening illness, but has been blessed to overcome that sickness, and is still living. I guarantee you that person will tell you once they realized there was a possibility that they could depart earth in the very near future, their entire perception about life changed. Material things shrunk to their proper sizes and each day became a gift. Their children became precious in their eyes and each day they were able to behold them as such. The things that they would previously get upset about were then petty and insignificant in retrospect. The things that created wedges between them and other people had also seemed petty and foolish as they realized how much time had been wasted. They began to live each day as if it were their last. There is nothing that can humble a person faster than to lose all physical mobility and have to have others care for them. Sense of independence is gone and dignity is significantly diminished. Tomorrow is promised to nobody and we never know when we shall breathe our last breath. That is why we should greet each day with love in our heart and live today as our last day on earth.

FORGIVENESS

Healthy married couples argue occasionally, which is normal. But let's say that you had a terrible argument with your spouse who you love dearly. You said some horrible things and without apologizing, you both go off to work. What if you are the only one who returns home, but your spouse was killed in a car accident on their way home from work? Can you imagine the overwhelming guilt that you would feel for not having attempted to apologize for the argument? How long do you think that guilt would last? It would take some serious healing through prayer to get over that because you would first have to forgive yourself.

One problem with many of us is that we are still beating ourselves up over something that God forgave us for a long time ago. When we cannot forgive ourselves, we certainly cannot forgive others. Had you put into practice the love and forgiveness that we are called to extend towards one another, you would have attempted to apologize before you both went off to work. That is the true test of character, when you have a justifiable reason to get upset over an offense, but you force yourself into reciprocating with love. It is not easy, but there is a powerful force that crushes the head of the enemy when good is chosen over evil. Even if the apology was not accepted right away, at least you would have tried. In that manner, your spouse would have known that you were truly sorry, and that you still love them in spite of the argument. Your grief would not have been compounded by the guilt, from you not apologizing. Too many people let others leave this earth without making amends and telling them how they feel. Unfortunately, when the person dies, there is tremendous guilt and grief. We must swallow our pride and make peace with whom we need to make peace and only you know who those people are. When it comes to forgiveness, it does not matter whose fault it was. You are the bigger person who is striving to be like Christ, so *you* apologize. Apologies should not consist of "if… thens." "*If* I have done something to hurt or wrong you, *then* I'm sorry". That's not a genuine apology. A genuine apology sounds something like this: *"I am sorry for hurting you, I am sorry for mistreating you. I am sorry for… I was wrong, and I hope that you forgive me."* No buts after the apology, just *I am sorry for…* period! You have now taken responsibility for your actions, and even if the other person wronged you, forgive them, and tell them that you have forgiven them, sincerely. There would be no need to get into details; all that does is open old wounds. Apologize and go forward from there. You will feel a heavy load being lifted off of your shoulders. If your apology is not going to be sincere, then do not even bother. You are not ready yet. But remember, time waits for no one. Live today as your last day on earth.

~ LESSONS LEARNED ~

1. Time waits for no one. Sometimes we have to make small sacrifices of time to spend with loved ones in order to make precious memories. Tomorrow is not promised. A person may be here today and gone tomorrow. Make the most of each day.

2. We often think that things should have been different, but God knows the end from the beginning and everything is played out just the way He has planned it.

~~REFLECTION QUESTIONS~~

1. Are you taking the time to visit family members and friends to make those precious memories that mean so much to others and yourself?

2. When is the last time you sat at the feet of an elderly person and just listened to them talk to you about whatever it is they want to talk about?

Chapter 7

Believe That You are a Miracle
Complete in Christ

*G*od *danced the day you were born! Since the beginning of time there has never been another with your mind, your heart, your eyes, your ears, your hands, your hair, your mouth. No one who came before, no one who lives today, and no one who comes tomorrow will walk and talk and move exactly like you! You are rare, and there is value in rarity, therefore you are valuable!*

Don't look for miracles because you are a miracle. Don't compare yourself with others because you are a unique and beautiful creation. Don't let yesterday's accomplishments be sufficient for today's commitments, nor should you indulge anymore in self-praise for deeds, which in reality are too small to even acknowledge.

You are here for a purpose and that purpose is to grow into a mountain, not to shrink to a grain of sand. Henceforth, you will apply all your efforts to become the highest mountain of all, and you will strain your potential until it cries for mercy!

Seek constantly to improve your manners and graces, for they are the sugar to which all are attracted.

Your problems, discouragements and heartaches are really great opportunities in disguise. You should no longer be fooled by the natural garments they wear because your eyes are open wide. Look beyond the natural and do not be deceived.

THE SUPERNATURAL FALL

When I reflect over my life, I thank the Lord for how far He has brought me. My self-destructive behaviors were leading me down a path of failure, misery, destruction and death. I could have been dead in my grave had it not been for the Lord who has kept me. At a very young age, my life started down the wrong path, but because somebody had prayed for me, the hand of God and the mercy of God were with me.

When I look at my son, I can't help but praise the Lord because I count occasions when the forces of evil tried to take his life. Two stand out vividly in my mind. As I write this chapter, my heart is filled with gratitude because the memories of how the hand of God was upon my child flood my mind. When my son was nine months old, we were temporarily living with a friend because I had left my husband and was in the process of getting a divorce. She had a room that she had converted into a small office where her computer was located. Also in the room was a futon that sat very high. This particular day, I was using her computer while my son lie asleep on the futon behind me. Something made me turn around to check on the baby, and as I turned, all I could see was my baby falling on the floor very fast – head first. Since he had already begun falling, I knew that I could not get to him in time to catch him. All I could think about was the hard tile floor and my baby's head hitting it. All of a sudden, as the baby was falling, he began to move in slow motion. It was as though some unseen entity had come and placed its wings under my child's body and then gently laid him on the floor. The child had awakened without me hearing a sound and he was about to crack his head open on that floor, but a supernatural intervention happened, and I witnessed it! My baby was gently placed on the floor, and he began laughing excitedly. When I saw that, I began praising and worshiping God right then and there. The scripture in Psalm 91 where it says ... *for he will give his angels charge over thee, to keep thee in all the ways. They shall bear thee up in their hands...* became alive and real in my life at that very moment. The angels held my son in their hands. I will never forget that day, and as I write, the tears flow down my face because of how God protected and covered my son. I think that through that experience, God was telling me that he was not going to allow me to go through the pain that I endured with the loss of Stephanie. I think that deep down inside, I was afraid that I would lose my son prematurely as I had lost my daughter. After this experience however, I knew that God was protecting my child and all fears of him being taken away were erased from that day on. My child is a miracle, and God is keeping him here for His divine purpose.

THE LITTLE CLIMBER

After my divorce from Victor, the Lord blessed us with our first home. My son and I had our own house. It was a modest two bedroom, two bathroom home in a quiet neighborhood. I was blessed to be able to furnish every room in the house - my bedroom, my son's bedroom, and the living room, in a relatively short period of time. It was such a gratifying feeling to have purchased something that I could call my own. It was so peaceful coming home everyday and being happy. Stephan was almost two years old, in school, talking way too much, and was a happy little boy. One Thursday evening after he and I had come home, I asked him to get his pajamas out of his drawer in preparation for his bath. About 30 seconds later after he ran into his room, I heard loud crashing noises. I ran from the kitchen into his bedroom and the sight of what I saw caused me to panic. I saw his furniture chest on top of his little body and the huge 19" television that was sitting on top of the chest was on top of his head! I felt the energy leaving my body and I knew that I was about to faint, but as I got closer, I saw that the child had not been touched by neither the chest nor the television. I noticed that the edge of the bed had stopped the chest from falling directly on top of his body and the television was brought to a standstill at the edge of the bed where his head was. I could see how the chest was stopped by the bed, but there was nothing to be seen by the natural eye to explain how the TV was hanging *over* the child's head. Immediately, I lifted the heavy television and placed it on the floor. It appeared as though time had been frozen to where the chest and the TV could not complete their falls. Stephan was between them both lying on the bed with the chest at his feet and the television at his head. When I had asked him to get his clothes, he had a tendency to climb on the knobs of the chest to the top drawer where his underclothes were kept in order to reach them. In doing this on this day, it caused the television and the chest to both slide forward, knocking him onto the bed. What a miracle that he was not killed! If that chest did not crush him, the television definitely would have. Again, in looking at the positions of the objects, something unseen had to have been holding them in their places until I arrived. Needless-to-say, his underwear/pajama drawer is now at the bottom of the chest, so no climbing is necessary. My child is a miracle indeed. To God be the glory!

A BUCK 05

We live in a country where we initially accept or reject others based on their outward appearance. Physical appearances seem to take precedence over many things these days, including competence and skills. Much pressure is placed on beauty and weight that peer pressure among teenagers and adolescents to look like Barbie Dolls and Calvin Klein models is very prevalent. Many people are unhappy with some part of their physical appearance, and as a result of their dissatisfaction, they modify areas of their body in an effort to look better, feel better, and be accepted. People typically complain that they are overweight, underweight, too short, etc. I know from experience what that is like because for years I was totally dissatisfied with being so very thin. I hated being skinny. From the age of 19 to the age of 30, I tried gaining weight while everyone else was striving to lose weight. I took all kinds of weight-gaining pills, shakes, SSS Tonic, and many other things in an effort to put on pounds. Of course, people would tell me that my weight was just fine and that I needed not to gain a pound, but when I looked into the mirror, all I could see was skin and bones. It never did take much food to fill me up, so no matter how much I would eat, I just could not gain weight. Regardless of what anyone told me, I was still self-conscience about this, and it lowered my self-esteem. After my breakup with Robert, I lost even more weight. I stayed home as much as I could. I hated seeing anyone I knew because I was embarrassed that I was so skinny.

I went to the daycare to pick up my Goddaughter one day and I ran into someone I knew from high school. We were fairly good friends, so I really expected a pleasant greeting from her. Instead of greeting me happily, she said,

"Isn't your name Mia?" I said, *"Yes, and your name is Shauntelle."* She then said, *"What happened to you, you are so skinny?"* We did not hug and there were no pleasantries exchanged. She had a repulsive look on her face as if I had a contagious, infectious disease. I was hurt because we were very close in high school and she used to call me her big sister. One would have thought that we were die-hard enemies after that encounter. I went home and cried like a baby. After that, I remained secluded in my apartment with the exception of going back and forth to work and places I absolutely had to go. I know first hand what it is like to be unhappy with one's appearance.

LOOKING PAST APPEARANCE

Ideally, we should be content with our appearance because God, in His wisdom, purpose, and creativity has made us each unique. In fact, His word says that we are "fearfully and wonderfully made" (Psalm 139:14). Our life and all it entails is not about physical appearance, because our spirit is so much deeper than mere looks. Our physical bodies are only shells that hold our spirit and the spirit of a person is what makes him or her who he or she is. That is what it is really about, the spirit of a person, what is deep inside the heart. There are beautiful spirits in this world, and if we took the time to look past the physical appearance, we would discover the most precious people in the world.

When God looks at us, He looks beyond the appearance and directly into the heart. When Isaiah prophesized about the coming of Jesus, he said in Isaiah 53:2 *"...and when we shall see him, there is no beauty that we should desire him."* Jesus was rejected because He *looked* like an ordinary man. There was no majestic or powerful supremacy emanating from His person. He was not wearing the finest of garments, nor did He come wearing a crown of gold. Jesus Christ suffered the ultimate rejection. He was jeered, spat on, threatened, and finally put to death. Everywhere He went, He faced rejection. But man's view of Him never altered His focus. If the people knew God, they would have recognized Jesus by the spirit of God that was in Him. We judge the outer appearance way too much and often make critical, life-changing mistakes because of our superficial judgments.

I am not saying that appearance does not matter. Your appearance does matter, and we should strive to look our best at all times because our appearance is the first basis for evaluation that other people have. People look at us, make a quick and often subconscious judgment, and then treat us accordingly. But most importantly, we should strive to display those precious attributes that have nothing to do with outer appearance. These qualities can never be purchased with silver or gold. Love, humility, wisdom, integrity, compassion, understanding, and purity are but a few. Coincidentally, when we display that kind of fruit, our outer appearance is reflected and the glory of God makes us beautiful. Do you want to be attractive? Put on the garments of praise, humility, grace, excellence, love, joy, peace, patience, kindness, goodness, faithfulness, gentleness, and self-control. As we begin to walk with God, we begin to walk in His nature.

ACCEPTING YOURSELF

Yes, you are a miracle, which is why you are *"fearfully and wonderfully made" (Psalm 139:14)*. You are valuable in God's sight and He loves you deeply and cares about every aspect of your life. There is a reason that you have the personality that you do, the abilities that you do, the aspirations that you do. There is a reason that you are different from everybody else. He made you different for His own purpose. One of my favorite quotes written by Marianne Williamson is the following: *"A tulip doesn't strive to impress anyone. It doesn't struggle to be different than a rose. It doesn't have to. It is different. And there's room in the garden for every flower."*

If you are not content with the person that God has made you to be, inside and out, then you will never truly be content or able to accept anyone else and their flaws. Why? because you do not truly love yourself and all that you are. We see in others what we see in ourselves. Until you are able to accept who you are, how you look, and how God has created you to be, you will always find fault in others. T.D. Jakes wrote in his book, The Lady, Her Lover, and Her Lord, that *"when we don't value ourselves, we tend to attract people who support that devalued image."* Respect and love yourself. Have a healthy love and respect for who you are, and when you do, you will be able to love others for who they are and all that God created them to be. Self-approval is essential to healthy living. It is the catalyst from which your goals are emanated, pursued, and accomplished. Self-hatred, guilt, shame, and unforgiveness block your growth. It is time for us to forgive ourselves and move on. Practice loving yourself, pampering yourself, and forgiving yourself. Watch how that new self-perception will carry over into your relationships, your job, and ultimately the world around you. By loving yourself, you open up the possibility for others to love you too. Having confidence in yourself and all that you are is not being arrogant. It is being self-assured and it is very necessary in order to have healthy relationships with others. Walk in this world with humility and grace, yet be confident and fearless!

Do not be fooled into believing that when you find someone to truly accept and love you, then you will be complete. You will never find that person because he or she does not exist. Until you love, understand, and accept yourself for who you truly are, you will always pursue external relationships with hopes of finding love and acceptance from other people. Find that love and acceptance inside of you. If you don't, your relationships will not last because of the weight that you are putting on another person to give you those things that you should find within yourself. It becomes too much for anyone else to bear, and it's not fair to the other person. You are not an incomplete person looking for someone to complete you. You are already whole and complete in God. What complete man wants an incomplete woman? Even the incomplete man wants a complete woman. There is no void that God can't fill to make you whole again.

DEVELOP SELF-CONFIDENCE

People with self-confidence are inner-directed and self-assured. Their validation is not a function of people liking them or treating them well. They are validated from within. One of the most dominating fears afflicting humans is the fear of rejection. This fear compels one to become the person he or she believe will be accepted or recognized, which will vary from some degree with each new group or situation. A person with self-esteem issues is always looking for acceptance from others. These individuals are looking for others to validate who they are. These people are affected by the way others treat them. If people treat them well, they feel well. If they are not treated well, they become hurt and sometimes depressed, pondering over and over in their minds what they could have done that caused that person not to like them. Their sense of worth comes from other people liking and accepting them. When we get a complete revelation of who we are to God and in God, there will be no need for validation from others because inner strength and tenacity will emerge from confidence in God. As long as God approves of you, that is the only validation you need.

Life's experiences are the reason that many suffer with low self-esteem and low self-confidence. Things that have happened to them as children, things too shameful and embarrassing to mention, leave many feeling as if they deserve whatever comes their way and nothing better. They feel undeserving of success, and it is not unusual for such people to unconsciously set about sabotaging their own success. As a result, people use them and abuse them. If you are carrying the weight of a negative experience that has happened in your past, you may be hindering your ability to live fully in the now. Hurtful memories can impede your personal and spiritual growth. It is okay to remember those painful memories in your life in order to make you stronger, but you must control them. If you view all the things that have happened to you, both good and bad, as sources from which to draw strength, you will think and live a higher level of consciousness. Do not let them control you any longer. In his book, The Lady, Her Lover, and Her Lord, T.D. Jakes writes: *"There are some things that can happen to you that leave you disfigured. I do not mean outwardly, but inwardly. Many women in this country are bowed down under the weight and pressure that comes from deep, dark secrets and traumas that have left them twisted and misfigured. Issues, relationships, and incidents leap out of their past and hold them hostage, forever chained to emotional pain."* This is the reason why many do not step out on faith and let their gifts come into fruition. They, meaning men and women, are too haunted by things they want to forget, but just can't seem to.

FINDING FULFILLMENT

Many, many people in this world are living their lives unfulfilled. The enemy of our faith wants us to step out before the appointed time or not move in time, or be in the wrong place at the wrong time, so that we will miss our calling and be unfulfilled. There is nothing more frustrating in life than being unfulfilled in your purpose. God has individually given each of us a purpose. Before you were born, He wrote in the Lambs Book of Life what your assignment was to be on earth. Many people think that after they give their life to the Lord, their purpose is to preach. They feel that if they are not preaching or pastoring, then they are not accomplishing their purpose. That is why so many people are preachers today, even though they have not been called to do so. Your purpose in this life is in direct proportion with the gifts that God has placed inside of you. It could be something that you view as insignificant. We tend to call things insignificant if those things are not glamorous or in the limelight. Your gifts may be sewing clothes or crocheting blankets. It could be that you are a skilled mechanic or plasterer. You may not be able to sing, but maybe you can dance. You may be a creative writer or a meticulous and quality painter or carpenter. Some people can play an instrument by ear and do not even know how to read music. You could be brilliant with numbers, excellent with encouraging other people, an outstanding singer, or a first-rate cook. You may have a gift for cleaning, building things, or writing poetry. God has given each of us at least one

gift to be used for His glory. God seeks expression through us each and every day, every hour, every minute, every second, and He expresses Himself through men, women, and children. The variation of gifts we have are all for God. He wants mouths to sing beautiful songs for Him and to speak His truths. He wants hands to play harmonious music for Him, to draw beautiful pictures for Him and to build magnificent skyscrapers for Him. He wants eyes to behold his beauties and to experience His miracles. He wants to express Himself through us because it is him that enjoys all these things. Most of us have many gifts, but we all have at least one. The key is to take your particular talent to a level where it has never been taken before. With the gifts you have been given comes the responsibility to use and develop them. Keep your effort on the areas where you shine. Some of the things other people find boring will actually energize and enrich you if its your gift.

God even gave Adam, who was in the garden of utopia, a purpose. Adam had to rule and subdue. He had to take charge of the garden and be a dresser for it. He had to name each of the animals and keep order. Adam was a perfect man, but he too had to have a purpose. God's purpose for our lives is larger than our plans, goals, or desires. *"Eye hath not seen, nor ear heard, neither have entered into the heart of man, the things which God hath prepared for them that love Him. But God hath revealed them unto us by His Spirit ."* (1 Corin 2:9-10).

I know that you have seen men (and even women) who hang out at the corner store drinking beer all day talking trash and doing nothing productive. They have lost their identity, and are living unfulfilled lives. No one is here by accident. You are not here by chance. God gave you an assignment to complete while on this earth. There is something that you are to do that no one else in this world can do. Even if your mother tried to abort you, the fact that you are here means that you have purpose. There is a reason why you can eat, drink, see, and hear. Develop a sense of urgency in your life and commit yourself to walking in your purpose. Many know what their gifts are, and in knowing what your gifts are, you can sometimes easily find your purpose because your gifts and your purpose coincide with each other. For instance, I know beyond a shadow of a doubt that God gave me the gift of teaching. I love teaching! I am good at it, and when I do it, I am in line with what my purpose on this earth is. I teach children. I teach young adults in Sunday School. I teach college students at the University, I teach when I give presentations and workshops to organizations and corporations. I was sent here to teach. Now, I believe that there are so many other gifts inside of me that have yet to be discovered, but at least I know that when I teach, I am on the path that God has destined for me. My destiny unfolds and expands when I teach. Only through God, can we know all that we are.

The enemy of God and man does not want us fulfilled. Satan even wanted Jesus to be unfulfilled. He wanted him to abort the Calvary, the Golgotha experience. He wanted Jesus to fall down before His appointed time. He told Jesus to jump off the apex and even quoted scripture to Him in an effort to persuade Jesus: *"And saith unto him, if thou be the Son of God, cast thyself down: for it is written, He shall give His angels charge concerning thee, and in their hands they shall bear thee up, lest at any time thou dash thy foot against a stone."* (Mathew 4:6). He tempted our Lord, the Emmanuel, the Prince of Peace, the maker and creator of heaven and earth. The devil tempted Him! Jesus' main mission on earth was to die an agonizing death for our sins. *"For this cause he came into the world and for this cause, He died."* (Mathew 26:53). Jesus knew His purpose and the devil knew that if Jesus had thrown Himself over that pinnacle, he would have caused Him to abort His calling. That is what the forces of evil wants for you too. He wants you to abort your calling, deviate from your purpose, be unfulfilled, and wander to and fro, aimlessly, seeking for things and situations that do not belong to you. When you strive for positions and things that do not rightfully belong to you, there is failure and dissatisfaction. When a person can truly say, *"I desire only that which God desires for me"* (Florence Shinn), all false desires fade out of the mind and a new set of desires is given by the Lord Himself. The enemy of your faith does not want you to be fulfilled.

What is fulfillment? Well, I will first tell you what fulfillment is not. It is not earning a lot of money, achieving materialistic things, being around elite people, achieving certain goals, holding a powerful position or obtaining various degrees. Many people have attained all those things, but are still not fulfilled. Some have earned two and three PhD degrees and are still not fulfilled. Some are currently working on a fourth or fifth degree in search of the "feeling" of fulfillment, still trying to fill a void. Do they think that earning degrees will give them the fulfillment they are searching for? The answer is "no."

Fulfillment is not found in degrees, wealth, worldly success, pleasure, family and friends, good teachers, or even reading scripture. Fulfillment is found in righteousness. The person who finds refuge in true righteousness (not self-righteousness), has a wise understanding and a loving heart, and is already fulfilled. He or she is contented and stable whether in success or failure, wealth or poverty, with friends or without friends, educated or uneducated, or in health or sickness. Fulfillment is found in the will of God. It is found in the Word of God. Fulfillment is walking on the path that God has preordained for your life before you were born. It is found when you work on the assignment that God gave to you while you were still in your mother's womb. When you take the time to pray, read the Word of God, and establish a close, genuine relationship with God, He will keep you on the path that leads to fulfillment. It will be revealed to you why you are here. You do not have to search for it. It will come to you. What you seek, is also seeking you.

THE GREATNESS WITHIN YOU

You showed up on this planet with a seed of greatness inside you! When you were born, your possibilities were endless! There is greatness in all of us, but until you find your purpose and let the gifts that God has placed inside of you flourish, you will never be great. The only way to live a rewarding and fulfilling life, is to spend time with God in prayer. You cannot be fulfilled without accomplishing what God has ordained for your life. Winston Churchill said, "To each there comes in his or her lifetime a special moment when they are tapped on the shoulder and offered the chance to do a very special thing, unique to them and fitted to their talent. What a tragedy if that moment finds them unprepared or unqualified for that which could have been their finest hour." The more you pray, the clearer His will for your life will become. Until then, you will have a void and will constantly search for that feeling of contentment, fulfillment, and the peace that passes all understanding that only God can give. One of my favorite motivational speakers is the inspirational Les Brown. He is the epitome of how having a strong will to be great, a motivation to be successful, a desire to overcome other people's negative predictions, and a strong unwavering faith in God, will bring you to the point of surmounting even your highest expectations. In his book, Live Your Dreams, Les Brown quotes, as it relates to gifts and talents, the following: "*Most people never nurture their gifts, skills and abilities. Each of us has a unique offering. No one else is going to produce your product, write your book, open your academy. And if you don't bring your gift forward, if you die with it inside of you, then we will all suffer from being deprived of your particular genius.*" He further writes, later on in the chapter the following: *...the richest place on the planet is not some diamond mine or an oil field. It is a* *cemetery, because in the cemetery, we bury the inventions that were never produced, the ideas and dreams that never became reality, the hopes and aspirations that were never acted upon.* How sad. Most people die never having shared their gifts with the world, thus never being fulfilled. Do you remember the Bible parable of the talents? God gave each man a different amount of talents, and all but one came back with more talents than he gave them. But, the one who was given only one talent, did absolutely nothing with that talent. In fact, he hid it, and when the master came back looking for his profit, the wicked servant had no profit for him. When you don't use the talent that God has given you, you are called wicked. Can you imagine having to face your Lord on judgment day, and He says to you, *"You did not use any of the talents that I gave to you to bless others."* And you say, *"But master, what talents? I did not know that I had talents in me, please show me."* And the Lord shows you the many books that you were supposed to write, the songs that you were supposed to sing, the poems that you were to publish, the businesses that you were to establish, the inventions that you were to create, the people that you were to help, etc. Wouldn't that be a sad situation? You have a unique message to deliver, a unique song to sing, a unique act of love to bestow. This message, this song, and this act of love have been entrusted exclusively to the one and only – you! Don't let your dreams die within you rather than letting them blossom in your lifetime. When I read Les Brown's book, and reached the part where he said, *"No one else is going to write your book,"* something inside of me propelled me to get this book that I had already begun to write and do what was necessary to get it published, because no one else can tell *my* story and I do not want my contribution to the world to die inside of me. The feeling of completion, accomplishment, and gratification will not emerge until you complete that, which you and only you are required to do. Thank you Mr. Brown, for that push. There is nothing worse than starting multiple tasks and not finishing any of them. When you start things and never finish them, you are operating in a spirit of incompletion and failure. Your subconscious gets into the habit of not completing. Remember Chapter 2; Work in a Spirit of Excellence? Not many things indifferently, but one thing supremely, is the demand of our world. If you scatter your efforts, you cannot expect to succeed. As the within, so the without. I was committed to writing and completing this book the second time around.

KNOW YOUR PLACE

Are you in your right place? Ponder on this for a moment: Think about what it is that you do for a living? Is it in line with what you think your purpose is? Is there fulfillment for you at the end of the day? You may be very busy, but busy doing what? Do you like what you do or do you think that there is something else out there that you ought to be doing? Are you in the right place for God to bless you? Dr. Martin Luther King, Jr. knew his place. When it was time for him to die, he said, *"I'm not worried about anything. I'm not fearing any man. Mine eyes have seen the glory of the coming of the Lord."* He knew why he was here. He knew that he was here to bring liberty in the 1960s. He came here to sing, "We shall overcome." Many think that he died before his time, but in the time that God gave him, he did what he was sent here to do. He was able to close his eyes and rest in peace because his assignment was completed. His life, all that he did with his life showed that he was indeed a miracle. When it is time for you to close your eyes and go to your final resting place, will your assignment be completed? Find your purpose so that you may live a fulfilled life. Spend time with God so that He will guide you and keep you on the path that leads to the unfolding of your destiny. You are a miracle, so start acting like it!

~~ LESSONS LEARNED ~~

1. When we begin to truly love ourselves and everything about us, self-confidence will emerge, and we will develop the wherewithal to accomplish every goal that we set for ourselves.

2. Until we find our purpose and begin walking on the path that God has pre-ordained for us, there will never be fulfillment in our lives. There will always be a void.

3. The seed of greatness is within you. You must cultivate and nurture that seed in order for it to blossom in the earth and bring forth fruit.

~~ REFLECTION QUESTIONS ~~

1. Are you validated from within or do you place emphasis on outer appearances instead of feeding your spirit?

2. Have you identified your purpose on this earth? Are you living a fulfilled life?

3. What have you done to bring out the greatness that is within you? Are you nurturing the gifts that God has placed inside of you?

Chapter 8

Plan for Prosperity and Abundance
Live a Life of Vision, Purpose, and Fulfillment

With persistence comes success. You must persist no matter how slow you have to move at first. No one enjoys great achievement without passing the persistence test. Those who can endure are greatly rewarded for their persistence. They receive as their reward, whatever goal they are pursuing.

Lack of persistence is one of the greatest causes of failure. You must labor. You must endure. You must ignore the obstacles at your feet and keep your eyes on the goals in front of you. You may still encounter failure, yet success hides behind the next corner. Strain your potential until it cries for mercy.

Dream big dreams! Reach for the moon, and even if you miss, you will land among the stars! It is better to attempt to do something great and fail, than attempt to do nothing and succeed.

Before success comes in your life, you will meet with temporary defeat and even some failure, but success will come just one step beyond that point at which momentary defeat tries to overtake you. Temporary defeat is NOT permanent failure!

A very large portion of your success will come from eating the bread of adversity, and drinking the waters of affliction.

IMPOSING ON THE MEETING

When I joined the Master Mind Women's Group (MMWG), it was totally by mistake in the natural eye, but it was orchestrated by God for His purpose. I went to the home of Ann McNeil for a college alumnae meeting that she was conducting. When I arrived, the meeting had already started, or so I thought. I pulled up a chair and joined the women who were already sitting and talking. I listened as one lady, Juanita, was giving her report. She was talking about the goals that she had set and the progress she had made toward the attainment of her goals. She began reporting in different areas of her life. She talked about what she was doing to keep her relationship with the Lord progressing, what she was doing health wise, the books she was reading, etc. After she finished her report, there were some questions asked by the other members relative to her goals and suggestions were made on how she could improve areas that she had been struggling in. It was as though she had to give an account of what she had previously told them relative to her goals. After her report was completed, another member began giving a report on the progression of her goals. While sitting there, I realized that I was in the wrong meeting, but I was too embarrassed and too interested to get up and leave. It would have been too obvious. After the meeting was over, Nifretta, a member of the MMWG, approached me and introduced herself. She handed me a book and said, *"This is the book that we are reading for the month, and these are the forms that we are using to write our goals."* She was very nice as she was giving me all the information, and she welcomed me to the group as though I was a new member. I went to Ann and apologized. I explained to her that I did not mean to impose on her meeting, but I thought that it was the alumnae meeting. I proceeded to tell her that Nifretta thought I was a new member and had given me

Plan for Prosperity and Abundance

a book and other information. I told Ann that I was very interested in becoming a member and wanted to know if and how I could become a member of the MMWG. Needless-to-say, she welcomed me with open arms and told me that all I needed to do was read the book that I was holding in my hand, which was, *Think and Grow Rich* by Napoleon Hill. She told me that after I read the book, I needed to give a report at the next meeting on how I will apply the principles to my life. I became a member of the MMWG, and I read every book that was required of me. I developed my personal affirmation, began setting my goals and gave a great report at every meeting. I was so motivated by being in Master Mind, and as a result, I have developed and achieved many goals that I never thought possible. I attribute my humble success to that group, headed by Ann McNeil. Had Ann not talked to me about the importance of goal-setting and planning, I may have been haphazardly doing things in my life that have little meaning. Master Mind has blessed me immensely and still is today. I am constantly working towards achieving my goals and setting new ones to replace the ones achieved. The women in Master Mind planted the seed in me to write this book. After reading many motivational books required by the group, I put together and gave each member a motivational packet consisting of excerpts from different books we had read. Someone suggested that I write my own book from those excerpts and everyone else agreed. The seed was cultivated, watered, and nurtured, and your hands now touch the manifestation of the seed.

WHAT ARE YOU WAITING FOR?

Take a moment to ask and answer these questions: What is one major goal that you always wanted to accomplish and never did? What would it take for you to start working towards that goal right now? What are the obstacles stopping you? Can the obstacles be overcome so that you may pursue this goal? Why haven't you done it yet? I had you ask yourself those questions because I had to ask myself the same questions regarding my life. I seriously reflected on where I use to be, where I am now, and where I want to be in the future. We have all heard the saying, *"You can be anything you set your mind to be."* But how many

Destined for Great Things!

people take that literally to heart? I do believe that if your mind can conceive it and your heart can believe it, then you *can* achieve it. How many times have you pondered on something you have always wanted to do, but never did? When that thought comes to mind, do you feel bad or guilty about not having achieved it? Why do you think you keep having thoughts and visions of it? The vision has been imprinted in your spirit for a reason. The desire in you is the power seeking to manifest. You are walking around with seeds of God's purpose inside of you, and you are not cultivating the seeds, nurturing the seeds, or watering the seeds so that they can grow and blossom. Why are you hiding your gifts from the world? It is not too late to go after that goal. Let's take an example. If I wanted to become a lawyer, could I pursue that goal right now? Would it be too late this far in the game? No. If I pursued becoming a lawyer today, I would need to earn the undergraduate degree, get accepted into a law school, study very hard, sacrifice sleep, pass the Bar Exam, and eventually become an excellent lawyer (I'm always winning arguments). Sounds easy? I know there is so much more in between, but my point is that whatever you want to do in life can be done with the start of a goal and the necessary steps taken to achieve that goal. Big accomplishments are only but a bunch of small accomplishments multiplied. It is very sad to have lived forty, fifty, sixty, or even seventy years on I coulda… shoulda… woulda.. Time is waiting for no one. If you desired to go back to school to earn that college degree you always wanted, what is stopping you? Your age? Okay let's say you are forty years old right now, but you say that you are too old to go back to school. It would take four years to earn a Bachelors degree, two years after for a Masters (with these accelerated programs, maybe less than that), and three years minimum thereafter for a Doctorate, but you decide not to go back at all. In four years, you will just be four years older *without* that degree, but in the same educational position you were in four years prior; whereas had you gone back to school, you would be four years older *with* that college degree, a sense of achievement, and an increased level of self-confidence. How old we are is not important. It is one's view towards age that makes it a blessing or a hindrance. Stop thinking, *"I should have done that years ago."* That is failure thinking. Instead think, *"I am going to start right now because my best years are ahead of me."* My point is that no matter what age you are or what your present circumstances may be, you are never too old to accomplish your dreams. You are special and still have something unique to offer. Your life, because of who you are, has meaning. When you multiply tiny bits of time with tiny bits of effort, you will find that you can accomplish magnificent things. It is never too late to do anything you purpose in your heart and mind to do. Your sacrifice of time and effort should serve the vision that God has given to you.

God outlined all throughout the Bible what we needed to do to be successful. We just don't apply the principles to our lives. A good example of how God outlined success for us is in the book of Joshua, Chapter 1:8 *"This book of the law shall not depart out of thy mouth; but thou shall meditate therein day and night, that thou mayest observe to do according to all that is written therein: For then thou shalt make thy way prosperous, and then thou shalt have good success."* Good success is attaining total peace and fulfillment in every area of your life. God plainly told Joshua how he and the Israelites could have not just success, but "good success" and be prosperous. He said for them to meditate on the Word day and night and do what the Word says. Seems simple enough right? Then why was it so hard to do, and still is today? Because it takes discipline to meditate on the Word of God day and night. It takes discipline to *"do according to ALL that is written therein..."* It takes discipline to do anything that is worth something. Unfortunately, most of us keep our lives so jammed with junk food for the soul and amusement for the flesh, that the cost for good success and prosperity is too expensive for us to pay. God reiterates this same principle in Psalm 1:2, *"his delight is in the law of the Lord and in his law does he **meditate day and night**; and he shall be like a tree planted by the rivers of the water that bringeth forth fruit in his season; His leaf also shall not wither, and whatsoever he doeth shall prosper."* There it is again. God says to meditate on His Word day and night and we shall be prosperous. Prosperity is an ongoing, progressing state of success. God wants us to have prosperity and have "good successes," and He told us what we needed to do to have it. You can have it. I can have it. Discipline and obedience is the key.

THE EFFECTS OF LOW SELF-ESTEEM

Self-esteem refers to how you feel about yourself on the inside. The thoughts and feelings you have regarding yourself may be positive or negative. The more positive your thoughts and feelings about yourself are, the higher your self-esteem will be. On the contrary, the more negative your thoughts and feelings about yourself are, the lower your self-esteem will be. Feeling good, no, feeling great about yourself is imperative, as it gives you a sense of power over your own life, helps you feel satisfied in relationships, allows you to set realistic expectations, and enables you to pursue your *own* goals. Notice I said "own" goals. I place emphasis on this word because it is so important. One main characteristic of those with low self-esteem is that they go over and beyond to help others achieve their goals and seldom work on achieving their own. They do this so that they will be accepted, so people will appreciate them, recognize them, and praise them for their efforts and hard work. Yet, they leave their own goals and dreams on the backburner and never get around to pursuing them because they are constantly helping others fulfill theirs. Feeling good about yourself gives you that motivation required to achieve goals and reach dreams. Feeling bad about yourself, on the other hand, contributes to a distorted view of yourself and a distorted view of others. The limitations that you think you have, and the negative thoughts that you internalize are given to you by the world, but the possibilities that you envision for yourself come from within you by the spirit of God residing in your soul. Ralph Waldo Emerson states, *"What lies behind us, and what lies before us are tiny matters compared to what lies within us."* What a profound statement! There is so much greatness within us! Therefore, in order to be great, you must believe that you are great, expect great things in your life and be ready to receive them when they arrive.

People are looking at you and wondering if you truly believe in your vision, your goals, and your dreams. If you are not positive, if you are not confident, if you are not excited about your OWN dreams, how can you expect anyone else to be excited about your dreams? When you work with diligence towards your dreams, people notice, and they will support your vision. Everything you do will make an impression on others, good or bad. Therefore, it is of the utmost importance that we begin to value ourselves as individuals worthy of accomplishing great things.

One with a low self-esteem does not have the inner strength and fortitude to develop goals and pursue them with persistence and unwavering faith. Think about it. Is it characteristic for a person with low self-esteem to believe in himself or herself and pursue his or her goals? No, it is not. It may sound harsh, but unfortunately, it is true. He or she is too insecure and deep down inside they believe that they are not worthy enough to be great, although he or she may dream of greatness. If one asks for success, but prepares for failure, they will get the thing they have prepared for.

BELIEVE IN YOURSELF

There is power in believing in yourself. According to Les Brown, a man who had to dig deep within himself to find the value that he possessed, *"When people have a sense of their self-worth, a sense that there is greatness within them, the payoff comes in the increased value they place on their own lives and the lives of others. They are more likely to have an agenda for their lives, a mission that keeps them focused and shields them from the distractions and peer pressures that knock others off course."* Success in this life is not determined so much by the size of one's bank account as it is the size of one's belief. If you really believe that you can move a mountain, you can. But you must believe, really believe, and do not doubt. When you begin to have strong belief in yourself, your mind will start formulating ways to help you achieve your goals and your dreams. When you have a high level of self-confidence, others will have confidence in you as well. Once we have accepted and love who we are, recognized the gifts that God has placed in us, and walk in the belief, confidence, and knowledge that we are worthy of pursuing our dreams, we will never expect anything less out of life.

GOAL SETTING

You only get out of life what you invest in it. I once read that only 3% of Americans develop goals and strive to achieve them. Three percent! More often than not, people with goals and plans succeed in life, while people without them fail. If you have no goals to strive for and no plans for improving yourself, then what are you living for? This is certainly not to say that people cannot be successful if they do not develop goals, but life is much more meaningful when you are always striving to grow and working toward a goal. It is extremely important that you begin to accept yourself as a person worthy of accomplishing great things. Goals are like a road map, they show you where you want to go and tell you approximately how long it will take to get there. Plans are the "how" of goal setting. Plans delineate the steps you need to take along the way to arrive at your destination. For you who are visual learners like me, you need to see things written down on paper. Not only does writing your goals down help you to see clearly what it is that you aspire, but seeing them written down motivates you. Once you have taken the time and effort to write specifically what you want to achieve, the desire to accomplish those goals emerge from within you. There is power in writing things down on paper. The Bible puts it this way: *"Write the vision, and make it plain upon tables, that he may run that readeth it. For the vision is yet for an appointed time, but in the end it shall speak, and not lie: though it tarry, wait for it; because it will surely come, it will not tarry."* (Habakkuk 2:2). There is a resurgence of taking on the world that overwhelms you once you see your vision on paper.

However, once you get your goals down on paper, you must not file them away, never to look at them again. Spend time examining and memorizing your goals. Do not let the motivation die. If the obstacles that I have overcome are not enough motivation for you, then read the words of Les Brown, who states the following in 'Live Your Dreams', *"With a powerful hunger for your dreams driving you, you will be surprised at the ideas that will come, at the people you will be able to attract, at the opportunities that will unfold. You will be able to see things that you won't believe you couldn't see before – things that may have been right there in front of you the whole time."* You have everything you need inside of you to accomplish your goals. The only thing that can stop you from pursuing your goals is YOU! You are the master of your own destiny. You are the captain of your ship.

Properly setting goals can be incredibly motivating. As you get into the habit of setting and achieving goals, you will find that your self-confidence increases quickly. A sure way to increase self-esteem is by setting and achieving goals. Goal setting techniques are used by many successful individuals and achievers in all professions. Goals give you long-term vision and motivation. They focus your acquisition of knowledge and help you to organize your time and resources so that you can make the very most of your life. Cherish your visions. Have faith in your goals, for out of them will flow all delightful conditions and surroundings. Dream big dreams and as you dream, so you shall become. Falling into your hands will be placed the exact result of all your thoughts. You will receive that which you have created, no more, no less. Remember to dream BIG! Norman Vincent Peale said it best when he stated, *"When you affirm big, believe big, and pray big, big things happen."* Keep in mind that how big you think determines the size of your accomplishments. You are bigger than you think you are. People who dare to aim high and work towards accomplishing their goals are big thinkers. They are experts in creating positive, forward-looking, optimistic pictures in their minds, and in the minds of others. Don't concern yourself too much with *how* you are going to achieve your goals after you have written an action plan for reaching them. Leave that completely to God. Look at things not as they are, but as they can be. Visualization adds value to everything. A big goal-setter always visualizes what will be done in the future. A big goal-setter is not concerned with the present. The challenge of competing with yourself and winning is very rewarding. Don't give up. The reward is great if you persist until you succeed.

Destined for Great Things!

However you decide to plan is up to you. The key is to plan. When you fail to plan, you plan to fail. The majority of people meet with failure because of their lack of persistence in creating new plans to take the place of the ones that have failed. When they don't see instant results, they become discouraged and quit. There will be some failure, but that is okay. Temporary defeat is not permanent failure. It is in you to succeed. No one succeeds without overcoming obstacles and opposition. There would be no <u>test</u>-imony if there were no <u>test</u>. Out of every adversity comes an equal or greater opportunity. When setting goals, I always begin by defining who I am and who I aspire to be. I call it my personal affirmation. Others call it their mission statement. They are basically the same. I recite my affirmation at least twice per week. On the next page is an example of my affirmation:

Mia's Personal Affirmation

I Mia Yvette Merritt, am a prosperous, spiritual, humble, and faithful woman of God with character and integrity. As a child of the most high and powerful God, I meditate on the Word day and night. I pray without ceasing and I worship God in spirit and in truth. I exhibit a quiet and meek spirit, which in the sight of God is of a great price. I walk in this world with humility and grace, and yet I am confident and fearless. Out of my mouth departs wisdom, power, and the law of kindness. I control my emotions in every situation, I practice good habits on a daily basis, I attract and magnetize to me the people, circumstances, money, and conditions that I require in order to fulfill and achieve my highest ideals. I am great! I come from greatness! I attract greatness, and I am the kind of person I want to attract into my life.

I am a lender, not a borrower. I am above and not beneath. I am the head and not the tail. It is my birthright to live in prosperity, peace, harmony, and abundance and my life is a reflection of that birthright. I speak with perfect self-expression and my words rapidly perform those things
which I speak.

I keep my mind, my spirit, and my soul healthy by reading books that feed me in an effort to increase in knowledge, wisdom, and understanding. All of my positive thoughts are being established. My daily mindset is one of constructive thinking, ingenuity, and absorbing the power and wisdom
of the mind Christ.

As a mother, sister, friend, and wife, I encourage, uplift,
and speak life into the situations of others, and bless them with the fruit of my lips. I speak what the spirit of God gives me to speak, and I do it in season, and in love. My children arise and call me blessed; and my husband also, and he praises me. Favor is deceitful, and beauty is vain, but a woman who loves the Lord, she shall be praised!

Yes, my affirmation is long, but since I recite it at least twice per week, I cover every aspect of my life. Words have power and as I speak into the atmosphere, my words manifest themselves in the earth realm and return back to me with astounding accuracy. You should want all of your desires to come into fruition. Speak it into existence!

An affirmation/personal mission statement is basically a snapshot of how you see yourself in the very near future. Some people have much shorter ones, some have longer, but what is most important is to have one. Once written, you are consciously aware of the person you aspire to be, and therefore are compelled to begin acting like that person. It is so real. From your affirmation/mission statement, come your goals. Every year, I set goals in various areas of my life: spiritually, financially, educationally, recreationally, personally, family, business wise, and health. Many people set goals in only a few areas, but as I stated earlier, I like to have all areas of my life covered. Below is a brief example of how I set my goals:

SPIRITUAL GOALS
- Become more sensitive to the voice of God through prayer, fasting, praise and worship.
- Rise no later than 4:30a.m daily to pray and read the Word.
- Meditate on *at least* one Bible scripture per day.
- Sow into the kingdom of God by giving 12% tithes instead of 10%
- Give a monthly "sacrificial" offering.
- Fast at least twice per month to hear the voice of God concerning my life.

FINANCIAL GOALS
- Pay off at least half of my student loans
- Save $30,000.00 in checking account
- Pay off all credit cards
- Purchase at least five stocks

- Renew membership with the Chamber of Commerce
- Renew membership with International Mastermind Association.

PERSONAL GOALS
- Speak positive in all manner of conversation. Eliminate vain talk and gossiping
- Meditate daily
- Learn a minimum of 20 sentences in Spanish
- Maintain my nails and hair twice monthly
- Do 55 sit-ups a night
- Write and publish my second book
- Book at least three speaking engagements per month
- Send birthday cards to friends and family
- Tell my son that I love him every day
- Do at least one random act of kindness every week
- Call Grandma more often

EDUCATIONAL GOALS
- Learn to speak Spanish fluently
- Increase my vocabulary and enunciation
- Reinforce learned skills with my son
- Renew my teaching contract with the university

FAMILY GOALS
- Invite at lease 10 people to church
- Organize monthly family outings
- Have Sunday dinners at my home
- Take Stephan on a summer vacation
- Visit Grandma in Madison, FL
- Go to the movies and/or a concert or play at least 3 times with family and friends.

- Go bowling with nieces and nephews

HEALTH GOALS
- Take multivitamins
- Drink at least 3 pints of bottles of water daily
- Get annual physical
- Lose 5 inches around my waist
- Get a mammogram
- Take Stephan for his dental appointment
- Take Stephan for his eye appointment
- Take Stephan for his annual physical
- Exercise at least four times per week

CHECK AND BALANCE

As mentioned previously, your motivation is increased when you write your affirmation/personal mission statement. Writing an affirmation is time consuming. It requires you to look deep inside yourself and identify your strengths and weaknesses. Going deep inside and bringing out the less attractive stuff can be a humbling, yet beneficial and worthwhile undertaking. It requires soul-searching. Write down your strengths and weaknesses. However, after writing your affirmation, your yearly goals will be a bit easier to develop. Learn yourself and write down what you find out. Then, identify what you want out of life and what role you want to play in the lives of those whom you love and interact. Your motivation increases after you actually sit down and write out your goals. Your goals must be clearly defined, realistic, meaningful, and acted upon. In an effort to assist in the most important areas of my life, I use a Goals Form when developing one-year goals, (see p. 152 in back). Once the mission statement and goals are written, there must be accountability. Therefore, I use monthly and weekly forms as a check and balance system (see p. 155 in back). Every month I look at the goals that I have developed for that particular year. I then look at the smaller goals that I need to achieve in order to reach my large-scale goals. In doing this, I identify what is realistic enough to accomplish within a month's time. They are then written on the monthly form. Everyday, I look at the form and check off what has been done for the day.

This next part may sound crazy, but at the end of the month I calculate the difference between the goals accomplished and the goals not accomplished. I then take out my grading scale and give myself a grade – the grade that I earned (this comes from the teacher in me). I write my grade at the top of the form, just as if I am grading an assignment. I do this on a monthly basis. It is a (sometimes sad) reality check. I am pleased to say however, that I have never gotten an "F", but I have gotten a few "Ds", but mostly "Bs" and "Cs". I am, however, steadily moving and striving for "As." Goal-setting may sound like a lot of work, but nobody is going to put more time into your goals than you are. When you want success bad enough you must be willing to pay your dues to achieve it. Taking the easy way is the surest way to be misled. In all human affairs there are efforts and there are results, and the strength of the effort is the measure of the result. Nobody cares as much about your life as you do. Remember that.

FEAR OF FAILURE & FEAR OF SUCCESS

Psychologists say that all humans are born with only two types of fear: the fear of falling, and the fear of loud noises. All other fears are learned. They come with knowledge or develop as a result of our experiences. They come from what we are taught or what we hear and see. In his book *The Magic of Thinking Big*, David Schwartz, PhD, writes on the subject of fear, the following:

> *Fear is real, and we must recognize it exists before we can conquer it... Fear stops people from capitalizing on opportunity; fear wears down physical vitality; fear actually makes people sick; causes organic difficulties, shortens life; and closes your mouth when you want to speak... Action cures fear. Indecision and postponement fertilize fear...Hesitation enlarges and magnifies fear... To overcome fear, act. To feed fear, wait, put off, postpone... the only cure for fear, is action.*

Oftentimes the only thing that holds us back from accomplishing great things is our fear – fear of failure, fear of what people might say or think, fear of how we are going to make it financially, and believe it or not, fear of success. When you overcome your fears, great and mighty things begin to happen for you. The most liberating, yet surprising thing about fear is that when you finally do overcome your them, you realize that they were not as big as you made yourself think they were. I once saw an acronym for the word fear that is so very fitting: **FEAR**= **F**alse **E**xpectations **A**ppearing **R**eal. Once you overcome your "false expectations" and go after your goals with running shoes on, you will begin to do things you never imagined were possible. Fearlessness removes all fear. I am an avid reader, and I love reading old wise quotes, which is why I like the book of Proverbs so much, but one of the most profound quotes on fear that I have ever read comes from Marianne Williamson in the following. You probably have heard it before:

"Our deepest fear is not that we are inadequate. Our deepest fear is that we are powerful beyond measure. It is our light, not our darkness that most frightens us. We ask ourselves, Who am I to be brilliant, gorgeous, talented, and fabulous?

Actually, who are you not to be? You are a child of God. Your playing small does not serve the world. There is nothing enlightened about shrinking so that other people won't feel insecure around you. We are all meant to shine, as children do. We were born to make manifest the glory of God that is within us. It's not just in some of us; it's in everyone.

And as we let our own light shine, we unconsciously give other people permission to do the same. As we are liberated from our own fear, our presence automatically liberates others."

Whew! Talk about getting to the very heart of the matter. Can you imagine? Our deepest fear is that we are powerful beyond measure. Let's just overcome our fears and strain our potential until it cries for mercy.

MONITOR YOUR THINKING

We are all today where our thoughts have brought us and we will be tomorrow where our thoughts take us. Our character is literally the complete sum of all our thoughts. Your life is what you make it by your thoughts and deeds. You have no personality, no soul and no life apart from your thoughts. When you think, your life appears. As your thoughts are modified, you change. Your life cannot be separated from your thoughts. You have become what you are but are becoming what you shall be by your thoughts. You, and only you, can change your character. There are a plethora of books and materials written on the power of the mind, and yet scores of individuals still do not understand the power that their "thoughts" have on their lives, their experiences, their destinies. Life is about cause and effect, sowing and reaping, going around and coming back around. If you lie, you will be lied to; if you cheat, you will be cheated; if you give hate, you will receive hate; if you give love, you will receive love; If you give criticism, you will receive criticism. Wherever there is an effect, there is always a cause. To change the effect, we must change the cause and if we trace the cause back far enough, we will see that it can be found in the mental attitude which created the conditions. It is also important to note that effects become causes, which become effects, which then become causes. It is therefore important how we react to the effects. The person that you are today, the way that you carry yourself, the things that you have accomplished, the way that you speak, the job that you have, the car that you drive, all originated in your mind. James Allen, often referred to as an unrewarded genius, wrote one of my favorite inspirational books of all time titled *As a Man Thinketh*. The book is small enough to fit in one's pocket, yet powerful enough to change the world. The inspiring writings of James Allen have influenced millions for good and have brought fame, fortune, and happiness to those who have applied his teachings. In *As a man Thinketh*, James Allen writes: *There can be no progress or achievement without sacrifice, and a person's worldly success will be in the measure that he sacrifices his confused, evil thoughts and fixes his mind upon the development of his plans. The higher he lifts his thoughts, the more positive, upright and righteous he becomes, the greater will be his success and the more blessed and enduring will be his achievements.* Notice how success is contingent upon the way one thinks? To live, is to act and think, and to act and think is to change. Even if you are ignorant of this fact, you are still changing for either better or worse. We must become masters of ourselves because we have the power to control our thoughts. We must get ourselves right by monitoring our way of thinking. When you find yourself focusing on negativity, which brings forth no good fruit, you must immediately switch your thinking to thoughts of a more positive nature. Once we begin to observe what we think about, we will discover that we oftentimes occupy our minds with petty insignificant details instead of letting it soar, as it was divinely designed to do. Positive and negative thinking cannot occupy the mind at the same time. One must dominate the other. Therefore, it is your responsibility to ensure that positive thoughts dominate your mind. If you fail to plant desires into your mind, if you fail to focus on things that are positive and constructive, if you simply neglect to plant the seeds that will yield positive fruit, your mind will feed upon the thoughts that reach it as the result of your neglect. All that you accomplish or fail to accomplish with your life is the direct result of your thinking. It is imperative that you monitor what goes into your mind. You absolutely must change the programming of your mind, bring hope and happiness into your life, and awaken the faith and inner conviction that you can change, overcome, and improve any situation through your thought process. Thoughts of doubt and fear will never accomplish anything. They always lead to failure. If you allow doubt and fear to sneak in, then your purpose, your energy, and your efforts all become futile. Guard well your thoughts reader, for what you think in your secret thoughts today, good or bad, will eventually manifest into action tomorrow.

At the bidding of negative, disappointing thoughts, your body sinks into sickness and disease. At the command of pleasant and righteous thoughts, the body becomes clothed with youthfulness and beauty. Strong, pure, and positive thinking build up the body in health and grace. Out of a clean heart, comes clean thoughts and a clean body. To renew your body, you must beautify your mind. Negative thoughts of unforgiveness, hatred, and bitterness rob the body of its health and grace. Clean thoughts make clean habits. You must monitor your thinking in order to be truly successful.

NATURAL LAWS OF THE UNIVERSE

Regardless of who uses them, the natural laws of the universe cannot be broken. For instance, anyone who consistently gives 10% of his or her income to donations or tithes will have that money returned back to them in great financial measures. An atheist can apply this principle and reap the benefits just the same as a believer. This is the law of reciprocity. The natural laws work for or against anyone who uses them. People, in ignorance of the laws bring about their own destruction. Christians typically pay 10% tithes to their local church. Others pay 10% of their income to charitable organizations. The key is to give back a portion of what has been given to you. In life, we get by giving. We grow rich by scattering. Many have asked God to give them peace, righteousness, and blessings, but still have not obtained these things. Why? Because they are not practicing or sowing those things in their life. Since everything has a value, that which is freely given is gained with accumulation. If you were to read the stories of great financial giants, a common element among most, if not all of them attributable to their success is their monetary giving. My point here is that the natural laws of the universe do work when applied accurately. You may fail to observe the laws, but they are infallible. There is the law of sowing and reaping and before you plant your seeds, make sure that you are going to be satisfied with what the harvest is going to be. Make certain that you are sowing the seeds that will sprout up good fruit, fruit of kindness, honesty, tolerance, wealth, time, service, etc. There is a time to plant and a time to reap. All of us have eaten fruit from trees that we never planted. It is therefore time for us to start planting seeds that will grow trees that will bring forth fruit that we may never eat from. Thoughts, words and deeds are seeds sown and by the infallible law of things, they produce after their own kind, good or bad. People may fail to observe these principles, but the principles are as mathematically exact as two plus two is four.

As you read this book, you might be in your reaping season. You may be in your planting season. You may be in your cultivating season. It is not difficult to discern what season you are in. You must know your season and continue working until harvest time. *"Be not deceived; God is not mocked: for whatsoever a man soweth, that shall he also reap. For he that soweth to his flesh shall of the flesh reap corruption; but he that soweth to the Spirit shall of the Spirit reap life everlasting"* (Galatians 6:7-8).

RESPONSIBILITY

With success comes responsibility. Through diligence, commitment, and a strong desire to succeed, many obtain success in this world. James Allen asserts that *some even reach lofty altitudes in the spiritual realm, but again, fall back into weakness and wretchedness by allowing selfish, arrogant and corrupt thinking to take possession of them. Your victories that are attained by right thinking can only be maintained by watchfulness.*
Many give way when success is assured, and rapidly fall back into failure.
Knowing how to remain humble and keep a level head at all times will maintain your success. Pride is a terrible and dangerous condition to be in. It often is very difficult for the one afflicted by it to perceive it because it sneaks up on a person. The more successful you become, the more vulnerable you are to becoming lifted up in pride. The more prosperity you obtain, the more time you must spend with the Lord. Only He can protect you from the pride that has caused many to fall. The enemy wants to see you lifted up so you can you fall back down and be humiliated. Unfortunately, pride will not allow a person to admit that they are lifted up in it, thus making it difficult to get freed from it.

I once read a quote that stuck with me, and whenever I receive too many compliments from those whose credibility is questionable, I remember the quote: *Don't be afraid of enemies who attack you, be afraid of friends who flatter you.* Stay grounded. Be very careful not to get "caught up" in people praising and lifting you up. Remember, what the Lord said, *"No flesh shall glory in my sight"* (1 Corin 18:31). God alone is to be lifted up and praised. Stay humble. Humility is a precious and valuable attribute to possess. In heaven, the more humble you are, the higher your position. The world says that the greatest one among you should be served. God says the greatest one among you should be your servant (Mathew 23:11). Greatness is measured by service, not status. Real success is found while

Plan for Prosperity and Abundance

bowing at the feet of others. If you stay at the feet of Jesus, you will remain humble. In discussing pride and arrogance with my mother one day, she said the **Plan for** following to me that really stayed in my spirit: *"The feet that you step on to get to the top, may be connected to the butt you have to kiss on your way back down to the bottom."* Man will lift you up on a pedestal today and throw you away like yesterday's garbage tomorrow. How can you face people whom you have mistreated once you have been regimented, demoted, downgraded, and no longer respected? When you mistreat or overlook people because they are "beneath" you, they wait for your downfall and then rejoice when it happens. You may be the most knowledgeable, competent, and experienced person that has ever held the position, but if you treat people like crap, they won't care about your skills or abilities. Many people get caught up into thinking that they are indispensable and can not be replaced. To get an understanding of just how much you will be missed if you were to leave that position, read the poem on the next page.

Sometime when you're feeling important;
Sometime when your ego's in bloom;
Sometime when you take for granted,
You're the best qualified in the room.

Sometime when you feel that your leaving
Would fill an unfillable hole;
Just follow this simple instruction,
And see how it humbles your soul.

Take a bucket and fill it with water,
Put your hand in it up to the wrist;
Pull it out and the hole that's remaining,
Is a measure of how you'll be missed.

You may splash all you please when you enter,
You can stir up the water galore;

Destined for Great Things!

> But stop and you'll find in a minute,
> That it looks quite the same as before.
>
> The moral in this quaint example
> Is to do just the best that you can;
> Be proud of yourself, but remember
> There's no indispensable man!
> *Author Unknown*

This poem applies to everybody, not just the "little people" like me, but ALL! If you are humble and genuinely good to people, they will do everything in their power to support you and make you look good. It is important to care about people. When you take time out of your day to ask the least among you how his or her weekend went, that speaks volumes, not only to that person, but to God. Smile at people, be genuinely interested in people and stay humble. It will carry you a very long way.

~~ LESSONS LEARNED ~~

1. Once you begin setting goals and making plans to accomplish them, you will discover that you can achieve those things you never dreamed of. It all begins with a personal mission statement, then the setting of your goals.

2. The only thing that is stopping you from being successful is YOU. Once you believe, and really believe that you have the seed within you to be successful through goal setting, you are on the path that leads to prosperity.

3. Humility is the key to sustaining prosperity. Ask for humility so that you will always remain level-headed.

~~ REFLECTION QUESTIONS ~~

1. Are you monitoring the thoughts that reach your mind or do you feed off the thoughts that enter as a result of neglecting to monitor your thinking?

2. Do you have a mission statement for your life that you are striving to accomplish or do you live your life from day to day with no goals to strive for?

3. Do you really believe that you are worthy of accomplishing great things or deep down inside do you believe that you are unworthy? How will you convince yourself that there is greatness in you that needs to be manifested in the earth?

Chapter 9

Reflect on Your Deeds of Each Day
One bad Choice can Change Your Life

At each day's end, I will carefully examine the progress and problems of my day's journey, and this will create in my mind a diary for today, and textbook for tomorrow.

In the evening before I retire, I will review the words and actions of every hour of the day, and I will allow nothing to escape my examination, for why should I fear the sight of my errors when I have the power to admonish and forgive myself?

Perhaps I was too cutting in a certain dispute. My opinion could have been withheld, for it stung but did no good. What I said may have been true, but all truths are not to be spoken at all times. I should have held my tongue, for there is no contending either with fools or superiors.

Am I guilty of omission? Was there something I could have done to help someone or a situation, but I neglected to do so? Am I guilty of commission? Did I deliberately do or say something that was not appropriate, nor fruit bearing?

Let me review my actions. Let me observe myself as my greatest enemy might do, and I will become my own best friend. I will begin right now, to become what I will be hereafter. Darkness may fall, but sleep will not cover my eyes until I have reviewed in full the events of my day.

THE VISITS TO HOMESTEAD

When my mother would take my sister and me to Homestead to visit relatives, we would be so happy. My mother's two sisters and their children lived in the low-income housing projects down there, which was 45 minutes south of where we lived. We loved it there because we played outside all day and into the night and did what we wanted to do while there. My mother also had cousins who lived in the same housing projects, so it was like a big family reunion when we went. Our cousins lived literally doors away from each other, and we would go from door to door playing and eating food. We had so many cousins, so there was always someone to play with.

As a fourteen year-old girl, I envied the way my cousins were able to do what they wanted to do. They had no curfew, stayed out all night, sometimes even for days, did not have to complete homework, did not have to go to school if they didn't want to, and had no one really telling them what to do. They had boyfriends at eleven and twelve years old, and the boyfriends were allowed to spend the night with them. They had no discipline, no structure, no guidance. They used profanity freely around their parents, came in and out as they pleased and basically had it made in my eyes. Boy, how I envied that life back then. They did not seem to get in trouble for anything. When they would tell me about their lives, I thought they had it made. When I would say, *"Don't you get in trouble when you stay out all night?* Their response would be an emphatic, *"No! My mama don't care."* These were twelve, thirteen, and fourteen year old children.

On the other hand, I thought that my mother was the meanest mother in the world compared to the mothers of my cousins who lived in Homestead. We lived in the North area of the county where we were one of very few Black families in the neighborhood at the time. We were only allowed to play in the front or back yard when we went outside. If we did go to someone's house, it had to be someone on our block and my mother had to talk to their mother first. She would give us a time to be home and we had to be in the house before the sun went down or she would come and get us from wherever we were and embarrass us. We were not allowed to play with boys unless it was in the front yard where she could look out of the window and we could not spend the night at anyone's house. Girls could spend the night at our house, but I wanted to go to other people's homes and spend the night sometimes. When we came home from school, we had to do our homework and leave it out for mother to check. If it was not done correctly when she checked it, she would wake us up to re-do it. Boy, did I think my mother was mean. That's why whenever we went to Homestead to visit our relatives, Lisa and I would be so happy because we knew we were in for some freedom and some fun. There was always excitement going on in the projects - fighting, shooting, loud music, dance competitions on the basketball court, you name it. All the kids would be out late, even after 11:00 p.m. there would be children outside playing.

Boyfriends? Huh, I'd better not even think about having a boyfriend at fourteen. I did like boys, but they never knew it. I would always get nervous and shy around boys that I liked, so unless they approached me, I would never talk to them unless I did not like them. In that case, they were just my friends. My cousins had boyfriends, and they would try and set me up with boys who lived in the projects. I did like the attention. The only thing I did not like about going down there was when people would say that my sister and I talked 'White'.

MONKEY SEE MONKEY DO

I'll never forget this one particular time that we went to Homestead. We had been outside playing mostly all day. We were back and forth buying candy from the candy house, a place where this couple sold candy, chips, and soda out of their apartment. We had been playing all day long and going from house to house visiting relatives. On this particular day, I did not know where my mother was. When she would go to Homestead to be with her sisters and cousins they would hang out and she would leave us with our great aunt, a much older aunt, who let us do whatever we wanted to do. That was the only time my mother was not tight on us regarding our whereabouts. This particular day, I went to my aunt's apartment to look for my sister. I vividly remember walking into the house and seeing two of my cousins sitting on the couch with a boy beside each of them. There was a third boy sitting on the chair alone. They were all watching a triple X adult movie. The people on the tape were having sex. The first thing I said was, *"Ooh, I'm gonna tell!"* One of the boys asked who I was, and my cousin responded, *"That's our cousin, she's from Carol City."* He proceeded to say, "*What's wrong with her?"* and my cousin said, *"She square, they from a white neighborhood."* I closed the door and left. When I returned about an hour later, no one was in the living room, except the boy who was sitting in the chair by himself. So I asked him where everyone was. He said that they were in the back rooms. When I went to the bedrooms, my cousins were inside having sex with the boys they had been watching the movies with. One of my cousins was on the bottom bunk bed with a boy, and my other cousin was on the top bunk having sex with the other boy. I started yelling, *"Ooh, I'm gonna tell, I'm gonna tell!"* My older cousin, the one who was a year older than me, jumped up, started yelling at me, and said, *"Why don't you stop acting like a little girl."* By then, the other cousin had gotten up, and was a little calmer. She said that I should have sex with Ricky, who was in the living room. I exclaimed, *"I'm not doing that!"* The other cousin said that Ricky had told them that he liked me. Then she tried to convince me that sex was nothing, and that all I had to do was lay down and open my legs. She said it would feel good. After much debating back and forth, I was convinced to consider it. My cousin went to the living room and began talking to the young man about me. I was in one of the other bedrooms where she had told me to wait. I was so scared. I had never had sex before, nor had I ever seen a man's private part. As a late bloomer, I had not even had a menstrual cycle yet, and I was fourteen. Ricky came in the room where I was. He walked in slowly and said, *"You want to have sex?"* I said, *"I don't care."* Then he said, *"You have to take your shorts off."* I said, *"OK, turn around."* I slid in the bed and took off my shorts while under the covers. He began to take his shorts off as well. Then he climbed on the top of me and put his private part at the tip of my private part, but all of a sudden, a liquid came out of him before, we could do anything. He seemed to be afraid. I assumed that had never happened to him before, and I don't think that he had ever had sex before either. He did not know what the liquid was, and he never inserted himself inside of me. We both got up and put our clothes on. It did not work, at least I thought it hadn't.

A SHOCKING SURPRISE!

About four months later, my mother took me to the doctor for having stomach pains. The results came back. I was pregnant! Needless-to-say, my mother was devastated. She became sick and desperate and didn't know what to do. She wanted to know what had happened. She knew that I wasn't sexually active, and she could not believe that I was pregnant. I was too far along to have an abortion and they wouldn't give me one anyway since my little body had not fully matured to that of an adult (back then, fourteen year olds did not look like 20 year olds as they do today).

She ended up sending me away to a home for unwed pregnant girls who gave their babies up for adoption. My mother told family and friends that I went to California to live with my father. I was actually right in Miami-Dade County. The plan was that I was going to have the baby, put it up for adoption and then return back home to the normal life of a fourteen year old.

Informing the parents of the boy was completely out of the question. All that would have done was made me look like a fast girl and cause problems. The mentality of most people who lived in the projects during that time was apathetic and belligerent about everything except for drugs, sex, and welfare checks.

BYE BYE, MIA

So off I went to the home for girls. I was the youngest one there until a twelve-year-old girl came who had been raped by her stepfather. Shortly after that, an eleven-year-old came in. The home was very structured. We had three meals a day, home school, daily chores, and had to be in bed with lights off by 10:00 p.m. every night. We also took Lamaze classes three times a week. The only time we were able to leave the premise was on Saturdays, and we had to be back on the grounds before 11:00 pm or we would be penalized by not being able to leave the next weekend. I never went anywhere on weekends because I didn't have any place to go. All of my family and friends thought that I was in California. My mother came to visit me three times the entire time that I was there, and I received no other visitors because no one knew about the pregnancy.

I hated being pregnant. I would do things to try and have a miscarriage. I would do cartwheels, run, jump, and sometimes I would punch the area that the baby would move on. Why did this have to happen to me? I had never even had a menstrual cycle. I had never had sex before, and still hadn't! My medical file was proof of that. The very first time I went to the doctor for a check-up during the pregnancy, they were astounded. I remember my gynecologist calling other doctors in the room to examine me, and I felt so uncomfortable with so many people trying to look "examine" me. I remember one doctor saying, *"It's as though she's never been touched."* They asked me how I became pregnant because my body was that of a virgin. I explained to them that the boy did not enter inside of me, but that his tip was on the entrance of my private area. They were very cautious of my pregnancy, and also concerned that I wouldn't be able to have a vaginal delivery because of my fragile body. My pregnancy was always an issue with the doctors, and I had more doctor visits than the other girls because of it. I believe they were afraid that if something went wrong, they would be sued.

THROUGH THE WINDOW

The time came for me to have the baby, and I will never forget that day. I was lying on the bed watching *The Jefferson's*. When the show went off at 4:30p.m., I got up to use the bathroom when all of a sudden water came rushing down my legs. I notified the housemother on duty, who then notified the hospital, which was walking distance from the facility where I was living. They did not take me over right away. In fact, they made me walk around the premise, take a shower, and practice breathing exercises. Hours later, when my contractions were minutes apart, I was finally able to walk to the hospital with one of the housemothers. I had a normal vaginal delivery and the baby boy was born at 10:50 p.m. that night. I was not supposed to see the baby. After the birth, the baby was supposed to be immediately taken away, and I was to be taken to another floor. Obviously, one of the medical personnel did not know that because after the baby was cleaned off, someone wrapped him in a blanket and brought him to me. All of the hatred I had for the baby was immediately gone, and an overwhelming sense of love for that child was poured into my heart. He was a handsome little fellow with a head full of beautiful black hair. I held him for about five minutes and then they came and took him. I was taken to another floor and they never brought him to me again.

I would walk to the maternity ward to see him several times a day while I was still in the hospital. I would notice that all of the babies were positioned in front of the glass window for people to see them, but my baby wasn't. He was the only baby that was not displayed in front of the window. His little incubator was in the back of the room, so I would have to strain to see him. Once I was released from the hospital, I walked back there everyday to get a view of him. I would stare at him from the outside of the glass window.

One day when I was staring at him from the window, a young Hispanic girl approached me and began talking to me. She must have been about eighteen or nineteen years old. She obviously had seen the sadness in my eyes as I would stare inside the window. She approached me and was so gentle and sweet to me. She asked me my name, and after I told her my name, she said, *"Which baby are you here to see?"* I pointed to the baby that was in the back of the room away from the other babies. Then, she asked me *"Is that your baby?"* I shook my head yes. She said, *"Tell the nurse that you want to see your baby."* She proceeded to call for one of the nurses to come out, and she was very insistent. She said to the nurse, *"That baby in the back is her baby and she wants to see him."* The nurse opened the door and asked me to come in. My new friend came in with me. The nurse took me to an area away from the view in the window, and I was able to sit down and hold him. I was crying the entire time. My new friend was sitting next to me and holding my hand. I'll never forget that day, nor will I ever forget that young girl who showered me with love and compassion. I still pray for her today. As I write this, I pray for her that God would bless her wherever she is. I wouldn't know her if she was to walk up to me and ask for the time, but God knows who she is and I'm confident that he blessed her for her kindness towards me that day.

My mother came to the hospital after the baby was born. When she saw him, I believe that she felt the same love towards him as I did. She asked me if I wanted to keep him. She said that if I wanted to keep him, I could. I declined. I knew that it would be a hardship on her as a single mother, and me as a young girl. We would have had a lot of adjusting, not to mention explaining to do. I was fifteen years old by then, but I was wise enough to know that a fifteen year-old had no business having a baby. I needed to finish high school and try to live the life of a normal teenager. I could not take care of a baby, and it was hard enough on my mother having to take care of three daughters. She was newly divorced and trying to provide for us alone. It wasn't easy on her, and I knew that. I really believe that she wanted to keep him however.

The following day, I went back to the hospital to see the baby, but he was gone. I inquired as to where he was, and they told me that a social worker came and took him to a foster home. I never saw him again, but I did write him a letter, and my social worker assured me that he would get it.

A WISE CHILD

My mother and I subsequently had to go to court. I really didn't know exactly what was going on, but I knew it had something to do with "the baby". As we entered the courtroom, the judge ordered everyone out except for my mother, my social worker, and a few other relevant parties. He asked me a few questions such as, *"Are you giving up this baby for adoption on your own free will?" "Did anyone influence you to give this baby up?" "Are you certain that this is what you really want to do?"* When the judge was convinced of my answers, he gave the order and the adoption was executed. I had to sign many papers. I left the courthouse and went back home to my family. After we came home, my mother never brought it up again.

It's been over twenty years as I write this, and she has still never talked to me about it. Whenever I would try and bring 'the baby' up, she would discourage me from talking about him. So, from that time until the present, I have never had a discussion with my mother about 'the baby', whom I never even named. His birthday is on September 5, 2007.

I thought about "the baby" often. Every year on his birthday, I would secretly sing him happy birthday and I still do. I have prayed for him over the years and I often wonder what his life is like. I pray that he is an upright and decent young man who isn't a big problem for his family. I know that if I diligently sought him, he could be found, but I don't know if I am ready for that right now. The experience of having that baby is one of those deep dark secrets that has been tucked and hidden down within my soul. It has been extremely hard writing all of this down because it brought forth many memories that I had to relive. I have had to stop writing several times just to cry because facing the details surrounding that situation has been sorrowful.

NEW MERCIES

God gives us new mercies with each day. We all have made mistakes in life, and we all have done things that we are now sorry for, regret, or ashamed of. When we examine our deeds of each day, we can plainly see the error of our ways, and strive to correct from them. When we ask God to show us the hidden things that are holding us back or keeping us from being all that we can be, He will. When we truly desire to be delivered from everything that is holding us hostage and keeping us bound, He will purge, wash, deliver, and set us free. As we continue to examine our deeds, we will find the strength to turn those experiences into confessions in order to be able to bless others. You will be surprised at how many other people you will find with similar, if not identical stories. As we continue to grow in the knowledge and wisdom of God the Father, we will walk in righteousness, and the actions and deeds from most days if not all will be that of joy and peace.

I believe that we as humans, imperfect by nature are guilty of passing judgment on individuals just by observing their actions. We have no idea what people have been through and more importantly, what they may currently be going through. Many times, people act in certain ways because of some traumatic life-experience, brutal act, or other painful incident they may have undergone. The wound may still be in their heart tormenting them continuously. We must reflect on our deeds of each day and determine if our decisions will bring on consequences that will last a lifetime. A split second can change the course of your life and affect your destiny. Less than five minutes of experimenting with sex caused me a lifetime of deep impact. Before succumbing to temptation, look ahead to what the repercussions from the temptation could be, and then ask yourself the question. Is it worth it? Let the results of your daily examination be positive and pleasing. They should be nothing that you have to be ashamed about, but if they are, just remember that you have the power to forgive yourself and your Heavenly Father will always forgive you when you sincerely ask Him. Tough times don't last, but tough people do. Walk in wisdom. Examine each night your deeds of the fading day.

~~ LESSONS LEARNED ~~

1. Be obedient to your first mind. Second guessing yourself can often lead to regret, shame, and disappointment.

2. As children, we don't always understand why our parents seem so strict. It is not until we are older that we can appreciate the sternness. Strictness always seems like bondage, but the end result works out for your good. Freedom always seems like fun, but the end result is usually failure and disappointment.

~~ REFLECTION QUESTIONS ~~

1. What regretful decisions in life have you made? What is the goodness that you can find in that decision to help you move on, be strengthened, and grow?

2. Do you reflect on your behaviors and actions at the end of each day? Were there any decisions that were made that you can resolve before they get out of control?

Chapter 10

Pray with an Attitude of Gratitude
He Hears Your Prayers

I will pray for guidance.

Heavenly Father,
I come to you in humble submission to honor, worship, praise, and magnify your holy and righteous name. I thank you for life, health, strength, and the wisdom to know that you are to be magnified and honored in my life. I thank you for putting the spiritual strength and fortitude inside me, which has enabled me to overcome every trial, tribulation, hardship and difficulty in my life. Each encounter has made me stronger, better, and wiser. Each victory has increased my faith in you to deliver me out of every seeming impossibility.

Lord, please continue to teach me how to live this life with faith, courage, integrity, grace, and confidence. Allow me a forgiving heart and mind that will lead me on the path that keeps me free and strong. Help me to always strive for the highest legitimate reward of merit, ambition, and opportunity; but never allow me to forget to extend a kind, helping hand to others who need encouragement and assistance.

Lord, I ask for wisdom to acknowledge rewards and recognition with humility. Let the spirit of excellence, understanding and patience take root in my heart, mind and soul manifesting through actions, words, and deeds.

Keep me forever serene in every activity of life. Allow me to possess a tranquil heart that will keep me calm regardless of unfavorable circumstances.

In sorrow, may my soul be uplifted by the thought that if there were no shadow, there would be no sunshine. Steady me to do the full share of my work and more with efficiency and effectiveness, and when that is done, stop me. Pay what wages thou will, and permit me to say from a loving heart, a grateful ……...AMEN.

GRATITUDE

I find it fitting for the last chapter of this book to be about gratitude. Why? Because after overcoming many challenges from my past, I am still here. I am still standing. I am still healthy, in my right mind and I am grateful. Each day is a new day, an unfoldment. The decisions that we make today determines how and where we will end up tomorrow. If I looked at the circumstances surrounding my past and sighed over them, feeling sorry for myself and asking "why me?" and all the while doing nothing productive to help get me through them, I would never have ended up where I am today. Today, I am happy, healthy, whole, strong, powerful, harmonious, loving, and happy. I can see now, as I look back, how every situation made me stronger. Each challenge awakened seeds inside me that grew and blossomed into powerful testimonies, which has blessed the lives of others. I don't regret a single experience. I am grateful that God chose me to use to bring glory and honor to His name through such challenges!

If we had no problems for God to solve, no difficulties to overcome, no challenges to face, and no obstacles to cross, then how would we know that God can bring us out, over, or through them? When we ask God for strength, He sends us the difficulties which make us strong. When we ask for courage, He gives us dangers to overcome. When we pray for wisdom, He gives us problems that require wisdom to solve them. A very large portion of our spiritual growth and worldly prosperity will come from eating the bread of adversity and drinking the waters of affliction.

When we find ourselves giving thanks for EVERYTHING, we open a floodgate of blessings to come pouring toward us. We place ourselves on a current that draws good things our way. There is always something to be grateful for. I once read the following quote said by Buddha, which really sums up the fact that there is always something to be grateful for: *Let us rise up and be thankful, for if we didn't learn a lot today, at least we learned a little, and if we didn't learn a little, at least we didn't get sick, and if we got sick, at least we didn't die, so let us still be thankful.*

When my daughter died after having lived for only 93 days, I gave thanks to God for giving her to me for that period of time. She could have died at birth, and I never would have gotten to know her, love her, feed her, change her, care for her, but he allowed me to do those things, which I will always cherish in my heart. I give thanks.

PRAYING IN THE PRESENT TENSE

I find that when we pray as though what we ask for has already been received, the manifestation of what is desired comes faster. For example, if your desire is for a husband, your prayer should sound something like this: *Father, I thank you for my loving husband. I thank you for blessing me with a man who walks in wisdom, knowledge and understanding. He loves me dearly, takes care of our household and prays for us. Thank you for this beautiful man who puts you first and has truly taken his rightful place as head of the household. Lord, this man showers me with love and affection, honors me, and communicates with me lovingly and honestly. I thank you for sending this man to me. I am truly happy that he is in my life and I pray that you continue teaching me how to love, support, and honor him. I am grateful for my husband and I thank you for him.* Whatever you want God to bless you with, pray in the "present" tense as though you already have it! If it is right for you to receive it, it is right for you to pray for it. Your hands shall begin to touch, feel, and experience the manifestation of it through constant gratitude. Begin to *feel* the spirit of gratitude now. Your strong thankful emotion will draw your desire to you speedily.

As I look back over my life, I can't help but be thankful, humble, and appreciative for the many trials that God has brought me through. I know that there are many remarkable people who have surmounted challenges far greater than mine, but my struggles, my pain, and my sorrows are mine, and the magnitude of those trials caused me to be that much stronger in God and has allowed my intestinal fortitude to emerge mightily. All of us have a story to tell. YOU have a story to tell, and I believe that there is a book waiting to be written in everyone. Put God first, pursue your dreams, discover your purpose, monitor your thinking, and everything in your life will fall into place just as it should. Start living your dreams today because you, like me, are *Destined for Great Things!*

EPILOGUE

In the Foreword, I said that this book was written and completed in August 2002, but never published. At that time, it was not the season for me to publish and disclose this book to the world. It was a time for therapeutic healing for me. Expressing my difficult life's experiences in writing was needed for me back then. Since then, God has delivered me completely and blessed me immensely. Now is the season for me to make known the things that have been written in this book. The five years that passed between then and the time that I finally published the book has been years of reaping the seeds that were planted in prior years.

When I wrote this book, I had been a teacher for nine years aspiring to become an Assistant Principal. Now, as I write this book I am in my fifth year as an Assistant Principal and am now aspiring to become a principal. From then until now, I have earned a Doctorate Degree in Education, opened a Motivation Consulting Firm, teach college students at the local university, and have published a book, this book. My son, Stephan is nine years old and in the fourth grade. He is a pleasant and delightful little boy who is in the Gifted Program at school, plays the piano and chess, talks a lot and asks lots of questions.

Who would have thought that a thieving child, who had a baby at 15, barely graduated high school, and been to jail, would amount to anything good. My life is an example of how God can take a sinner like me, activate His spirit inside of him or her, and use him or her as an example of His great grace and mercy. When we truly surrender everything to His will, mind, body, soul and spirit, He will make us into what He has predestined for us to be. We all have the capacity to deal with tragedy in our lives. It is just a matter of tapping into the inner strength and fortitude that we were given by God. We must learn from every lesson, and strive to bring out the greatness that is within us. No life is without complications and failures. You must expect tough times. If not you, then who?

Just remember that life is 10% of what happens to you, but 90% of how you react to it. Every pain we suffer brings us nearer to the knowledge of divine wisdom. May the wisdom, knowledge, and understanding be in your soul and when you have found them, there will be a great reward, and your expectations will not be cut off. May God bless you abundantly!

SUCCESS VOW

Taken from Napoleon Hill's Book
Think and Grow Rich

I know that I have the ability to achieve the object of my definite purpose in life, therefore I demand of myself persistent, continuous action towards its attainment. I realize that the dominating thoughts of my mind will eventually reproduce themselves into outward, physical action, and gradually manifest themselves into physical reality; therefore, I will concentrate my thoughts daily upon the task of thinking of the person that I intend to become, thereby creating in my mind, a clear mental picture.

I will devote time daily to demanding of myself the development of self-confidence, and I will never stop trying until I feel that I have developed sufficient self-confidence for the attainment of my purpose.

I will succeed by attracting to myself the forces I wish to use, and the cooperation of other people. I will induce others to serve me because of my willingness to serve others. I will eliminate hatred, envy, jealousy, selfishness, grudge holding, anger, and cynicism by developing love for all humanity because I know that a negative attitude towards others will never bring me success. I will cause others to believe in me because I will believe in them and in myself. I can do all things through Christ who strengthens me.

-Napoleon Hill

About the Author

Dr. Mia Y. Merritt is a single, divorced mother of one son. She was born and raised in Miami, Florida and matriculated in the Miami-Dade County Public School System. She is an Assistant Principal, College Instructor, Motivational Consultant, and Author. She accepted Christ as her Lord and Savior at an early age, but developed an intimate relationship with Him in her late twenties. Her Christian walk has not been easy, in fact, it has been a struggle, but she walks by Faith. Her challenges and experiences in life prompted her to write this book. Through the book, she shares the trials, tribulations, hardships, and difficulties that have strengthened her character and made her a stronger person. Writing this book was a part of her healing. She knows that there will be more tests and temptations, but feels that she is strong enough to handle them with the help of God.

I thank you for taking the time to read my book. I pray that you have understood how my hardships and difficulties have made me a stronger person and have drawn me closer to God. But most importantly, I hope that you understand that you too, posses the inner strength and tenacity to overcome every obstacle in your life that will draw you closer to greatness.

You were created to praise and worship, and when you consciously decide to worship God, He will guide your steps so that you will walk on the path that has been predestined for you. Find your purpose and you will find fulfillment in this life. You are never alone. You are very precious in His sight. He wants you to live an abundant life full of success, prosperity, love, peace, and joy. With God, all things are possible. Just believe and receive.

Mia

Yearly Goals

Name _____

SPIRITUAL GOALS

1. _____
2. _____
3. _____
4. _____
5. _____

FINANCIAL GOALS

1. _____
2. _____
3. _____
4. _____
5. _____

HEALTH GOALS

1. _____
2. _____
3. _____

4. _____
5. _____

PERSONAL GOALS

1. _____
2. _____
3. _____
4. _____
5. _____

EDUCATIONAL GOALS

1. _____
2. _____
3. _____

RECREATIONAL/FAMILY GOALS

1. _____
2. _____
3. _____
4. _____
5. _____

CAREER/WORK GOALS

1. _____
2. _____
3. _____
4. _____
5. _____

Weekly Goals Form

(Taken from Yearly Goals)

_____Goals _____Accomplished _____Not Accomplished

Spiritual
1. _____
2. _____
3. _____

Financial
1. _____
2. _____
3. _____

Educational
1. _____
2. _____
3. _____

Health
1. _____
2. _____
3. _____

Family

1. _____
2. _____
3. _____

Personal

1. _____
2. _____
3. _____

Prayer List

1. _____
2. _____
3. _____

BOOKS TO READ

1. _____
2. _____
3. _____

ACT OF KINDNESS

_____
_____
_____

Books That Have Inspired Me

10 Spiritual Principles of Success Women *Victoria Lowe*

Acres of Diamonds *Russell Conwell*

As a Man Thinketh *James Allen*

Battlefield of the Mind *Joyce Meyers*

God Chasers *Tommy Tenney*

Greatest Salesman in the World Part I *Og Mandino*

Greatest Salesman in the World Part II *Og Mandino*

How to win Friends and Influence People *Dale Carnegie*

Invest in Yourself Dr. *Marthenia Dupree*

Live Your Dreams *Les Brown*

Love and Law *Ernest Holmes*

Matters of the Heart *Juanita Bynum, Ph.D*

Success *Glenn Bland*

The Lady, her Lover, and her Lord *T. D. Jakes*

The Magic of Believing *Claude Bristol*

The Magic of Thinking Big *David Schwartz*

The Master Key System *Charles Haanal*

The Prayer of Jabez *Bruce Wilkinson*

The Secret of the Ages *Robert Collier*

Think & Grow Rich *Napoleon Hill*

Remember that you are:

Destined for Great Things!

www.destinedforgreatthings.com

Words of Inspiration

Golden Nuggets for the Wise at Heart

Quotes by:

Dr. Mia Y. Merritt

Taken from the book
PROSPERITY IS YOUR BIRTHRIGHT!

Copyright © 2010
by Mia Y. Merritt, Ed.D
WORDS OF INSPIRATION
Spiritual Nuggets for the
Wise at Heart

All biblical references/scriptures are
taken from the
King James Version of the Bible

ISBN # 978-0-9720398-5-7

First Printing June 2010

Merritt, Mia Y.

Printed in the U.S.A.

Other Books by Mia Y. Merritt:
Destined for Great Things!
Destined for Great Things Workbook
Prosperity is Your Birthright!
Prosperity is Your Birthright Workbook

FOREWORD

You are only given one life and the way you play the game of life determines your successes and failures, ups and downs, good and evil and joy and sadness. Remember that the application of certain laws and principles will help this game called life get played with a winner's attitude.

Remembering some of these quotes and implementing them will put you ahead of the game that will lead you down the road that leads to happiness, peace, prosperity, and wealth.

Enjoy these quotes and live life to the fullest. You only have one!

ABUNDANCE

There is plenty in the world for everyone. Just look around and notice the profusion everywhere. Look at the number of trees in the world, the amount of sand on the seashore, the quantity of water in the ocean, the number of fish in the sea, the amount of animals on the land, and the vast amount of plants and flowers everywhere. There is enough of everything for you too!

There is more than enough of everything in this world. Things are always being replenished and always will be. Man has been taken care of from the beginning of creation until the present age. There is never a limit of anything.

ASSOCIATIONS

Great people hang around great people, attract great things and exude great confidence. Show me the kind of people you hang out with and I will tell you the kind of person you really are. It is better to be alone than in the wrong company.

You become like those with whom you associate. Those who don't increase you will eventually decrease you. Wise is the person who enhances his life with the right friendships.

If you show me the caliber of friends you have, I can tell you a lot about the kind of person you are. You must be watchful of the people you choose to make your friends. They will either help or hinder you as a person. Your friends will enhance or take away from your image and quality. Birds of a feather do flock together.

ATTITUDE

Maintaining a positive attitude is about choices in emotional responses. People with this ability choose their focus instead of allowing circumstances to dictate their focus. They tend to remain in a rational state of mind, and make the most of whatever life offers them. These individuals know how to seize the day and create good memories by projecting a positive future.

Our attitudes must be positive regardless of what we may be thinking, feeling, or what circumstances we may be facing. Attitudes parallel with what is in the mind, and attitudes do reflect thinking.

ATTRACTION

Positive thinking and positive speaking is a sure way to attract goodness into your life.

Focus your mind on things that make for greatness and notice how you will begin to attract all that is desired through your laser sharp focus.

Whatever is being sent out from your thought world is what attracts things, people and situations to you.

You attract what you talk about. When you change your conversation to reflect positive things, you change your conditions, your situations and your reality. The more specific you are when speaking positive, the quicker the manifestation, the greater you feel, the more powerful the materialization. You decree your life one word at a time. Specific statements produce specific results.

We are all made of energy and are always giving off a certain kind of vibration that magnetizes people and situations to us.

When you are truly ready to rise to greatness, you will begin to attract all sort of wonderful, influential, wealthy, and prosperous people into your life who will help you get where you desire to go. Do you want to know what kind of "vibe" you are sending out? Look at the people and situations around you.

BALANCE

Some would not agree that money is necessary to be happy, but it is a fact that a sufficient amount of money is needed for effective living. All must agree that health is a necessity because how can you be happy and at peace if your body is in pain? Most would say that love is the most important of them all, but in my opinion, all three: money, health, and love are absolutely necessary for happiness, peace and balance.

Many Christians have an imbalanced spiritual life, which often leads to frustration and confusion. This is because they are connected to the body of Christ only, the Head of Christ only, or neither. There is a disconnect. There must be a balanced connection between the two.

Keeping a balanced life is essential to walking in prosperity. The mind, body, and spirit must be adequately nourished. An excess in any one area causes a deficiency in another.

BEHAVIOR

Always let your light shine. Someone is always watching you. Be sure that what they see coming from you is light and not darkness. You could just be having a bad day, but that one bad day could leave a lasting impact on someone's life in a negative way. Train your mind to think positively, and as you think on positive things, you act in positive ways, even on bad days.

Watch your actions and reactions at all times. Your actions and reactions reveal what is inside of you. People respond to your actions more than they respond to your words. If the reaction is worse than the action, then the problem usually gets bigger, but if the reaction is less than the action, the problem usually gets smaller.

Once a person behaves in a foolish, outlandish, out-of-control manner, that image can not be taken out of the minds of those who witnessed that behavior, no matter how many times an apology is given. To be ill-mannered is to be unlearned and unwise.

BEING POOR

Some have the false belief that being poor is walking in humility and serving God to the fullest. Jesus said, "I am come that they might have life more abundantly."

When you are wealthy, you are in a better position to serve God and bless others. How much can you bless others if you are broke? Being poor is not the will of God for your life. Remember that!

BELIEF

The size of your belief determines the size of your accomplishments.

Faith is the key that expands your belief.

Your faith that your desire will be accomplished is the power of belief that will bring it to you.

You must always believe that you have received even before you have physically received what you desire.

You manifest what you believe.

CAUSE & EFFECT

There is never a cause without an effect nor an effect without a cause. There will never be one without the other. If the cause is good, the effect will be good. If the cause is bad, the effect will be bad.

When you act, you are initiating a cause. The law will bring the effect. The law has no motive. It is a blind, powerful force that simply acts upon what has been initiated.

The thoughts and pictures you see in your mind are causes and the experiences that you encounter are the effects. If your thoughts are peaceful, harmonious, constructive, and positive, the effect shall be good. If your thoughts are destructive, discordant and negative, the effect shall be evil.

CHARACTER

You never know what's inside a person until they are squeezed. If you squeeze a lemon, you will get lemon juice. If you squeeze an orange, you will get orange juice. When life puts the squeeze on you, what is going to come out? If there is cursing in you, then cursing will come out. If evil, then it will come out. If praise and worship is in you, then no matter what happens, you will praise Him through it all.

What you do when no one is looking is the true test of character.

CHILDREN

Children are gifts from God, given to adults to teach them how to take care of the world and the people in it in order to keep creation moving forward harmoniously.

We can create monsters through children or develop great men and women while raising them. They feed off of their environment and they become like those they see and hear on a daily basis.

Children are like long-term investments. In time, you will reap the benefits of what you have invested in them or get back the results of neglecting to invest in them.

Children need the same things that adults need: to feel loved, to be able to give love, to feel safe and secure, accepted, appreciated, and respected.

COMPETITIVENESS

When you refuse to share what you have or what you know, you are operating in a competitive spirit.

We must learn to share what we have. When God blesses you with knowledge, gifts, money or material possessions, they are to be shared with others, not to keep to yourself. You will never keep anything for long if you hoard them.

CONCENTRATION

Concentration and self-discipline are the sacrifices that you make in order to receive the desires of your heart.

Concentration on your desired goal is what freezes it into your mind until it manifests into the earth realm.

When you focus on the task at hand, you do that task in a spirit of excellence.

When you are working on a project, but your concentration is divided, your efforts will reflect a half-finished, mediocre result. Always concentrate wholly on what you are doing at that moment.

It is those who concentrate on but one task at a time who advance and progress in this world.

CONFIDENCE

With confidence, you pursue your goals and dreams with boldness. With confidence, you tackle life's challenges with the faith that you will always be victorious in the end.

Confident people "believe" that they are important and they know that their lives matter, therefore they face challenges with boldness and faith.

Having confidence in yourself is not being arrogant. It is being self-assured in your potential and your abilities.

True confidence comes from knowing that you are worthy and deserving of the things you seek and through self-reliance, you pursue those things with faith.

Confidence depends on the type of thoughts you habitually allow to occupy your mind. If your thoughts are dwelling on your self-worth, your abilities, and your potential, then your confidence level will increase.

DESTINY

Until you understand your true destiny, you will be walking in a false destiny. Your true destiny is to manifest your gifts, talents and abilities in the earth through serving.

You were made by God for God. It is only in Him that you discover your purpose, your meaning, your destiny.

God will show you the path to your destiny, but He will not force you to walk it. You must choose to walk that path. You have free choice to walk on the path leading to your destiny or you can take another path leading to uncertainty.

Your destiny is in line with your purpose in life. Your purpose will lead you to your destiny.

When you seek the face and guidance of God, He will show you your destiny as well as the people, situations and circumstances that are not in line with your destiny. It is up to you to remove yourself away from those hindrances.

EDUCATION

Educate yourself. It does not matter whether you do it by way of the classroom or by way of self-knowledge.

You never stop learning. Education should be an ongoing continuous process for every person. Continuous learning stimulates your mind and enhances you as a person.

The application of an education will get you much farther than an education that is not being used.

A college degree is definitely an asset and advantage, but not having one should never be used as an excuse for a person's lot in life or justification for poverty or lack.

EXCELLENCE

An excellent spirit clearly means working with pride, optimism, precision, and focus in all one does.

One who has a spirit of excellence does everything to the best of his or her ability whether others are watching or not.

When you are committed to a project, focus diligently on it in a spirit of excellence to ensure that the end result has quality, is accurate, meaningful, and fully complete.

Only God can give you an excellent spirit and it comes by spending time with Him.

EXPECTATION

You must live in a state of expectancy, knowing that good things are continuously flowing into your life.

When you are expecting good things to arrive, you must make room in your conscientiousness to receive them so that you may properly place them where they belong in your life when they arrive.

Hope and expectation are positive feelings and as your mind resonates on those feelings, you attract the essence of what you feel back to you.

When you expect the best, you get the best.

FAITH

Faith is the key that expands your belief.

Without faith it is impossible to accomplish anything meaningful. In order to please God, you must have faith.

Faith is the unwavering belief that you will have whatever you are desiring to have.

FEAR

Do not allow thoughts of doubt and fear to enter the field where you have planted your seeds of success and prosperity.

You attract what you fear. Therefore you must overcome your fears!

Self-hatred, fear, guilt, shame, and unforgiveness block you from moving forward.
When there is doubt and fear, you attract people who will do things causing you to continue doubting people and fearing the worse.

FOLLOW-THROUGH

You must finish what you start. I don't care if the planets fall! If you are in a healthy state of mind and body, you must finish what you have started until it is fully and accurately completed. I once heard the following quote: *"If a task is once begun, never leave it til it's done; Be the labor great or small, do it well or not at all."* (author unknown)

Many people start multiple tasks and do not finish any of them. Their projects are worthy, have merit, and the ideas great, but without completing them, the world will never know of the benefits that the completed projects would have had on society.

When you start something and do not follow through until it's completed, you have formed the habit of failure and your subconscious mind gets into the habit of never allowing you to complete anything. Always finish what you start. This is the beginning of greatness.

Decide on your goals and hold them constantly in your thoughts until they have been effectively achieved.

The smallest task well done becomes a stepping stone to greater prosperity.

FORGIVENESS

Let us forgive as God has forgiven us.

When you cannot forgive yourself, you certainly cannot forgive others.

Forgiveness is not a feeling. It is a decision.

It is time for you to also forgive yourself, love yourself, and move forward with confidence in yourself.

When God asks you to forgive others, He understands that there may not be instant reconciliation with the person who has hurt you.

Forgiveness is one-way and does not require the other person's response in order to forgive them.

Forgiveness is a personal decision on the part of the victim regardless of the offender's behavior. Reconciliation requires a change in the offender's behavior, but forgiveness requires nothing at all from the offender.

Always forgive. No matter what has been done to you, forgive.

FRIENDSHIPS

The world loves you, puts you on a pedestal and praises you when you are up, but they also kick you, ridicule and criticize you when you are down. True friends love you at all times, not just when you are on top of the world.

There is a need for discernment when it comes to people that you allow into your inner circle of friends. Genuine friends are very rare and you must use discernment to know who is truly sincere with no motives.

Acquaintances and associates come a dime a dozen, but true friends will be there when everybody else is gone.

FUTURE

Your future is determined by the diligence, hard work, and effort that you put into the present moment. Create a delightful future by living fully in the present.

It is wise to prepare for the future, but do not get caught up in the future so much that you lose the momentum of the present. Always live fully in the present moment.

GIFTS

God has placed gifts, talents and abilities inside every one and He wants to see them used to their greatest potential. You must use your gifts to bless the world and in return bring supplemental income for yourself. God has given you the abilities to do what you love. Now use your gifts!

God wants hands to play harmonious music, draw gorgeous pictures, and build magnificent buildings for Him. He wants eyes to behold His beautiful creations and to experience His miracles. He wants feet to dance for Him and run His errands. He must express Himself through you.

There is more than enough room for you and your talents, but you must compel that room.

The world is sometimes cruel to individuals who do not make room for their gifts. Whatever your decision may be concerning the strengthening of your gifts, that decision must be made right now. Your gifts must be expressed in the earth while you now live, otherwise they will die with them inside you never having been expressed and never again having the opportunity for you to express them.

> When you expect the best, you get the best.

Your gift is given to you to be exercised to the greatest potential. If you have a gift for encouraging people and lifting their spirits, then you need to do this every opportunity you get. If someone calls you at two o'clock in the morning, you need to wake up and use your gift of encouragement to make them feel better. With practice, every talent gets better and grows stronger.

GOAL-SETTING

Do you have goals for your life? Are they written down? It is extremely important that you begin to strategically plan out your life in a courageous manner and execute your goals fearlessly.

Recognize yourself as a person worthy of accomplishing great things through goal-setting and strategic planning.

When you develop goals, you are actually planning how you want your life to unfold in terms of what you want to see manifested.

Setting goals helps you to visualize clearly what it is that you aspire to do, have, or be, but seeing them written also motivates you and strengthens that power within you that causes those goals to come into fruition.

GOD'S WILL

Living in God's permissive will is not always for your ultimate good, but because you have free will and self-choice, He allows you to live in that will for a while until you become wise enough to ask for his perfect will.

When you pray for God's *perfect* will to be done in your life, He guides you and detours you from things that are not in line with His divine plan for you. He removes people and situations in your life that are unfruitful, He uproots you from places and circumstances that are contrary to your

divine purpose, He leads you to where your destiny can be fulfilled, and He begins to reveal your purpose to you.

GRATITUDE

There is always something to be grateful for. When you give thanks for everything, you open a floodgate of blessings that come pouring toward you. You place yourself on a current that draws good things your way.

GUILT

Guilt is a negative emotion that will rob you of fulfilling your true destiny because it makes you feel that you are not worthy of anything good.

Take any guilt that you have, give it to the Lord and then leave it there. Guilt is a poison that will manifest into your body in the form of disease and will eventually kill you if you let it. You must learn to release yourself from all destructive emotions such as guilt. The siblings of guilt are shame, unforgiveness, and bitterness.

GREATNESS

Greatness is measured by service not status. When you do all things in a spirit of service and go over and beyond that which you are required to do, you are on the path that leads to greatness.

HAPPINESS

Is money the key to happiness? Financial happiness is a temporary thing. Once you have bought all the material things your heart desires, are you truly happy?

We are spiritual beings and material things can not satisfy the spirit within us. Only the spirit of God can satisfy the spirit in humanity. We make many mistakes when we think that financial independence equates to happiness.

Many people think they should seek happiness, but joy is much more fulfilling. Happiness is dependant upon the "happenings" whereas joy is an internal deeper feeling that remains no matter what the circumstances are.

HARD WORK

When we see powerful manifestations appear in other people's lives, never forget that no big achievement came easy. There is always hard work, labor, some sleepless nights, a few failures, some disappointments, hurts, and obstacles behind those successes. After persistence comes success.

Going over and beyond and never doing less than your best is a habit that will bring great rewards to the consistent soul who works in this manner. Hard mental work is always rewarded.

Continue to go over and beyond the call of duty. You will see how the law of compensation will reward far in excess to the consistent hard work that you have put in.

HUMILITY

Humility is one of the greatest personality traits that one can have. The humble person never tries to be in the spotlight. He or she does good deeds without needing to be noticed. This person is rewarded by God Himself.

The world says, "The greatest among you should be served." God says, "The greatest among you should be your servant (Mathew 23:11). If you stay at the feet of Jesus, you will remain humble.

If you stay humble, you won't get caught up in the glory and pride of the world.

Knowing how to remain humble and keep a level head at all times will maintain your self-control and peace of mind.

"I AM"

When you say, "I am" you are confessing God's nature in you. When God told Moses that His name was "I am," He was telling Moses that He is everything Moses needed Him to be. God says, I am your strength, healer, comforter, deliver, guide, light, counselor, rock, fortress, lover of your soul. He is everything you need Him to be!

When you say, "I am," make sure that whatever comes behind that "I am" is good, because you are affirming God's nature and He is ALL GOOD.

Never say, "I am" miserable, unhappy, tired, broke, discouraged, sick, depressed, frustrated, inadequate, etc. God is none of those things, but He is, "I am" and so are you.

INTEGRITY

Do not compromise your integrity. Hold on to your morals. Always be ethical and remain honest.

With time, a person's integrity builds back up again if they consistently strive towards doing right and becoming right.

Integrity guides a person to give out good will towards every soul they meet.

When you let integrity guide your actions, it is difficult to walk contrary to God's will.

JUDGING

If you dislike something about a person, it is because that which you hate in them is a part of yourself. What isn't a part of you does not bother you.

Before you decide to open your mouth to criticize, judge and ridicule others, remember your own faults, vices, and shameful deeds.

KNOWLEDGE

If knowledge is applied and guided strategically, it leads one to successful achievements.

Knowledge is only latent power if not used. Knowledge acquired must be used for personal growth and development or it is useless.

Having knowledge of the Word without the Spirit of the Word is ineffective.

LOVE

Love is the strongest force in the universe. It is God in manifestation when expressed.

If we look at all people and things with love, we become renewed.

Genuine love is unselfish and free from fear. Its joy is in the joy of giving.

There is perfect peace, courage, and power in love.

If you are committed to walking in love, speaking in love, and encountering others with love, then when facing difficult people, the spirit of love in you will break down their hard exteriors and penetrate to the goodness inside them, causing them to love in return.

MAKING MONEY

People who make excuses don't make money and people who make money don't make excuses. If you really want to make money honestly, you'll find a way.

When you work with your hands, you get the salary that is set by your employer. When you work with your mind, you set your own salary. A salary means the same thing as "allowance" which allows you to make only the money that others have set for you to make.

When you work your mind, there is no limit to the money that you can make because you set the limit. There is no allowance except for the allowance that you put on yourself.

If working with your hands could make you rich, then every construction worker in the world would be a millionaire.

Set the amount that you want to make in life, then use your mind to create and originate in order for you to receive the wage that you have set for yourself.

MANNERS

Good manners are the sugar to which people attract themselves to you. A smile enhances your beauty and attractiveness. A pleasant attitude magnetizes others to you.

To be rude and impolite is to be unwise. Rudeness is the outward expression of inward deficiencies. A person is what he or she does.

Good manners, a pleasant attitude with no money will get you much farther in life than ill-manners, a nasty attitude and plenty of money.

MANIFESTING

Our duty on this earth is to manifest. Your duty as a human being is to be a creator through God's spirit, then manifest things on the earth. MAN-IFEST. Notice the word begins with "man". You must manifest your goals, your desires, your dreams!

You must be very careful of what you say when experiencing strong emotions. The manifestation could be instantaneous.

MEDITATION

Successful people tap into their creative powers through being alone in the silence, which is where all the power is. Managed solitude pays off. When the mind is peaceful and still, it taps into the greater good and the higher self.

It is vital that those who desire to tap into their power spend considerable time alone with nothing but their own thoughts.

Many people fail to arrive at practical solutions to their problems because they confer with everybody else except themselves. If they only communed with themselves in the silence, they would clearly receive the answers they seek.

Meditation requires strict self-discipline and sacrifice. It is a healing, soothing, healthy practice.

MOODS

One of the mysteries of life is that we sometimes go to sleep feeling just fine, but then wake up in a horrible mood the next morning, not understanding why. These are days of testing to see just how you will handle your mood.

When you learn how to change your action regardless of how you feel, you change your mood. Never allow your moods to control you. Become a master of your emotions!

NAMING

When you call something by name it comes closer to you. When someone calls your name, don't you respond? What do you want? Prosperity, wealth, health, success? Call it forth by name. Affirm it and claim it everyday!

PAST

If you allow yourself to live in past regrets, guilt, shame and remorse, you will never fully live in the present.

Living in the past will not change one thing that happened there. All you can do is live your best in the present so that the negativity and hurt from the past will fade away.

You are continuing to make a past for yourself as each day goes by. Live in the present moment so that when you do look back, all you can see is the beauty of your past.

Leave the past in the past.

PATIENCE

We live in a microwave, fast-paced world. Everybody wants instant results and immediate solutions to problems, but nature teaches that things must take time. Some things just can not be rushed.

Even when you know that you have been called to do a specific task, there is a season for when you are to step into the position.
The time between the calling and the actual commission is an essential time of preparation.

There is a time and a season for everything. Have patience and wait for your season before you step out into your role. Stepping out before the appointed time may obstruct God's plan for your life.

PERCEPTION

Things are not always what they appear to be. Things may look one way in the natural but could have a totally different outcome working in the spirit. Trust in faith and look to God for answers. He has the last say so. Your destiny is always in His hands when you place it there with faith and assurance.

Be open-minded enough to realize that just because you see things a certain way does not mean that is the way it really is. Understand that everyone sees things differently. You are not always right and everyone else is not always wrong.

PLANNING

Planning ahead is a major attribute of wealthy, successful, organized, productive people of the world. It requires commitment and has many benefits.

When you develop goals, you are actually planning how you want your life to unfold in terms of what you want to see manifested.

PRAISE

God is not a respecter of persons, but He does give favor to those who praise and worship Him.

God desires your praise & worship, so give to Him what He desires. Praise is due unto His holy name. He is your maker and creator and will never leave you nor forsake you. God will be with you always.

If praise and worship is in you, then no matter what happens, you will praise and worship Him in and through all things.

When you are connected to Christ the Head, you have a strong prayer life, a consistent praise and worship life, constant time for study, and a designated time for fasting with the Lord.

PRAYER
Your prayers do make a difference

Prayer should be the foundation upon which every aspect of your life is predicated upon.

Prayer is keeping the lines of communication open to God, casting all your cares upon Him, praising and honoring Him, and confessing your offenses to Him.

Many are malnourished in their soul because of deprivation of prayer.

God hears you because He listens to your heart. When your prayers come deeply out of your heart, they go directly into His ears.

You must have a lifestyle of prayer.

PRESENT

You must start living in the present moment. Now is all you have. Tomorrow is not promised. Do the very best you can in "this" moment.
The future is not guaranteed and the past is gone. It is time to start living in the present.

There is great power in speaking in the present tense. The present means having what you need right now and things are happening right now. When you speak in the future, you are always waiting for an arrival, but the present means you already have what you need.

We should never take away from our present by worrying about the future or crying over the past. Live in the present moment.

PREPARATION

If you ask for, pray for, desire for and meditate for success, but you subconsciously prepare for failure, you will get what you "prepare" for.

You must prepare for the thing that you have envisioned when there isn't any sign of it in sight. Keep in mind that everything has two creations: a spiritual creation (first), then the physical manifestation (last).

In order to prepare for something, you must make room for its arrival. If there is no room for it in your life, then it will not come because preparation has not been made.

PROSPERITY

Prosperity is a mindset.

Abundant prosperity is waiting to break forth in your life in a mighty and powerful way!

Prosperity most often does encompass money, but it also includes peace, good health, affluence, love, joy, happiness, and abundance.

You do not hinder or offend another person when you live in prosperity. If prosperity is the result of your own sacrifice, hard-work, and commitment to your vision, then you owe no-one an apology for what you legitimately earned. Enjoy the fruit of your own labor.

SELF-CONTROL

Practice self-control and good manners.

Self-control is the evidence of ripened experience and a knowledge of the correct use of positive thinking.

It is not always easy to be calm and positive in stressful or frustrating situations, but if you will exercise self-discipline, you will see how it will work out much better for you in the end.

SERVICE

Money comes as a result of the degree of service you render.

This is why you exist – to contribute, to serve, to give of yourself, to reach towards your highest good, and to make a difference in the world.

When you begin to share your gifts with the world with the intention to serve, you will receive far in excess to what you give.

SOWING & REAPING

Life is about cause and effect, sowing and reaping, going around and coming back around. No one is exempt from this.

You can not sow hatred, discord, conflict, and dissension and get back love, peace, happiness and harmony. You have no right to reap what you have not sown.

We must learn to stop judging by outward appearances of things and sow our own seeds of goodness, hard work and labor so that when the time arrives, our "harvest" will come in full bloom with no weeds.

SPIRITUAL AUTHORITY

You walk with power and authority within you.

When you walk in spiritual authority, external circumstances no longer dictate your actions, but you control your circumstances exactly the way you want them to be.

You have total power and authority over your environment and ultimately your destiny.

SUCCESS

Many people believe that you are successful if you earn a lot of money. The truth is that you can only earn money "after" you are already a success.

Success is not the result of making money. Making money is the result of being successful. The majority of the world has it backwards. How can a failure make money? You must be successful at what you do first, then the money will come.

You can not let your accomplishments from yesterday be sufficient for your commitments of today. Celebrate yesterday's successes, but strive towards higher and greater successes.

Success comes as a result of achieving high goals that you have set to their fullest potential and then reaping the benefits from the hard work and effort that you put into those goals.

VIBRATIONS

Attract extraordinary people to you by sending out the vibration that you are an extraordinary, influential, and great person.

When you freeze the images of what you desire within your thoughts and hold them there, your subconscious mind begins to pick up the vibration of the embodiment of the thing and creates the environment that manifests what you are envisioning.

TALENTS

Once you start using your main God-given talent, a domino effect begins to follow and you begin expressing other talents you never knew you had.
The key is to take your particular talent to a level where it has never been taken before.

You will discover that after using your talent, God has doubled it. Find a way to use all your talents for His Honor and your benefit.

THE POWER OF WORDS

The word that you release from your mouth determines your successes or failures. You are to speak only what you choose to see happening in your life.

Your words contain the power to kill or heal, bless or curse, tear down or build up, create or destroy. Your life is shaped by the predominant thoughts you entertain and the words you speak. Your own words shape your world and everything in it.

THE TWO BIRTHS

Just because you don't see your desires manifested in the physical realm does not mean they aren't manifested in the spiritual realm. Everything has two births, the spiritual then the physical. It is up to you to pull your vision out of the spirit into the physical. Focused attention, writing things down and meditating makes the manifestation quicker. Keep holding the vision in your mind until it comes into fruition. That's what you do.

THOUGHT

You are changing everyday and as your thoughts change for the better, your life changes for the better. Thoughts bear fruit and when your thoughts are good, the fruit of your life is good.

Your achievements today are the culmination of your thoughts from yesterday.

It is imperative that you become consciously aware of the thoughts, imaginations, and visions that you entertain on a daily basis because what you think about today shall become the reality that you shall experience tomorrow.

The thoughts that you entertain determines your mental attitude. If your thoughts are negative, you will exude a negative disposition and the words that you speak will be negative, thus attracting negativity to you. If your thoughts are positive, then your conversation will be of a positive nature, thus attracting good to you.

If your thoughts are peaceful, harmonious, constructive, and positive, the manifestations shall be good. If your thoughts are destructive, discordant and negative, the manifestations shall be bad.

Be careful of the thoughts you allow to spring up in your mind. If they are of an unpleasant nature, dismiss them immediately and replace them with thoughts of a more positive and productive nature.

All thought is creative according to the strength, power, conviction and vitality of the thought.

The quality of your thought is the measure of your power.

The thoughts you think and the images you focus on consciously or unconsciously bring to you certain kind of people, who bring certain kind of circumstances, which make the conditions you meet in life.

Negative, self-defeating thoughts minimizes your self-worth.

UNDERSTANDING PEOPLE

You must learn the art of listening, studying, and understanding people while making allowances for his or her ignorance relating to people.

If you treat others as God's children, you would never have to worry about being offensive to anyone.

Despite how others treat you, you are to respond with calmness and dignity. You must learn the art of listening, studying, and understanding people.

VISION

There is a resurgence of taking on the world that overpowers you once you see your vision clearly in your mind's eye.

Your thoughts, words and visions are magnets that attract things that are of the same nature of your thought.

WISDOM

There is a difference between common sense and wisdom. Having common sense means understanding things from a reasonable point of view. It is knowing what is politically correct to do and say.

With wisdom comes poise, calmness, and the power to dwell upon all that is pure, unselfish and right. Those with wisdom know how to think the right thoughts and avoids the pitfalls and troubles that accompany wrong thinking.
A person who has true spiritual wisdom also has integrity because wisdom guides a person by integrity.

We often expect wisdom to come with age, but the sad reality is that age sometimes comes alone.

Wisdom is the greatest desire that one should aspire to posses. If a person has wisdom, all other good things follow.

WORSHIP

When you lift up your hands to worship God, you usher in His presence and He comes and sits in the midst of your worship.

God placed inside of you the desire to worship. If you don't worship Him, you will worship something or someone else.

When we worship God, we tell Him that we adore, reverence and love Him. He is worthy to be worshipped.

WRITING

Understand the power of writing. When you put pen to paper to write down your dreams, goals and plans in detail, you pull the vision out of the spiritual into the physical and make it real. The manifestation then comes quicker but work is still required.

Writing crystallizes your vision and brings it out of the invisible world into the visible world.

Golden Nuggets for the Wise at Heart

From the Word of God Himself

Taken from the Original King James Version of The Bible

ABUNDANCE
(John 10:10)
The thief cometh not, but for to steal, and to kill, and to destroy: I am come that they might have life, and that they might have it more abundantly.

ASSOCIATIONS
(1 Corinthians 15:33)
Be not deceived: evil communications corrupt good manners.

BALANCE
(James 1:8)
A double minded man is unstable in all his ways.

BEHAVIOR
(1 Timothy 4:12)
Let no man despise thy youth; but be thou an example of the believers, in word, in conversation, in charity, in spirit, in faith, in purity.

BEING POOR
(Proverbs 10:4)
He becometh poor that dealeth with a slack hand: but the hand of the diligent maketh rich.

(Deuteronomy 15:11)
For the poor shall never cease out of the land: therefore I command thee, saying, Thou shalt open thine hand wide unto thy brother, to thy poor, and to thy needy, in thy land.

BELIEF
(Mark 11:24)
Therefore I say unto you, what things ye desire, when ye pray, believe that ye receive them, and ye shall have them.

CAUSE & EFFECT
(Galatians 6:7)
Be not deceived; God is not mocked: for whatsoever a man soweth, that shall he also reap.

CHARACTER
(Mathew 12:35)
A good man out of the good treasure of the heart bringeth forth good things: and an evil man out of the evil treasure bringeth forth evil things.

CONFIDENCE
(1 Philippians 1:6)
Being confident of this, that He who began a good work in you will carry it on to completion until the day of Christ Jesus.

DESTINY
(1 Corinthians 2:9)
But as it is written, Eye hath not seen, nor ear heard, neither have entered into the heart of man, the things which God hath prepared for them that love him.

EXCELLENCE
(Proverbs 17:27)
He that hath knowledge spareth his words: and a man of understanding is of an excellent spirit.

(Proverbs 12:26)
The righteous is more excellent than his neighbor: but the way of the wicked seduceth them.

EXPECTATION
(Psalm 9:18)
For the needy shall not always be forgotten: the expectation of the poor shall not perish for ever.

(Psalm 62:5)
My soul, wait thou only upon God; for my expectation is from him.

FAITH
(Hebrews 11:1)
Now faith is the substance of things hoped for, the evidence of things not seen.

FEAR
(2 Timothy 1:7)
For God hath not given us the spirit of fear; but of power, and of love, and of a sound mind.

FORGIVENESS
(Mark 11:25)
And when ye stand praying, forgive, if ye have ought against any: that your Father also which is in heaven may forgive you your trespasses.

FRIENDSHIPS
(Proverbs 17:17)
A friend loveth at all times, and a brother is born for adversity.

GIFTS
(2nd Timothy 1:16)
Stir up the gift of God, which is in thee by the putting on of my hands.

(Psalm 50:14)
Offer unto God thanksgiving; and pay thy vows unto the most High.

GOAL-SETTING
(Proverbs 26)
Ponder the path of thy feet, and let all thy ways be established.

GREATNESS
(Genesis 12:2)
And I will make of thee a great nation, and I will bless thee,
and make thy name great; and thou shalt be a blessing:

GUILT
(Romans 6:21)
What fruit had ye then in those things whereof ye are now ashamed?
for the end of those things is death.

HAPPINESS
(Job 5:7)
Behold, happy is the man whom God correcteth: therefore
despise not thou the chastening of the Almighty:

HARD WORK
(Proverbs 13:4)
The soul of the sluggard desireth, and hath nothing:
but the soul of the diligent shall be made fat.

HUMILITY
(Luke 14:11)
For whosoever exalteth himself shall be abased;
and he that humbleth himself shall be exalted.

"I AM"
(Exodus 3:14)
And God said unto Moses, I AM THAT I AM: and he said,
Thus shalt thou say unto the children of Israel,
I AM hath sent me unto you.

INTEGRITY
(Proverbs 11:13)
The integrity of the upright shall guide them:
but the perverseness of transgressors shall destroy them.

JUDGING
(Mathew 7:1)
Judge not, that you be not judged.

KNOWLEDGE
(Proverbs 1:7)
The fear of the Lord is the beginning of knowledge: but fools despise wisdom and instruction.

LOVE
(Proverbs 10:12)
Hatred stirreth up strifes: but love covereth all sins.

(Luke 10:27)
Love the Lord your God with all your heart and with all your soul and with all your strength and with all your mind ; and, Love your neighbor as yourself.

MAKING MONEY
(1 Timothy 6:10)
For the love of money is the root of all evil: which while some coveted after, they have erred from the faith, and pierced themselves through with many sorrows.

MANIFEST
(Luke 8:17)
For nothing is secret, that shall not be made manifest; neither any thing hid, that shall not be known and come abroad.

MEDITATION
(Psalm 104:34)
My meditation of him shall be sweet: I will be glad in the LORD.

MOODS
(James 1:8)
A double minded man is unstable in all his ways.

NAME
(Genesis 3:20)
And Adam called his wife's name Eve; because she was the mother of all living.

PAST
(Ecclesiastes 3:15)
That which hath been is now; and that which is to be hath already been; and God requireth that which is past.

PATIENCE
(James 5:10)
Take, my brethren, the prophets, who have spoken in the name of the Lord, for an example of suffering affliction, and of patience.

PLANNING
(Proverbs 6:6; 30:25)
Go to the ant, thou sluggard; consider her ways, and be wise: The ants are a people not strong, yet they prepare their meat in the summer.

PRAISE
(Psalm 150:6)
Let every thing that hath breath praise the Lord. Praise ye the Lord.

PRAYER
(James 5:16)
Confess your faults one to another, and pray one for another, that ye may be healed. The effectual fervent prayer of a righteous man availeth much.

(Colossians 4:2)
Continue in prayer, and watch in the same with thanksgiving;

(Psalm 5:3)
My voice shall thou hear in the morning, O Lord;
in the morning will I direct my prayer unto thee, and will look up.

PRESENT
(Mathew 6:34)
Take therefore no thought for the morrow: for the
morrow shall take thought for the things of itself.
Sufficient unto the day is the evil thereof.

PROSPERITY
(Job 36:11)
If they obey and serve him, they shall spend their days
in prosperity, and their years in pleasures.

SELF-CONTROL
(Ecclesiastes 7:9)
Be not hasty in thy spirit to be angry: for anger
resteth in the bosom of fools.

(Proverbs 16:32)
He that is slow to anger is better than the mighty; and he that
ruleth his spirit than he that taketh a city.

SELF-EDUCATION
(Proverbs 4:13)
Take fast hold of instruction; let her not go: keep her;
for she is thy life.

SERVICE
(Mathew 23:11)
He that is greatest among you
shall be your servant.

SHAME
(Psalm 35:26)
Let them be ashamed and brought to confusion together
that rejoice at mine hurt: let them be clothed with shame and
dishonor that magnify themselves against me.

SICKNESS
(James 5:14)
Is any sick among you? let him call for the elders of the church;
and let them pray over him, anointing him with oil in
the name of the Lord:

(Deuteronomy 7:15)
And the Lord will take away from thee all sickness, and will put
none of the evil diseases of Egypt, which thou knows, upon thee;
but will lay them upon all them that hate thee.

SPIRITUAL AUTHORITY
(Mathew 18:18)
Verily I say unto you, whatsoever ye shall bind on
earth shall be bound in heaven: and whatsoever ye shall
loose on earth shall be loosed in heaven.

(Psalm 8)
What is man, that thou art mindful of him? Thou madest him
to have dominion over the works of thy hands;
thou hast put all things under his feet.

SUCCESS
(Joshua 1:8)
This book of the law shall not depart out of thy mouth; but thou shalt meditate therein day and night, that thou mayest observe to do according to all that is written therein: for then thou shalt make thy way prosperous, and then thou shalt have good success.

THE POWER OF WORDS
(Proverbs 18:21)
Death and life are in the power of the tongue: and they that love it shall eat the fruit thereof.

THOUGHTS
(Jeremiah 29:11)
For I know the thoughts that I think toward you, saith the LORD, thoughts of peace, and not of evil, to give you an expected end.

(Philippians 4:8)
Finally, brethren, whatsoever things are true, whatsoever things are honest, whatsoever things are just, whatsoever things are pure, whatsoever things are lovely, whatsoever things are of good report; if there be any virtue, and if there be any praise, think on these things.

VISION
(Proverbs 29:18)
Where there is no vision, the people perish.

WORSHIP
(Exodus 4:31)

And the people believed: and when they heard that the Lord had visited the children of Israel, and that he had looked upon their affliction, then they bowed their heads and worshipped.

WISDOM

(Proverbs 16:16)
How much better is it to get wisdom than gold! and to get understanding rather to be chosen than silver!

(Proverbs 2:7)
For the Lord gives wisdom: out of His mouth comes knowledge and understanding. He layeth up sound wisdom for the righteous.

(Proverbs 4:7).
Wisdom is the principle thing. Therefore get wisdom and in all thy getting, get understanding.

(Proverbs 3:13)
Happy is the one that findeth wisdom, and the one that getteth understanding.

WRITING

(Habakkuk 2:2)
And the LORD answered me, and said, Write the vision, and make it plain upon tables, that he may run that readeth it.

My prayer for you:

*So shall the knowledge of wisdom be unto thy soul:
when thou hast found it, then there shall be a reward,
and thy expectation shall not be cut off.*

Proverbs 24:14

Love,

Mia

Author:
Dr. Mia Y. Merritt
www.miamerritt.com

M&M Motivating
President/CEO
Dr. Mia Y. Merritt

1-866-560-7652

Other books written
by Mia Merritt:

Destined for Great Things Workbook
Prosperity is Your Birthright Workbook
Prosperity is Your Birthright Journal

You are Destined for Great Things because Prosperity is Your Birthright!

www.ingramcontent.com/pod-product-compliance
Lightning Source LLC
Chambersburg PA
CBHW080331170426
43194CB00014B/2518